# A GRAND OLD TEAM

## TO REPORT

— by David Prentice —

Reach Sport
www.reachsport.com

# A
# GRAND
# OLD
# TEAM
## TO REPORT

45 years following
Everton Football Club
— by David Prentice —

## Reach Sport

www.reachsport.com

First published in Great Britain in 2020 by
Reach Sport, 5 St Paul's Square, Liverpool, L3 9SJ.

www.reachsport.com
@reach_sport

Reach Sport is a part of Reach plc.
One Canada Square, Canary Wharf, London, E15 5AP.

ISBN: 9781911613855
Ebook ISBN: 9781911613916

Edited by Roy Gilfoyle
Artwork by Rick Cooke & James Maluchnik

Photographic acknowledgements:
David Prentice personal collection, Reach plc, PA Photos.

Printed and bound by CPI Group (UK) Ltd, Croydon, CR0 4YY.

# Contents

# A MEMORABLE INTRODUCTION

"I WAS just telling my friend here, you're that shit from the Echo."

As introductions go, it wasn't up there with, "Dr Livingstone I presume."

But then Everton chairman Peter Johnson was no Henry Morton Stanley, either.

Just three years earlier we'd been sipping white wine together on the deck of his yacht in the Mediterranean, bobbing idly off the coast of Saint-Tropez.

Now we were standing eye to eye at an Echo Sports Personality of the Year function at the city's now demolished Moat House Hotel.

Well, not exactly eye to eye.

A drunken fan was swaying in between us and had been haranguing the former Everton chairman, prompting PJ's decision to call over a passing reporter he treated like faecal matter.

I was clearly a decoy. Somebody to distract the shouting supporter.

To say I was apprehensive was an understatement. We hadn't spoken since I'd penned an article about him headlined "Blundering, Inept and Crass."

But any ice was quickly broken by the drunk, who turned, slurred and spilled the contents of an entire glass of red wine down my shirt – and didn't notice.

I'm sure Peter smirked, although he hid it well.

But as I had learned many times in the past, PJ had a fortune-winning poker face.

We first met when he was chairman of Tranmere Rovers and I was the Echo's Tranmere correspondent.

That was a period when I wrote nothing but good about him.

He'd rescued a club on the brink of dropping out of the Football League, injected significant funds on players like Eric Nixon, Neil McNab and Steve Cooper.

Then sat back and reaped the rewards – emotional not financial – as he took Rovers to Wembley six times and into the second tier of English football.

Enthused by that success, he then injected even more – on Premier League-class players like John Aldridge, Pat Nevin and Gary Stevens. And three times Rovers came within a hair's breadth of the top flight.

In my role as the Echo's first full-time Tranmere correspondent I covered the first failure – against Swindon, but by the time Tranmere faced Leicester and then Reading, falling short each time, I'd landed my dream job and was following Everton's fortunes.

Peter made exactly the same switch.

I became the Echo's Everton correspondent in March 1993,

barely a year before PJ crossed the river to become Everton's chairman, owner and guardian of the supporters' hopes, dreams and aspirations. He briefly lived up to that onerous responsibility. But that's all for later.

We enjoyed a strange relationship – rendered a little more intimate than an average reporter-club chairman rapport might have been by the identity of Peter's then girlfriend.

This was the era of Everton's first proposed ground move. Everton had polled their supporters on whether they would prefer to remain at a dilapidated, tired, and arguably unsafe Goodison Park, with some supporters enduring views like watching a match from inside a postbox and continuing to use toilet facilities akin to the black hole of Calcutta.

Or alternatively move to a brand, spanking new state of the art stadium with a wealth of leisure facilities, themed pubs, restaurants and the opportunity to watch the players train there three or four times a week.

It was a heavily loaded poll.

Myself and my colleague Paul Joyce had driven over to Peter's house on the Wirral to interview him on the outcome.

It was a surreal experience.

A welcoming woman of a similar age to myself, hair tied up and sporting a bright apron, opened the door and ushered us into the kitchen. We were offered a glass of cold, crisp white wine and sat down at the kitchen table.

Peter started to talk, so we duly took notes. This was 1997, remember, and notepads, pens and 100 words a minute Teeline were still the order of the day rather than dictaphones or mobile phone videos.

As he spoke, the woman I'd presumed was his house assistant started to look quizzically at me.

The more she stared, the more uncomfortable I became.

Was I slurping my drink? Were my questions poor? Perhaps I should have accepted a cup of tea, not wine?

Then she spoke. "It's David Prentice, isn't it?"

The penny dropped. In fact cascades of coins poured into the collecting basin.

"Lorraine?"

The 'house assistant' was actually Lorraine Rogers, and she was Peter's partner.

We knew each other.

We'd been classmates at Formby High School, in fact we'd walked home the same way together many times. I passed her house at the top of Flaxfield Road before continuing on towards Byland Close, but had lost touch since leaving school.

I'd moved into journalism, Lorraine had embarked upon a financial career which had taken her onto the Football League board, the FA council, CEO of tourism body the Mersey Partnership. And into PJ's boudoir.

He was clearly horrified by the revelation.

"You know each other?" he stuttered. Peter had a habit of stuttering and blinking furiously when stressed.

And right now he was blinking like a prisoner of war with an arc light blazing directly into his eyes.

Perhaps it was the knowledge that I was, obviously, acutely aware of the 23-year age gap between them which concerned him.

There was no 'perhaps.' Before we left he tugged at my sleeve and murmured: "Will a picture of me accompany this article?"

"I would imagine so Peter," I replied. "But I don't make those decisions. It's the sub-editor who is designing the page who will make that call."

"Well do me a favour then," he said. "Ask them to use a young-looking one if possible, in case her mother buys the bloody paper!"

I told you our relationship was surreal.

On one occasion I had to call him from a pub in the Lake District on a day off, looking for a quote about a potential signing – no day off is ever a day off in sports journalism. He acted like a petulant schoolboy, telling me to ask 'your old friend Lorraine'.

If I didn't know better I'd have sworn he was jealous that I'd made his partner's acquaintance before he did.

But he could also be entertaining company.

On Cup Final day 1996 we enjoyed a long lunch in Dublin together. I say lunch, it consisted entirely of Guinness, and we were thrown together by accident rather than design.

Joe Royle had taken his squad to face Home Farm in a Friday night end-of-season friendly – then allowed them Saturday to unwind, watch that day's Cup Final between Liverpool and Manchester United and generally do what a group of football-ers would do at the end of a long, hard season.

And in 1996 that meant drink. Drink monumental quanti-ties of beer. And drink some more.

I'd travelled with the squad and had it in my head to join them on a Saturday all-dayer. Peter clearly had the same idea.

Joe had booked the players into a separate hotel to the staff, maybe as a reward for finishing sixth and maybe to allow them to unwind without the authoritative eyes of the coaching staff overseeing them.

So I'd walked the short distance from the staff hotel to the players' hotel at 10.30am on Saturday morning – to find Peter having done exactly the same thing.

Except every single player had taken the phrase 'all-dayer' literally. They'd gone out on the lash at 10am and were already hard at it. No lie-ins. No late breakfasts. They were nowhere to be seen.

So Peter was reluctantly forced into watching the Cup Final build-up with me – in a Dublin pub.

The conversation was pleasant enough. We kept our intake to around four or five pints, then Peter wisely said: "I need to go back to the hotel otherwise I won't make it out tonight."

So we returned to our respective rooms. The lack of meaningful incident in the White Suits final was such that I'd actually nodded off on my hotel bed until the sound of Barry Davies shrieking "Cantona..." woke me with a start.

Jolted into action I called Joe Royle's room to see what the plans were for the evening and Big Joe replied: "Come on up! We're having a party to celebrate United's victory!"

So I did. That was the beginning of a long night, which I'd like to say was memorable but the events are understandably sketchy.

It involved a nightclub called Lillie's Bordello. It included the sight of Dave Watson in trainers and jeans – only FA Cup-winning captains were allowed such casual attire in a capital city nightclub in 1996 – still standing, drinking and conducting coherent conversation after having consumed something approaching a barrel load of Guinness. And it also included a bizarre incident including pop star Lisa Stansfield.

Joe Parkinson was a lively young buck in 1996 and he'd spotted the Rochdale singer in the club. So he repeatedly loitered in her general vicinity, belted out the first few chords of her hit single: "I've been around the world and I, I, I…" in broad Lancastrian, then disappeared.

He repeated the trick over and over again.

When you've been drinking Guinness all day such high jinks are hilariously funny.

Lisa whirled around every time, but Joe was in his Premier League prime and his speed off the mark was deceptive.

He wasn't once caught and I still wonder what poor, puzzled Lisa made of the experience.

Joe, his room-mate Matt Jackson and myself then hired a horse and carriage to take us to our hotel to watch Lennox Lewis outpoint Ray Mercer in a heavyweight boxing contest which proved infinitely less entertaining than the earlier events of the evening.

The journey was barely 100 yards, and cost about 30 euros, but it wasn't a night for rational behaviour.

Matt has since told me his overriding memory of that evening was of me leaving their bedroom at around 4am, cramming my pockets full of the club sandwiches they had ordered for their room – "for the journey back to my hotel."

Looking back now it all seems so normal, so ordinary.

But it was probably the high point of my time as Everton correspondent.

Everton were the FA Cup holders, I had a close, if strange, relationship with the club chairman, the manager was one of the most engaging and honest individuals it has ever been my good fortune to work with in football and I could describe some of the players in the squad as personal friends.

I was allowed to travel, mix and engage with virtually everyone at the club, the football club I had grown up supporting.

So delivering stories for the paper I worked for, the Liverpool Echo, was like shelling peas.

Looking back, I'd come into journalism just before the football club drawbridge started to raise.

Everton had no formal press officer then. Now they have a media department numbering almost a hundred.

Back then I visited Everton's training ground every morning for tea and toast with the manager, and returned at lunchtime to try and persuade a player to be interviewed. Now a barrier and a security hut bars access to Finch Farm, access to which is by invitation only.

And before the turn of the millennium I ghost-wrote the manager's notes, an assistant-manager's page, the captain's column and penned the Youth Academy reports for the match programme. The programme for the first match of the 1997-98 season contained 40 pages. I wrote 18 of them.

I was an Everton reporter, programme writer, players' pal and old schoolmate of the chairman's girlfriend.

That was all going to change. And not always for the better.

## Chapter One

# MILES APART

ACCORDING to the AA's Route Planner, Roby Street in Bootle lies precisely 2.7 miles from Goodison Park.

You could walk to the atmospheric old stadium I've now visited more than 1,000 times in less than an hour – past the gas works at the end of the street, along Marsh Lane, up Hawthorne Road and then on to County Road, before entering a stadium which when I lived in Bootle was considered one of the most palatial in the country.

England played an international there in 1973, an FA Cup semi-final replay was staged under its floodlights in 1979; and when Nottingham Forest and Newcastle were ordered to replay an FA Cup tie in 1974 because of fighting amongst both sets of supporters, Goodison was chosen as the venue.

Not that I ever made that walk in the 10 years I spent living at number 18 Roby Street.

Not once.

In fact football barely crossed my mind as a small child, which is unusual because Bootle is a hotbed of football.

Andy Rankin, the Everton goalkeeper who saved the decisive

penalty in the first ever European Cup penalty shoot-out, was born there.

So, too, was West Ham hero Alvin Martin, former Liverpool boss Roy Evans and one-time Evertonian, full-time Liverpool legend Jamie Carragher.

I was born in nearby Walton Hospital, a wind assisted goal-kick from Goodison's Gwladys Street End.

But the first 10 years of my life were filled more by dinosaurs, Marvel comics, Enid Blyton and How and Why Wonder Books.

Yes, I was a nerdy child who loved to read.

I actually told amused teachers at Linacre County Primary school I intended to become a paleontologist when I left school – and they fuelled that enthusiasm with a steady stream of reading material.

But reading actually provided my first introduction to the assorted wonders of association football.

And George Mushrow was the man who first ignited a flicker of enthusiasm in an eight-year-old's heart for the sport, a flame which would soon become a raging inferno.

Our family regularly visited my Uncle George and Auntie Lauraine at their home in Enid Street, Toxteth, and when I was at that impressionable age my Everton-supporting uncle gave me a huge collection of Everton programmes.

Maybe he wanted a bit of peace and quiet. Perhaps he secretly intended to pass on the torch.

Whatever his intentions, I was gripped.

While those magazines were from the unrelentingly miserable 1971/72 season, that made no difference to a young boy gripped by images of men like Alan Ball, Howard Kendall and Colin Harvey – and bemused by the presence of others like Bernie Wright and Rod Belfitt.

I still have those programmes.

And they sparked a sense of intrigue about the world they encompassed.

I started to wonder about football.

That intrigue hadn't extended to playing the game just yet.

Roby Street was one of those typical labyrinthine terraced streets off Marsh Lane, a gasworks at one end of the cobbled street, St Matthew's Church at the other.

Football was rarely played on the street, and there wasn't much interest in the sport at home.

My dad, a former merchant seaman, had swapped the seaways for motorways as a long distance lorry driver – and he preferred Saturday afternoon wrestling for his sporting kick on the rare occasions he was home at weekends.

Football, weirdly, didn't feature on the Linacre Primary School syllabus either.

So my love of kicking a football, which I still indulge at the age of 57, lay dormant for a few years longer.

The nearest grass was in the nearby North Park, just across Stanley Road, which was bandit country to naive nine and seven-year-olds as my brother Stephen and I discovered when we once ventured across there to play. Our planned play-time was interrupted by a teenage mugger wielding an ugly kitchen knife who tried to steal my brother's bike. A passing dog walker witnessed the grim incident unfolding and ordered his dog, a beast which wouldn't have looked out of place in a

Hammer version of The Hound of the Baskervilles, to chase the would-be thief.

As a result, whenever I hear the name 'Chopper' I think of a wonderful animal with that evocative moniker, rather than the Chelsea defender of the 1970s who enjoyed the same nickname.

As a result, any enthusiasm to take a football over to the North Park for a kick around was swiftly extinguished.

Football remained an alien concept to me for a little longer. An Evertonian school pal called Robert Millington once told me he was going to Goodison Park. I envisaged a public park, a bit like the North Park but without the would-be assailants: although as this was the 1970s, the era of away match firms and Stanley knife-wielding thugs, I was probably half right.

It was only when my little sister Gillian was born in 1972 that my mum Laura persuaded my staunchly working class dad Eric, by then a shop steward at the Duke Haulage firm he drove for, that it was a good idea to move; and the quintessentially middle-class town of Formby became my home.

We moved in the summer of 1974, just as a bearded behemoth called Bob Latchford was about to kick off his first full season as Everton centre-forward.

Just 10 miles separate Bootle from Formby. But the towns exist in different stratospheres. They may both be part of the same metropolitan borough of Sefton, but that's all they have in common. Formby has a beach. It has pinewoods. But most importantly of all, it boasts grass. And everybody there played football.

At the bottom of Byland Close there was a patch of green,

a recreational space with convenient trees which quickly doubled up as goalposts.

Mark Kearney, who lived round the corner, was always up for a kick around and honed skills there which led to him joining Everton and forging a proper football career with Mansfield and Bury. He even scored a penalty in the shoot-out which saw The Stags win the Freight Rover Trophy at Wembley in 1987, by which time I was writing about the Blues for the Daily Post.

I like to think he practised that unerring eye from the spot which led him to lift silverware at Wembley, by clipping shots past me off the inside of saplings at the top of Byland Close.

By this time I was writing about football at every opportunity.

My new junior school, Redgate, was just around the corner and had the real thing – football goalposts.

So myself and my brother Stephen, and new pals Robert and Brian Hurst, Scaz, Tony Connolly and Sean Stevens, played football at every available opportunity. Cuppies, three-and-in, even five-a-side when the numbers allowed.

If no-one was available there was a handy Co-Op wall with a goal painted on it to practise finishing.

Even Christmas Day was spent on Redgate school field, breaking in my new Beckenbauer Super football boots before Christmas dinner.

Oh, and lots and lots of footballers lived in Formby, too.

Not about-to-be footballers like Mark Kearney, but already established stars.

They still do. But now they live in gated mansions, behind

security walls monitored by cameras and with driveways which leave you blowing for tugs simply walking up them – that's if you could ever get beyond the securely-locked gates. Which you can't. Modern footballers are a protected species you can only observe infrequently, at a distance.

Back then footballers lived in regular semi-detached dwellings.

And the chances of bumping into a real life football star were frequent.

On the morning of Sunday, August 22, 1976, while walking to Elson Road to the house of some friends, Steven and Bryan Whitehead – who were actually red-headed twins, what were the chances? – I spied Emlyn Hughes pushing a young child in a pram.

Yes, the Liverpool captain, an England international, a man who would be crowned Footballer of the Year later that season, was pushing his daughter in the sunshine without a care in the world.

Until I spotted him that is. Unfortunately for Emlyn, Everton had unfeasibly and unexpectedly won 4-0 away the previous day at the home of the team which had pushed Liverpool all the way to their ninth league title just three months earlier. And we'd thrashed QPR with 10 men, David Jones having been sent off after 17 minutes.

Liverpool, on the other hand, had scraped past Norwich 1-0 at Anfield. It was clear to this 13-year-old that a seismic powershift was taking place on Merseyside, so I did what any self-respecting teenage Evertonian would do.

I squeaked, probably several octaves higher than even

Emlyn's notorious falsetto, "Hey Emlyn, Everton 4 QPR 0, suck that!"

If 'Suck that' sounds like an unusual choice of phrase today, back in the 1970s it was a regular term of challenge, like 'In your face,' or 'Take that' or 'Put that in your pipe and smoke it.' But more succinct.

Emlyn might have ignored me. He might have shook his head in disgust.

But, no, his reaction underlined the times – and the nature of the man.

"Behave yourself son," he squeaked. "Where did you finish last season? 11th was it? (He was spot on). We're champions! Champions of England! What was the score last time you played us? One-nil was it? (It was). You'll do nothing again!" (He was right. We followed up that spectacular opening-day success by drawing 1-1 at home to Ipswich on the Tuesday and then losing at home to Aston Villa).

I was chastened. And unable to think of a crass retort like, say, 'Everton are magic, Liverpool are tragic'. So I shuffled off to call for Bryan and Steven.

By this stage I'd become a Goodison Park regular.

Again the circumstances are vague. To coin an old Everton advertising slogan, maybe I really was chosen. Another school pal, a few years older, called Gareth MacLardy, was an Evertonian – and wanted to go to the match.

Intrigued by the contents of my Uncle George's programmes and keen to experience the real thing, I took the plunge and accompanied Gaz to Goodison.

It was Easter Monday, March 31, 1975. We took the train

from Formby to Bank Hall, which cost 21p return, walked the half mile or so along Rumney Road – tagging onto the coat-tails of a couple of grown-ups to evade the teenage would-be muggers who lined the streets on matchdays – and paid 50p to enter the old Enclosure, now the Family Enclosure. And obviously I bought a programme for 8p – a cherished souvenir of the visit which I would tuck down my midriff to try and keep as uncreased as possible.

That was a sum total of 79p to go to the match, at a time when I was paid £2.15p for my seven-days-a-week paper round at Redgate newsagents – a shop where Alan Hansen's future wife, Janet, marked up the papers. Told you football influences were everywhere in Formby.

That meant I could spend the rest on the Pink Echo, magazines like Shoot! and Goal, Marvel comics – a passion which has never dimmed – and vinyl discs, which back then were simply known as records.

Such was my unbounded wealth I actually splashed out on FOUR hit singles on my first visit to Quirk's record shop in Formby Village. Bachman Turner Overdrive's 'You Ain't Seen Nothing Yet' suggests my teenage tastes weren't overly immature, but that rock-tastic classic was also joined by Mud's 'It'll Be Lonely This Christmas', Gary Glitter's 'Oh Yes You're Beautiful' and 'Tell Him' by Hello.

Well, one out of four ain't bad.

I don't think I've ever had so much disposable income again.

We arrived early at Goodison on that Easter Monday afternoon. Bachman Turner Overdrive might actually have been one of the discs pumping out of the tannoy speakers from

Goodison's resident DJ, Billy Butler. We were very early, in fact. Early enough to actually see the players walking across the pitch in their flared trousers, jackets with absurdly-wide lapels and ties with knots bigger than my head.

That was because the Enclosure then was a standing terrace, and if a 12-year-old wanted to actually see anything he needed to either haul a milk crate to the match and stand on it against the pitchside wall or, my preferred option, leap precariously onto a crush barrier and perch there.

A matchday programme was a vital element of passing the hour or so before kick-off. And it enabled you to get players' autographs on it as they walked down the tunnel to prepare.

Once the match had kicked off there was an elaborate ritual to follow to ensure a reasonable view of the action was enjoyed – and you remained free from injury.

Every time there was even a hint of excitement there would be a crowd surge (yes, even in the Enclosure) and you'd be sent hurtling from the crash barrier I was perched atop. So to avoid being sent flying I would anticipate a surge, every time there was a goal or a near miss, and leap to the concrete terrace floor. As a result I'm not even certain that I saw Martin Dobson's winning goal that afternoon.

Dobbo, an upright, elegant midfielder who now works in the lounges on matchdays at Goodison, struck seconds before half-time.

That goal took a Billy Bingham team labelled 'Robots' by the London press top of the old First Division, with just five matches of the season left. Two were against sides who would be relegated, Luton and Chelsea, one was at a poor Newcastle and the remaining two were both at home, to Burnley, who finished tenth, and a decent but unexceptional Sheffield United.

Surely a glorious introduction to Goodison Park beckoned?

No. We finished fourth. The Burnley match was played on a Friday night because of the following day's Grand National, and ended 1-1.

We actually led Sheffield United 2-0 at half-time, thanks in no small part to a penalty from the gloriously gifted but wildly unpredictable Gary Jones, and a sublime strike hooked over his shoulder from the talented but injury-plagued David Smallman.

We lost 3-2.

"And Smallman's first First Division goal is a honey!" screamed ITV's Gerald Sinstadt on the Sunday lunchtime highlights show.

But if that strike was sugar sweet, Dai Davies' goalkeeping was as sour as month-old milk and contributed to our demise. It would be a recurring theme throughout the 1970s.

Davies was replaced for the start of the following season by the equally erratic David Lawson – and we opened with a 4-1 home defeat to Coventry.

In the Coventry goal that afternoon was a young goalkeeper called Bryan King who I'd later encounter as a players' agent. About 20 years later.

But back in 1976 I had gravitated to the Gwladys Street End. It was five pence cheaper for a start (45p), although given my junior Rockefeller status that wasn't a primary inducement. More significantly you could cling to the outside of a crash barrier on the raised ledge in the centre of the terrace and be sure of an uninterrupted view without having to leap to safety every time there was a surge.

But most important of all for a 13-year-old, it was cool.

It was where the hard core fans stood, where the singing started and where a character called Fozzy Bear clung to a pillar and started chants which suggested that substances more mind bending than Brown Mixed or Mild were surely being consumed before kick-off.

There was the Goodison Boot Walk.

"I'm a knock-kneed chicken and a bow-legged hen, I haven't had a wank since I don't know when, I walk with a wiggle and I talk with a squawk...doing the Everton boot walk! La la la la la la la la la!"

There was the frankly rather convoluted attempt to reword Lena Martell's number one chart hit to fit Bob Latchford's bid to score 30 league goals in 1978.

"One goal at a time Bob Latchford, that's all we're asking of you. When you hit the bar, we all say aaah, one goal at a time."

Then there was the wonderful ditty composed in homage to the idolised Andy King.

"Olly, olly, olly with your balls in a trolley and your dick wrapped up in string. Sitting on the grass with a bottle of Bass ...singing Andy is our King, Andy is our King, oh Andy is our King."

The seventies grey and miserable?

Don't believe a word of it.

And don't believe that Everton were awful in the 70s either.

There were disappointments, sure. But Billy Bingham and

Gordon Lee both came agonisingly close to delivering the glory that supporters just a little older than me had enjoyed in 1970.

After my first match against Coventry an insanely tight First Division table looked like this on March 31, 1975...

**1 Everton Played 37 Points 46 Goal Average 1.43**
**2 Liverpool Played 38 Points 45 Goal Average 1.43**
**3 Stoke City Played 38 Points 45 Goal Average 1.33**
**4 Ipswich Town Played 37 Points 44 Goal Average 1.49**

The eventual champions?

Derby County, lurking in fifth with only 36 games played!

The following season – 1975/76 – offered little to commend it, other than the signing of a bubbly teenager from Luton Town called Andy King, the man celebrated with the afore-mentioned ditty.

But 1976/77 saw Everton twice come close to cup glory, in separate competitions.

That hardy perennial, an unreliable keeper, cost us in the League Cup – the only time in English football history that a Cup final had taken three matches to resolve.

I went to all three.

Wembley saw a grim goalless draw with Aston Villa enlivened only by the match being halted early in the second half because a half-time bandsman had lost one of his spurs.

But I was used to hours of tedium in the pursuit of Everton success by then.

Just to buy a Wembley ticket I queued for 12 hours outside Goodison Park.

Yes. At the age of 14 I missed morning registration at school to take the train to Bank Hall, run up Rumney Road and queue for a League Cup final ticket clutching my precious priority voucher.

I arrived at 8.30am to join the back of a queue which already reached where the ticket office now is on Goodison Road.

In 1977 tickets were dispensed from a portacabin around the other side of the stadium on Bullens Road. With one door in and one door out.

When fans today complain about tickets getting lost in the post or scans not loading properly on their iPhones, I'm reminded of that old Monty Python Yorkshiremen sketch.

You know, the one which concludes with Eric Idle complaining: "Right, I had to get up in the morning at 10 o'clock at night, half-an-hour before I went to bed, drink a cup of sulphuric acid, work 29 hours a day down t'mill, and pay mill owner for permission to come to work, and when we got home our dad and our mother would kill us, and dance about on our graves singing 'Hallelujah.'"

And Michael Palin delivers the punchline: "But you try and tell the young people today that…and they won't believe ya."

Well, I did queue for 12 hours. With no food or drink.

Fortunately for my mum and dad, in the days before mobile phones, my match-going mate Gaz had spotted me in the queue as he walked back clutching his precious ticket – he'd arrived an hour earlier than me – and narrowly escaped being lynched by increasingly frustrated fans in the queue after shouting to me: "You'll be lucky mate. They're nearly all gone!"

But at least when my increasingly-concerned mum telephoned his house to ask if he'd seen me he was able to tell of my whereabouts.

My mum even agreed to write a sick note to take into school the next day to explain my absence.

Getting a ticket for the Hillsborough replay four days later was much easier – and the second replay at Old Trafford easier still.

I sat in the front row of the South Stand for the first replay when the ecstasy of seeing your team score a goal in a domestic cup final was graphically delivered.

After Roger Kenyon had scored an unfortunate own goal 10 minutes from the end, the beautiful, bearded, bustling, barnstorming Bob Latchford did what big beautiful Bob always did and leathered a last-minute equaliser in from a yard.

He jumped for joy, so did the away end and so did the South Stand. I think the common parlance today is 'limbs.'

Such was the state of nirvana that goal produced that the large bottle of coke I had in the pocket of my parka had slipped out and smashed on the floor. And myself and the supporters around me had been leaping insanely up and down on shards of glass capable of slicing through even Dr Marten boots and severing several toes.

Those around in the 1970s will know that coke bottles then were heavy, and the glass they were made from was thick. Jason Bourne could easily have utilised the shards we were dancing on as lethal weapons.

Somehow we escaped injury. Further evidence that God was on our side that night.

I only became aware of what had happened when a steward

finally tapped me on the arm and gestured down to the debris on the floor.

He actually seemed more concerned about that than preventing me from scrambling over the low wall at the final whistle to run up to a sweaty Andy King and squeak "Great game Andy."

The Echo's Charles Lambert penned an evocative piece of writing the following day about the backing the Everton fans had given their team that night which struck a resonant chord with me.

Underneath Alex Goodman's match report, Charlie wrote a comment piece, unusual at the time, about the Everton fans.

He wrote: 'This League Cup final. This incredible story of sweat and effort and some of the most committed tackling I have ever seen, is the vehicle through which Everton are forming a communion with their supporters.

'So many times in the past Goodison Park has worn an air of detachment, the spectators looking on politely like ancients watching the youngsters at play.

'Goodison would hardly have recognised the scenes at Hillsborough last night, just as it would not have recognised those at Wembley on Saturday.

'There is a new spirit on the terraces – and in the stands too – for last night the chant of 'Everton are Magic', a chant which looks like becoming their new theme song, came from the stands as much as from the other parts of the ground.

'It is a spirit which is not easily related to the days, not so very long ago, when Goodison echoed not to the hymns of adulation but to the thuds of cushions landing on the turf.

'The point is, Everton have still not won anything. The fans are not waiting for success before making themselves heard, they are weighing in with their contribution in a bid to achieve that success.

'Last night proved it. They out-shouted the Villa clans from before the start, but did they pack up when they went a goal down? Did they sidle away when the last seconds were running out? Did they hell! They kept up the chorus of 'Everton Are Magic' and Bob Latchford proved they were right.'

My heart stirred. It was as if Charles was speaking directly to me, and my desire to follow his lead and write about Everton for a living was reinforced.

That same crowd backing was in evidence a month later when Everton and Aston Villa met for a third time at Old Trafford, in the only English cup final to require three goes to conclude.

But while the crowd did their bit, and the ever reliable beautiful, bustling Bob did his, David Lawson did not. The Everton goalkeeper was beaten by a hopeful 40-yard drive from centre-half Chris Nicholl, then came haring unnecessarily out of his goal to allow Brian Little to slide in another goal.

The Blues keeper could actually do little about the winning goal, scored in the final minute of extra-time – but his erratic interventions earlier in the evening meant the cup was on its way to the Midlands.

Everton's goalscorers that night were Mick Lyons, who I admired, and Bob Latchford, who I adored.

Bob and I were made for each other.

Bob even celebrated his birthday on January 18th, the same

day as my little sister Gillian – although my dad would always growl: "Bob Latchford's birthday is the same day as your sister's, you mean."

I remained unconvinced.

My adoration of Bob even extended to once spending half-an-hour standing outside the fashionable gentleman's outfitters he owned on Piercefield Road in Formby, plucking up the courage to walk boldly in with my collection of posters clipped from the pages of Shoot and Goal, for him to sign.

It may seem curious now for an England international footballer, the leading scorer in the top division in 1977/78, to actually serve behind the counter of a shop he owned, but in the 70s it was regular behaviour.

L.P. Hartley was spot on. The past is a foreign country. They do things differently there.

Bob dutifully signed all of my pictures. And he signed them 'R. Latchford', rather than Bob – in a perfectly recognisable signature unlike today's unintelligible squiggles – which merely underlined how classy the great man was.

That class even extended to turning a blind eye to the pictures which had been blu-tacked to my bedroom wall, and to which my brother had thrown darts at…leaving neat holes all around the club crest on his shirt.

But that was Bob. He always had a touch of class about him.

We 'met' again in 1988. Well, I stalked him again in 1988, at a celebration of Everton centre-forwards at the Clifton Hotel in Southport.

It truly was a remarkable gathering of Goodison goalscorers.

The signed programme I have from the night indicates that

Dave Hickson, Gary Lineker, Tony Cottee, Graeme Sharp and Derek Temple were also present…a gallery of goalscorers responsible for plundering 629 Everton goals.

Gary Jones only scored 15 in his Everton career, but his presence there was responsible for me enjoying an audience with the great man.

I had left our table to head to the gents, when I spotted Bob at the bar trying to extricate himself from a conversation with a clearly very, very drunk Gary Jones.

We made eye contact. My heart skipped a beat. I even offered to buy Bob a drink. "No, you're alright son," he said. "I'll buy you one." My heart pounded out the opening drumbeat sequence to Z-Cars. I was about to have a pint with Bob Latchford.

We stood and chatted idly about some of the goals he'd scored in his Everton career. Jones slurred something and then wandered off to pester another former team-mate.

I remembered more of the goals than Bob did, which was the only dismaying moment of the entire experience.

"What? You don't remember that header off the floor into the roof of the net against Man City? It came from a Davey Thomas corner? At the Street End? It was great!"

His dubious memory apart – after all, when you've scored 138 Everton goals it must be impossible to remember every single one of them (although Joe Royle CAN vividly recall each of his 118) – Bob was charming company.

As we stood and talked I became slowly aware of a small crowd assembling behind me. It was the friends I'd come to the dinner with. And I could hear them murmuring in reverential tones "Prenny's talking to Big Bob." I was – and it was great.

We eventually left him in peace – and returned to my flat in nearby Birkdale where we ended the evening by watching videos of Bob Latchford's greatest goals and toasting his greatness. That header against Manchester City wasn't one captured on camera.

During the course of my job I met and spoke to Bob many more times. And his demeanour always defied that old saying about never meeting your heroes.

He was always charming, always gracious, always classy. And I was always just that little bit in awe.

After attending an informal lunch in Liverpool city centre organised by my good friend James Corbett, who had just published Bob's autobiography, I eventually got up to leave.

Bob also rose and made to give me a hug. I froze. A man hug from my idol? I halted, simply shook hands, and left.

When I later related the tale to Peter Coyle, one of the friends who had assembled behind me in that Southport hotel almost 30 years earlier, he was appalled.

"You turned down a man hug from Bob Latchford? Are you insane?"

Maybe I was, but my Everton insanity had long since been diagnosed.

Uncle George's programme gift, and the influence of another family member, Uncle Sid, confirmed that I would become a Blue.

The reasoning is still difficult to decipher because Sid Nabb was a Liverpool fan. One of those armchair, non-match-going, in-your-face Liverpool fans, but a Liverpudlian nonetheless.

And when he heard I was contemplating a life following the Blues, the scorn and ridicule he heaped upon me was intense.

If he thought his zealous tirades would convert me he was mistaken.

I dug my heels in. And became even more entrenched.

At least Uncle Sid's broadsides prepared me for the trials of becoming an Evertonian in the 1970s – a decade when Liverpool won four league titles, one FA Cup, two UEFA Cups and two European Cups and Everton won…a solitary league title when I was too young to have any conscious recollection of it.

It was a tormented existence my family were soon to become aware of.

When Liverpool won their first European Cup in 1977, I sat in the front room fervently wishing, praying and hoping for a Borussia Moenchengladbach victory.

When Allan Simonsen equalised Terry McDermott's early goal I cavorted wildly around the front room, until my puzzled dad slapped me down and demanded to know how on earth I could be supporting a German team against a local side featuring four Scousers?

His answer came at the final whistle, when a tribe of Liverpool fans gathered outside my front door waving scarves and flags chanting: "Prenny, Prenny show us your scarf!"

To be fair, Eric William Prentice was just as angry with them as he had been with me an hour earlier and sent them packing.

It put a faint smirk back on my face, which quickly evaporated when Emlyn Hughes' neon smile lit up the TV screen as he raised Europe's most famous trophy for the first time.

What was it Alan Ball said? Once Everton has touched you nothing will be the same.

Nothing ever was.

Chapter Two

# THE SCHOOL
# OF SCIENCE

I WANTED to play for Everton Football Club.

I really did. Like every other Everton-supporting schoolboy.

But anybody who ever saw me lead the line for a team called Leisure Sport (we were sponsored by Formby's leading/only sportswear store) in the Southport and District League, or had the good fortune to mark me, will know it was only ever a forlorn pipedream.

I did score goals. Twenty-seven was my best in the 1984/85 season. But there was a whippet playing up front for Birkdale Crown back then called Andy Mutch who put that statistic firmly in the shade. He actually ended up enjoying a career with Wolves and Swindon Town – and even played at Goodison Park a couple of times.

So did I. Several times. But never in front of anything resembling a crowd of paying spectators. And with nothing like the dash or vim Andy displayed.

I was once asked to make up the numbers in a charity match, where a very good Liverpool Sunday League team had earned a reward of playing against a team of ex pros including Kevin

Sheedy, Kevin Ratcliffe, Graeme Sharp, David Johnson, Arthur Albiston. And me.

After slamming the phone down at the Echo's Old Hall Street offices I couldn't get to Goodison quickly enough.

But every time I made the kind of hopeful run I'd made for Leisure, the ball would miraculously arrive at my feet. And such was the quality of the Sunday League team we were playing – and my lack of it – the move would break down instantly.

That pretty much confirmed what I'd already known.

If playing for Everton was never going to be a realistic option, writing about them was the next best thing.

So I decided from a relatively young age that I was going to be a sports journalist. Not just any old sport, either. I decided that my ultimate goal was to write about Everton. And get paid for it.

Even now it all seems so straightforward. Yet in hindsight so many slices of good fortune fell my way in order for me to realise that dream.

Not least stumbling through school.

I always felt that English was one of my stronger subjects at Formby High School. Unfortunately my English teachers didn't share that optimism. Well, one of them in particular.

I loved creative writing. The analysis of other people's work, less so.

I actually attempted to answer questions during my English A Level exam on Charles Dickens' Dombey and Son, having failed to actually read more than half of a volume which makes an effective doorstop, but actually takes an enormous effort just to lift, let alone finish. Only the examiners can explain how I passed.

I loved the review a reader once left on Amazon: "Dombey and Son is, I fear, exactly the kind of novel that prevents people from reading Dickens and other 'classics.' Overlong, filled with long passages of moralising prose, painfully slow moving at times, sentimental, relatively humourless – strikingly so for Dickens – and, I regret to say, often boring."

Quite. Why it was on the 1980 A Level syllabus only Mr Kirby could answer.

If Mr Kirby had opted to ask his pupils to study the frankly wonderful Wuthering Heights, a decent Dickens read like Great Expectations or, say, anything by Raymond Chandler, I could have been an 'A' star student.

But he didn't. We read Dombey and Son. And I wasn't.

That wasn't the only thing Mr Kirby misjudged.

When I visited my careers teacher at the age of 16 to discuss my future career options, I stated, quite purposefully, that I was going to become a sports journalist.

The careers teacher's brow furrowed.

"Really?" she said, quite perplexed. "Your English teacher doesn't seem to think you're going to get your O Level, which would be a pre-requisite for a career in journalism."

The earth shifted under my feet.

It was as if someone had told me that Bob Latchford had been sold to Liverpool.

Really? Hadn't Mr Kirby read my essay detailing quite evocatively the night Everton won the European Cup? A work of fiction, obviously, but a work of sparkling imagination.

Clearly not. Because the proposed career path suggested to me was…book-keeping.

I still don't even know what book-keeping is. But I do recall the slightly puzzled expression on Mr Kirby's face when I returned to Formby High in the autumn of 1980 to start my A Levels, after achieving a B in English Language and a B in English Literature in my O levels.

"Hello David. I believe you did quite well in your exams," he murmured, then shuffled away.

Fortunately I had a different teacher for A Level English. But equally as fortunately the magnificent Mrs Manning was still my French teacher.

With the benefit of 40 years of hindsight, and just a fraction more maturity, I could understand Mr Kirby's reluctance to endorse my credentials as a solid student. Looking back I suppose I could be, how should you say, a little cocky in class?

I was more interested in trying to impress the alluring class hottie, Ali McCulloch, with witty one-liners than absorbing the lessons in front of me.

But Mrs Manning – who had been Miss Mattinson when I first started at Formby High – had an incredible ability for managing stroppy schoolboys.

I had somehow achieved an exam result of 96% in my first High School French exam, and Mrs Manning and co. believed – wrongly – that they had some kind of linguistic savant on their hands.

She indulged me, she nurtured my genuine love for the French language and she put up with my occasional arsiness.

"You were all fine," she told me years later, when I learned with absolute glee that she was still at Formby High School and was teaching my daughter, Scarlett. "You were part of a class with character. There's not so much of that around today."

I adored her so much I even agreed to study German. And briefly, Swedish.

I probably only possess a handful of words from those lessons. But I still love speaking French today. And I'll always be eternally grateful to Mrs Manning for that.

English, however, was always the primary subject, because it was a means to an end.

Passing my English exams meant I qualified to take an NCTJ (National Council for the Training of Journalists) exam to study journalism at Preston Polytechnic.

Passing that exam meant I qualified to sit in front of a panel of journalists and be assessed for my suitability for that one-year course.

And coming through that successfully meant that I moved to 55 Albert Road in Preston for a year – to study Newspaper Law, Shorthand, Public Administration and Newspaper Practice.

It was an intense course, but exciting. I still had the occasional moments of arsiness in class – lecturer John Hudson once growled at me, "Prentice. Go out and make some contacts."

But my sassiness in class was nothing compared to my best pal on the course, Graham Dudman. Neither of us were model pupils, but I ended up as sports editor of the Liverpool Echo while Graham became managing editor of The Sun.

Sometimes a little spikiness – or character as Mrs Manning would call it – isn't such a bad thing.

Former Everton boss Gordon Lee was convinced I was on the right career path when we met in his manager's office at Preston North End's Deepdale in 1983.

I was actually at Preston's ground to interview board member Barney Campbell for the Poly newspaper about directors digging deep into their own pockets to try and stave off financial hardship. When he heard my accent he asked: "Blue or red?"

When I replied with the former, he said: "Well you'll want to meet our manager then, won't you?" and marched me straight to Mr Lee's office.

It was mid-afternoon, and if Gordon was discomfited at being asked to entertain a local student for a few minutes he didn't show it.

He showed genuine interest in my choice of career, although his reasonings for backing my decision were basic.

"What does your dad do, son?"

"He's a long distance lorry driver," I replied.

"Very good," he declared in that thick Brummie brogue. "People will always want goods transporting."

"And what does your brother do?"

"He's a trainee butcher," I replied. Our Stephen had moved on from using Bob Latchford pictures as makeshift dartboards, to carving up sides of beef.

"Good choice. Very good choice," said Gordon. "People will always want to eat meat.

"And you want to be a journalist…"

Now he seemed less certain. He deliberated for a moment,

then he pronounced: "Yes, yes, I suppose people will always want news."

And they do. But the manner in which they acquire that news has changed dramatically since we chatted in the Preston manager's office.

We spoke for a long time. It actually went dark and Gordon didn't bother to turn the lights on.

Well, the club was in a financial crisis. But I valued his generosity of time and spirit. I valued his advice. And I even told him how I'd appreciated the exhilarating Everton side he had created just a few years before. This was a team which rattled 76 goals in 1977/78.

The final two seasons of Lee's Everton reign are usually the stick used to beat him with, but in those first two campaigns he oversaw a side which was easy on the eye and unlucky not to land silverware.

With jet-heeled Davey Thomas firing crosses for big, bad, bustling Bob Latchford to convert, backed up by freescoring midfielders like Andy King and Martin Dobson, they were the highest scoring team in the top division. They scored seven more than eventual league champions Nottingham Forest, and while they ultimately ended up with nothing more than a place in the following season's UEFA Cup, they were thrilling to watch.

Check out the YouTube videos of the 6-0 slaughter of Coventry, the 5-1 away wins at Leicester and QPR and the famous Goodison derby victory in 1978. That was a team worth watching.

The following season, my first as a Gwladys Street season ticket holder, Lee's team finished fourth and were also unbeaten against a Liverpool team which dominated the top flight like few teams had ever done before.

After that campaign it all started to unravel for Gordon Lee and two years later he was sacked.

But he'd given us some memorable high points.

There was the Andy King derby at Goodison, Everton's first victory over our fiercest rivals for seven years, and there was an FA Cup win over the same opposition in 1981.

Then there was the afternoon big, beautiful, bustling Bob became the first centre-forward in the top flight to score 30 league goals for six years and landed a £10,000 prize from the Daily Express.

The venerable Brian Viner interviewed me about that exhilarating afternoon for his splendid 'Looking For The Toffees' tome.

He quoted me accurately.

"Now that I look back on it," Prentice told me 35 years later, "it was actually quite embarrassing how we celebrated. There was a pitch invasion when he scored the goal and another one at the end of the match. By the time I got onto the hallowed turf someone had already pinched the penalty spot. So I tore up another bit of the pitch and stuffed it under my denim jacket. For a while I had it in a plastic container next to my bed, until my dad cottoned on to what I'd done and made me transplant it in the back garden. My sister had a swing with a scuffed bit of ground underneath. So that's where it went. We've long since moved out of that house, but number 6 Byland Close in Formby still has a piece of Goodison Park in the garden. Whoever lives there now, I hope they're Evertonians."

So there were some high points for Evertonians in the 1970s.

And but for a miserable, weasel-minded, self-centred, God-awful referee from Treorchy we'd have beaten Liverpool in a Maine Road semi-final and reached an FA Cup final too.

But that tosser's name is not going to sully this memoir. So let's move on.

## Chapter Three

# RHAPSODIES
# IN BLUE

MORRISSEY, the pop star not the winger, didn't do feel-good pop.

The Smiths' downbeat classic 'Every Day is Like Sunday' was reportedly inspired by a Neville Shute novel, about a group of people waiting for nuclear devastation in Melbourne.

But that 1987 hit might well have been about Southport.

Check out the lyrics…

*"Trudging slowly over wet sand*
*Back to the bench where your clothes were stolen*
*This is the coastal town*
*That they forgot to close down."*

Southport hasn't closed down. But it is struggling to recapture a past when it was a vibrant seaside resort vying with nearby Blackpool for the attention of tourists.

In 1984 I'd graduated from Preston Poly as the proud possessor of an NCTJ certificate in journalism, with 100 words per minute shorthand, had spent one year as a news reporter at the Formby Times and started my sports journalism career on the sportsdesk of the Southport Visiter.

The town had a huge fun fair, an open air swimming baths, a zoo, and rows and rows of elegant shops like Russell and Bromley, Broadbents and Debenhams, on a Lord Street thoroughfare modelled on a Parisian boulevard.

Now the fair is a significantly scaled down version, the zoo has closed, so has the open air baths, Broadbents and Debenhams have gone and Russell and Bromley is a Wetherspoons pub.

And the town's newspaper, the Southport Visiter, is now a website rather than a paid-for weekly which was published on a Friday and shifted around 20,000 copies a week.

Chain-pipe-smoking sports editor Alan Prole, my colleague Jon Ball, a young man who could accurately be described as a rugby-loving bon vivant, and myself were responsible for the sports pages then for the Vis, its Midweek counterpart, the Bootle Times, the Crosby Herald and the Formby Times.

I spent three blissfully happy years there.

I moved into a flat with my girlfriend, a news reporter called Christine Talbot, who went on to become a highly respected TV presenter with Look North and then Calendar in Yorkshire.

The Southport social scene was buzzing. And Everton were about to emerge from the considerable shadow cast by their neighbours and, under the inspirational management of Howard Kendall, become a side voted European Team of the Year by influential French football magazine L'Equipe.

During my solitary year as a news reporter with the Formby Times I even got to visit the great man's home in Argarmeols Road. Sadly Howard was out.

Years later he invited me in to share a bottle of wine on New Year's Day while Manchester United were entertaining Blackburn Rovers on TV.

We'd stumbled across from the nearby Freshfield pub and the frosty atmosphere created by Howard's then wife, Cynthia, suggested that Howard bringing 'a pal' home from the pub wasn't an entirely welcome surprise.

It shouldn't have been an experience Cynthia would have been all that unprepared for.

I was once told a tale, possibly apocryphal, of how Howard – as warm hearted an individual as you could ever hope to meet – had once bumped into a desperately upset Bobby Davro in a Liverpool city centre hotel on Christmas Eve.

The comedian was upset because he was in panto in Liverpool and was spending Christmas night on his own in a hotel.

So Howard took him home, offered him the services of his front room couch, and retired to bed, neglecting to inform his already-sleeping missus of the surprise awaiting her when she wandered in with her morning coffee on Christmas Day.

But on my first visit, in 1984, Howard was out.

I'd been asked by my news editor to interview Mrs Kendall and produce a lifestyle feature on what life was like married to English football's then pre-eminent boss.

Cynthia spoke articulately but guardedly – and sadly didn't divulge any anecdotes about Bobby Davro having kipped on her couch.

This was an era when a sizeable drinking culture existed in English football. And it was even more evident in journalism.

The El Tonel wine bar, Pizzeria Mamma Mia, the Sundowner nightclub, later to become the Kingsway Casino, and the Hesketh Arms and Bold pubs in Churchtown were all frequented frequently.

But the focal point was undoubtedly the Baron's Bar of the Scarisbrick Hotel.

Journalists, bankers, businessmen and players from Southport cricket, rugby and hockey clubs all congregated there most days, in the left-hand corner of the long bar.

But Friday lunchtime was undoubtedly the liveliest gathering of the week.

The Visiter was printed on a Thursday evening then, which meant that Friday was a very easy going day.

There would be a bacon buttie from Marie's Cafe on Tulketh Street, read the paper to check for any howlers, line up a few features for the following week, then head for the Baron's Bar.

Such was the throng who gathered every week that hotel staff decided it was a good idea to introduce 'Friday Club' sandwiches – free butties brought round on a couple of salvers to encourage the visitors to carry on drinking.

The Friday Club actually became 'a thing' – with embossed membership cards distributed and Rene and Renato's crass chart-topper 'Save Your Love' adopted as a club anthem. Whenever the song was played on the juke box a pint had to be held over the drinker's heart.

Membership cards had to be carried at all times – and if a member called a card-check and somebody didn't have their card on their person, fines had to be duly paid into a charity jar.

A card-check was once called during a lull in play in a Lancashire Hockey Cup final – and all bar one player had their card safely stuffed inside a sock or underwear!

An astonishingly alcohol-fuelled Friday Club Christmas dinner was always held on the first Friday of every December but that was all sensible fare compared to the weekly practice of bar diving.

The production of Friday Club butties every week usually convinced the drinkers to have 'just one more'. And the continuation of drinking led to weird and wonderful bar games.

None were weirder, or more wonderful, than bar diving.

The mahogany-topped bar along the Baron's was adorned with false medieval torches, the kind of things warriors would carry into battle.

They were mounted on the walls above the bar – at exactly the right height for a drinker to hold onto should he or she decide to climb up onto the bar, turn and face the room.

And plenty did.

Because then you could brace yourself like a downhill skier about to set off down the giant slalom, before launching yourself as far across the room as humanly possible like some kind of sozzled superman.

Don't wince. There would 'usually' be two teams of 'catchers' lined up like a guard of honour, hands clasped, ready to catch the human missile.

And as far as I recall, a local PE teacher called Colin Pimlott held the record, 18 beer mat lengths from the circular fire place in the centre of the bar room.

Now I said 'usually'.

Because one poor soul, who routinely arrived after a large

49

round had been started and always departed before it was time to stand his own, was punished ruthlessly for his parsimony.

Encouraged to make his bar diving debut he enthusiastically accepted.

Except this time the team of 'catchers' lined up either side parted like the Red Sea as he hurtled arrow-like through the air.

I can still see the look of horror on his face as he curled up into a foetal position to try to minimise the injury to his knees as he crash-landed.

And I can still recall the forced smile on his face as he hobbled out of the bar, trying to act like he was in on the big joke.

J.P. Hartley was spot on. The past IS a foreign country. They do things very differently there.

And drinking for prolonged periods on Friday lunchtimes can be a dangerous pastime.

Fortunately this was an era when pubs closed between 3pm and 5pm, so we either had to head back to work for two hours to dry out, or over zealous drinkers, and soaks, could visit an all-day drinking club called The Office – apparently so-named because you could sincerely call from there and say: "Where am I calling from? Oh, I'm still at the office."

It was down a side alley off Lord Street, a doorman genuinely slid back a peephole before allowing you in, and it was very sleazy, populated by the kind of people for whom drinking was not just a pleasure but a necessity.

Footballers would never be seen in there. Although they would occasionally pop up in Baron's Bar.

Shortly after Howard Kendall had decided to replace FA

Cup winning left-back John Bailey with the ruthless Pat van den Hauwe, a man for whom the nickname 'Psycho Pat' was entirely appropriate, the pair popped up together in the Baron's.

Bails did what Bails does, chatting and joking engagingly with everyone within earshot, while Psycho Pat did what Psycho Pat did, staring at everyone menacingly, like some kind of latter-day Lee van Cleef eyeing up a shoot-out rival.

Then somebody made the bizarre decision to inform Pat that we were actually a group of local journalists.

The eyes closed into sinister slits, the stare became even more intense – tumble weed may or may not have blown across the bar – and Psycho Pat marched intently over.

"Any one of you fackers writes anything about me and Bails being in here drinking today and I'll facking kill you. You got that?" he snapped in his curious blend of Bermondsey and Belgian.

We agreed instantly. We were Evertonians after all.

Then Bails ambled over to calm down his team-mate and tell us that Pat was an alright kind of guy, really. Just a little high spirited.

Anyone who witnessed him floor Simon Stainrod at Loftus Road in the title winning season of 1984/85 with a punch which would have floored a horse would entirely agree.

Queens Park Rangers were the opposition that day and even with 10 men – Van den Hauwe was correctly sent off along with the unfortunate Stainrod, who might as well have been carried off on a stretcher – Everton drew 0-0.

By the time Everton faced QPR again that campaign, the

Blues had played 28 matches in all competitions, won 23, drawn four and lost just once, a seven-goal thriller at home to Chelsea.

They had reached the FA Cup final, European Cup Winners Cup final, and were on the brink of being crowned league champions for the first time in 15 years.

Bizarrely, the day Everton clinched the 1984/85 league title against QPR was not an all-ticket game. And by this time, a period in my career when I often reported on Marine FC for the Crosby Herald, I didn't have a season ticket.

My matchday ritual then, in the days when I wasn't reporting on the Mariners, was to watch Football Focus at 12.20pm, get the train to Bank Hall, walk down Rumney Road and take my place on the Street End an hour before kick-off.

Except on May 6, 1985, for that match against Queens Park Rangers, I sat horror-struck as John Motson declared at 12.21pm: "And Goodison Park is already close to capacity as Evertonians cram into the old stadium where a win will see their team crowned league champions for the first time since 1970."

I rang my friend, John Coyle (Peter's younger brother). We both ran for the station. We alighted and ran down Rumney Road. And we arrived at Goodison Park barely 40 minutes later to discover that Motty hadn't been kidding.

While 32,085 had watched the previous home match against Norwich – and 32,657 were there for the next one against West Ham – most of the biggest gate of the season, 50,514, were already crammed into Goodison Park to see history in the making.

John and I surmised that there may be space in the away section in the Park End, as QPR fans surely wouldn't be travelling in numbers for this one?

Except the queue for this section was vast – and very few fans in the queue were from West London.

Sensing crowd disturbance possibilities, Merseyside Police were asking everybody in the queue for their address, and when it was my turn I muttered "24 Uxbridge Road, Shepherd's Bush" in the worst cockney accent since Dick van Dyke chirped jauntily for Mary Poppins.

But lumme, it worked. You'd better Adam and Eve it. I was ushered in. John, however, failed the Londoner test. Maybe he shouldn't have called the officer 'me old china'. Ironically John followed Norman Tebbitt's advice soon after, "got on his bike" and became one of the thousands of Scousers who actually did relocate to London, where he still lives to this day.

As soon as I found my way onto the terrace I sought out a police officer at the front, told him I was in the wrong section – and he shoved me through the gap in the metal fence into the Everton section alongside.

As a result I was behind the Park End goal when Derek Mountfield smashed a ball gleefully in off the crossbar to create another significant slice of Goodison history.

That was an era crammed with so many giddy highs.

Bayern Munich, victories over Liverpool, another league title in 1987.

But the one moment which will always stand out came at the centre-point of a memorable weekend in London in May 1984.

The last-minute FA Cup semi-final winner over Southampton at Highbury had sparked scenes of unprecedented delirium.

But at Wembley on May 19, 1984 I witnessed something I had never seen before. And I also experienced a sensation I had never felt before – or enjoyed since.

I had been to Wembley twice before. And I was still waiting to see a goal scored, by any side.

In 1977 Everton drew 0-0 with Aston Villa in the League Cup final. That was the final when a bright spark from the Football League decided it was a good idea to dispense with the need for extra-time. To be fair, Everton and Villa could probably have played until it went dark and not scored.

Then in 1984 I was in the Liverpool section at Wembley (long story – I'll explain later) for the 1984 Milk Cup final.

This time there was extra-time. But again it finished goalless.

So I was still waiting to celebrate a goal at English football's spiritual home when I made my way onto the West Upper Standing Enclosure on Saturday, May 19, 1984.

I made my way steadily. Unlike many of my travelling companions I was 'relatively' sober.

Watford were the opposition that afternoon and Evertonians were in the rare position of going into a big match without a sense of fear or fatalism.

Yes the Hornets had John Barnes, and Maurice Johnston, and a full-back in Lee Sinnott who could hurl throw-ins from the Wembley touchline to the moon.

But we KNEW we were going to win. Fourteen long years of hurt, schoolground taunts and fans turning up outside my house to ask to see the colour of my scarf were going to be ended.

And I didn't want to be so pissed that I couldn't appreciate it.

Mike Clarke, Kev Dowd, Chris Hartley, Pete and John Coyle and co. weren't so picky.

When the Sherpa van we'd hired for the weekend pulled up outside Clarkey's house at 5am he came out holding a half bottle of Scotch in one hand and a Frankenstein mask in the other.

Dowdy was carrying as many cans of beer as he could manage and an Israel flag. Well it WAS blue and white – and as I discovered years later when I published a picture of that motley crew on social media he'd just returned from a spell in an Israeli kibbutz.

Chris' dad had taken one look at the Sherpa van, one of the last to be hired that weekend, and politely enquired where we were all going to sit?

Such trivialities hadn't even crossed our minds, but we were later grateful for the garden deck chairs he had tied to the bar which ran along the inside walls of the van.

The van also had a driver's side window which wound down, but then refused to wind back up. Fortunately the weather was pleasant for most of that weekend.

The man enjoying the bracing motorway air as he hurtled down the M6 and M1 was called 'Drive.' I still genuinely have no idea of his real name – other than that he was a relative of Kev's and he was happy to drive all weekend.

I bumped into him years later when he worked at Marks and

Spencer and I somewhat embarrassingly had to introduce him to my wife as 'Drive'.

He didn't seem to mind.

And we didn't mind as he drove all the way to The Green Man in Harlesden, a pub where Kev's brother, a man who bore an uncanny resemblance to a young Brian Clough, was 'known' and we were able to safely abandon the van for the afternoon.

I had a sum total of three pre-match pints.

Like I said, I wanted to appreciate the moment, I wanted to remember it, I wanted to be acutely aware of every facet of what promised to be a famous afternoon.

But I still wasn't prepared for the experience which consumed me when Kevin Richardson whipped in a cross from the left, the ball glanced off Lee Sinnott's head and Gary Stevens half-scuffed half-connected with a shot from the edge of the Watford penalty area.

The ball was flying wide until Graeme Sharp killed it stone dead with one sure touch of his left foot and then ripped a precise right footed shot in off Steve Sherwood's right-hand post.

I visibly saw the net ripple. In the pre-VAR days I KNEW we'd scored at Wembley, and a physical shudder convulsed down the length of my spine as that end of Wembley exploded into a paroxysm of pandemonium.

It really was a surreal moment. Chris lost his glasses. He was lucky. Other fans lost shoes. I'd seen Everton score a goal in a cup final, right in front of me. We were leading at Wembley and this Everton team wasn't going to give up that lead easily.

Andy Gray added a hotly-contested second midway through

the second half when he headed the back of Sherwood's hand from a typically precise Trevor Steven cross and bundled the ball over the line.

Watford fans subsequently made an issue of the moment but at the time there was little controversy.

It really was a 'friendly' final. There was a strange lull in the crowd noise about 10 minutes from time as a dawning realisation began to filter into the Evertonian psyche – we were actually going to win the FA Cup.

You had to be around in the 70s and 80s to understand how big the FA Cup was, how glamorous that competition was.

And Kevin Ratcliffe was about to lift it. The first trophy an Everton captain would lift during my conscious existence as an Evertonian.

I wept when he hoisted that sparkling silverware into the sky.

As the triumphant Everton players showed the trophy to the Watford supporters at the end of the match they applauded. The Everton fans applauded the Watford fans for applauding. Then the Watford fans applauded the Everton fans for applauding their applause.

It was that kind of day.

Then the celebrations began in earnest.

'Drive' was still driving, and for some reason we decided to try and find an old friend of Peter's who lived in Balham.

For those of you who know your London geography, Balham is a long way from Wembley. We failed to find him.

But we had a rare old night, and around midnight parked the van up on a street which ran through the middle of Clapham Common and all got our heads down in the back of the van.

It was far from the most comfortable night's sleep anyone had ever had – but when you've just won the Cup it doesn't matter.

It didn't matter either that because we'd travelled south of the river, 'Drive' somehow found his way onto the M3 and it was only when someone spotted a motorway sign which read 'Southampton 48 miles' that we asked him if he really knew where he was going and perhaps we'd better head north?

He did and we arrived home on Sunday evening, well after the trophy parade around the city had ended.

Either way, your sacrifice that weekend is still appreciated 'Drive'.

## Chapter Four

# THE WAY WE WERE

THOSE three halcyon years in the middle of the 1980s was a period when Everton didn't just achieve parity with neighbours who had dominated Europe for almost a decade – and ensured my school years were tormented – they looked down on them.

During the calendar years of 1984 through to 1987 Everton faced their fiercest rivals 15 times (without counting the spurious Screen Sport Super Cup. And come on, how can you count a competition in which Howard Kendall had to field back-up players like Peter Billing, Warren Aspinall, Kevin Langley and Ian Marshall just to fulfil the two-legged final fixtures?)

They lost just four.

Everton beat Liverpool three times in the 1984/85 season alone – at Wembley, Anfield and Goodison – and won a couple more times at Anfield in 1986 and 1987.

And every match was contested with a neon-hot intensity.

But the atmosphere on the terraces was different to today. Yes there was tribalism, but there was little sick chanting masquerading as banter, or the need to segregate supporters at derby matches, as has happened in recent collisions.

I travelled to the 1984 Milk Cup final in a car evenly split with Blues and Reds. And ended up sitting on a bench in the Liverpool section of Wembley Stadium.

I don't recall any discomfiture or need to sit on my hands, neither did the young lad who sat next to me at Maine Road for the Wednesday night replay – in the Everton section – and leaped insanely to his feet after Graeme Souness volleyed a winner right in front of us.

He sat down again fairly sharpish afterwards but he needn't have worried. The most aggression he faced were a couple of stern looks.

The previous Sunday, for reasons which I've long since forgotten, I had a ticket for the Liverpool end of the ground, and wandered around Wembley Way pre-match that morning asking, "Any swaps?"

Eventually someone stopped and said: "Here y'are lad. I've got an Everton end ticket, I'll swap."

So we stood there in a footballing version of a Mexican stand-off, each holding our tickets tentatively out, neither wanting to make the first move.

If a movie director was filming the scene he'd have killed the music, stilled all the background movement and zoomed in on our eyes. Neither of us blinked.

Then I snatched his ticket at the same time as he snatched mine, but while I then looked down to scrutinise the ticket I'd just taken possession of, my duelling rival sprinted away with a turn of pace Kevin Ratcliffe might have been proud of.

The reason soon became clear. The ticket he'd given me was a fake. Not even a good facsimile. A fake ticket probably produced on a John Bull printing press. And even worse, it was STILL for the Liverpool end.

I had a dilemma. Did I try and gain entry with a clearly fake ticket, or try and buy another outside the ground?

Then I heard the greatest pearl of wisdom I think I'd ever heard uttered at a football ground.

"There's a turnstile round there taking cash, lads. He's taking fivers off anyone."

So I sprinted around to the designated turnstile and chanced my arm. I wasn't taking chances. I offered a tenner. I can still see the perplexed look on the young turnstile operator's face as he weighed up the risk versus reward, and then pressed his foot pedal and allowed me in.

I was euphoric. Until I realised that I had only gained entry to a concourse for a lower tier stand, and there were stewards also checking tickets before you gained entry to the seats.

Fortunately I was far from alone in my method of entry to the stadium – and when a group of fans surged past the stewards I smuggled my way in with them. As a result I squeezed on a bench designed for half-a-dozen fans along with at least a dozen others.

It was cosy – but it meant I had an unimpaired view of Alan Hansen blocking Adrian Heath's goalbound shot on the Liverpool goal-line with his arm midway through the first half.

Referee Alan Robinson's view was clearly very impaired because he gave nothing.

But there was no furore. No raging. And at the end of the

match both sets of fans really did join in with a chant of "Mersey-side, Mersey-side, Mersey-side!"

It was exactly the same in the two Charity Shield matches of the era. And the FA Cup final of 1986.

Ian Ross, a fine reporter who briefly shared the same sports desk as me at the Daily Post, was an impartial observer that afternoon and he reported: 'Long before referee Alan Robinson brought a nerve-jarring two hours of fiercely competitive football to a halt, officials at the famous stadium had dubbed this first-ever all-Merseyside showdown 'the friendly final' – and how right they were.

'A combined lap of honour in front of a sea of blue and red was confirmation, should it ever have been needed, that whatever divisions may exist in Liverpool the proud people of a much maligned city are united by their common love of sport.'

John Bailey, Everton's man of the match that afternoon in March 1984, recalled: "The moment I'll take to my grave is when I walked out of the tunnel. The noise, the cheering, the red and blue everywhere, no segregation. You couldn't see that anywhere else in the world.

"At the end of the game I ran around the ground with Alan Kennedy, with a blue scarf and a red scarf tied together above our heads. I remember the fans singing and it still brings a lump to my throat thinking about it now."

And mine.

Did the venue provide the motivation, a desire to prove to the rest of the country that Scousers weren't the volatile, aggressive types, years later caricatured by Harry Enfield?

Or did both clubs' domination of the domestic game nationally at that time ease the local rivalry?

It would take a sociologist to examine the cause and effect, but the mood undeniably changed after that – and it is difficult to pinpoint exactly when.

Five years later, the first post-Hillsborough derby match provided another ringing endorsement of mutual respect.

'LFC thanks EFC. We Never Walked Alone' was one banner typical of the mood that night.

But in the FA Cup final a month later there were suggestions the mood was subtly shifting. Pitch invasions at the final whistle prevented the triumphant Liverpool team enjoying a lap of honour.

Even so, subsequent derbies were still not accompanied by the level of hostility which later existed.

By the mid-90s, an air of resentment was evident on both sides. By the end of the decade the derby day atmosphere had soured poisonously.

Theories abound.

Many feel that as the historical significance of the Heysel tragedy on Everton's fortunes became apparent, their fans became increasingly bitter towards their rivals.

Some feel that Liverpool supporters, bred on a diet of almost unbroken derby success in the '70s, couldn't handle a brief period of Everton dominance.

Perhaps it's a lot more simple than all that.

A more partisan atmosphere was inevitable as soon as both clubs started slashing the allocation of tickets for visiting fans.

At the Wembley showpieces, the split was always 50-50.

In Anfield and Goodison derbies of the same era, away fans would always dominate at least one section of the stadium, with a healthy minority finding their way into other sections also.

Blue on the Kop? Red on the Gwladys Street? It happened more regularly than you'd think.

When Kevin Ratcliffe's daisy cutter somehow squirmed under Bruce Grobbelaar's body to break the deadlock in a vital 1986 Anfield derby, Liverpool instantly surged down the Anfield Road end to pressurise the Blues defence, while a sizeable chunk of Evertonians standing on the Kop chanted "You're a clown, you're a clown!" at the hapless Liverpool keeper.

There was no disorder.

But times – and the mood – were changing.

That outstanding Anfield administrator Peter Robinson remembers the time well.

"After Heysel and Hillsborough, ground capacities were reduced dramatically as all-seater stadia were introduced," he recalled.

"I think Anfield came down from 48,000 to 42,000. We were the first club to host a derby match after the changes and in order to satisfy our season ticket holders I think the only section remaining for visiting fans was a small standing area of 1,500.

"We reduced the allocation for away fans, but Everton did exactly the same."

All-seater stadia meant smaller capacities, smaller capacities meant smaller away allocations, and smaller away sections led to a small-minded mentality towards the now isolated away fans creeping in.

The derby day atmosphere deteriorated dramatically between 1994 and the following decade.

It used to be Anfield tradition for a fan to race from the Kop and hand Everton goalkeeper Gordon 'Honey' West a handbag before the derby.

Twenty years later, Evertonians dressed as jesters jogged onto the Goodison Park pitch and 'clowned' about with Bruce Grobbelaar.

Both sets of fans laughed.

Supporters in the nineties and noughties would have been more likely to scream for their ejection.

But it's not so long ago that relations were respectful. Look back again to the coverage of that historic Milk Cup final.

"Fans wearing red and blue travelled down together, shared the stadium together without having to be segregated, and returned home together.

"Everywhere was good humour and not a sign of the violence that has marred many cup final occasions in recent years.

"To consolidate the atmosphere of comradeship which showed a city united in adversity, the two teams did a combined lap of honour in front of the fans.

"Wembley boomed to the chant of 'Merseyside, Merseyside, Mersey-side,' as they did so.

"There were no cups or medals handed out, but there was one winner – the unique sporting spirit, witnessed by a worldwide TV audience, brought to Wembley by Merseyside."

Can that level of camaraderie ever be recaptured?

It's not a myth. It's not some sentimental, dewy-eyed view of how football fans used to be in this city.

The Merseyside derby was genuinely different.

It would be heartening if we could take a step back and reclaim that difference.

But I fear too many changes have taken place in football for that to happen any time soon.

Football, journalism, indeed society are very different now to how they were then.

## Chapter Five

# **THE FIRST POST**

IN a previous life Len Capeling had been a stand-up comic.

Using the stage name Tony Miller he performed on cruise ships, in cabaret clubs and small halls.

His humour during those days on stage must have been blacker than Dracula's cloak – and Sahara desert dry.

Because Len was the sports editor of the Daily Post when I started supplementing my income from the Southport Visiter by doing shifts on their sports desk.

And overseeing the sports desk of a regional daily newspaper was no laughing matter to Len.

Len took his job seriously. So seriously that he once insisted on filing his weekly column – a witty, well crafted and incisive read in which he took no prisoners – from his hospital bed just hours after coming round from open heart surgery.

When the surgeon who had performed the life-saving procedure demanded that Len rest, the stricken hack replied: "I am the sports editor of the Liverpool Daily Post. I wouldn't expect you to understand. It's a pressurised job. You wouldn't know what pressure is."

It was not a quickfire gag.

And you couldn't argue about the drugs in his system causing him to hallucinate because Len believed it.

When football and people's lives were concerned, Len Capeling was very much from the Bill Shankly school of thinking.

It was a seismic shift in outlook for me.

Writing for the Vis and the Crosby Herald I had been allowed to indulge my own writing style and technique, in what I hoped was a hybrid of local luminaries like Charlie Lambert and Ian Ross.

But when I started writing for the Post the requirements suddenly became much more stringent.

My first significant piece, a preview for the 1987 FA Vase final between St Helens and Warrington Town, was thrown back at me by deputy sports editor Trevor Peake. He snapped: "Look at what Albert Draper's produced for the Echo, that's what you should be doing."

Albert had quotes from former Manchester United star Tommy O'Neill, then patrolling the rearguard for Warrington, and some genuine insight from both camps.

I'd tried to get away with a bit of flowery prose. I learned quickly.

But there were lighter moments. There were plenty of what you may politely term 'characters' who revelled in that twilight existence of working 3pm until 1am shifts on Old Hall Street in Liverpool city centre.

There was a Daily Post features sub, let's call him Dai (name changed to protect his long suffering wife's reputation), who stood at his work station a couple of desks down from me. Yes, that's stood.

He believed it was poor for a person's posture to sit for a 10-hour shift so had his desk redesigned to enable him to stand while he worked. Stand in his brown felt trousers, stitched at home on a sewing machine, and blue T-shirt.

Dai commuted from deepest North Wales and during one particularly cold snap was found in the building's West Yard car park, asleep in his vehicle, having decided not to risk the icy North Wales roads.

The security guard who had popped out to check on his welfare couldn't help but notice that the front passenger seat had been removed from the vehicle.

"Have you had problems with the car?" he asked.

"Of course not," snapped the previously slumbering sub. "I had it taken out so my wife can't sit next to me. Can't bear that woman sitting by me when I'm driving."

It wasn't just his missus he couldn't bear alongside him.

Dai endured a fractious relationship with a fellow features sub called David Stuckey, a studious and inoffensive individual who for some reason rubbed his colleague up the wrong way.

Dai's revenge was palpable.

Underneath the leader column of every day's Daily Post a word game was published – a puzzle which involved an obscure word, with three possible definitions printed. The reader had to guess which definition was correct.

The word Dai chose shortly before he was due to leave the company was, a 'Stuckey'.

Check out any Oxford English dictionary and you won't find that word within, because Dai had invented it, as only Daily Post employees appreciated when they scanned through the possible answers:

A: A pompous know all.

B: A foolish oaf.

C: An interfering office busybody.

And the answer was revealed as: All three are correct.

But Dai was far from alone in the Daily Post character stakes.

There was the fabulously flamboyant theatre critic Philip Key, the cynical, world weary Scot Jim Lynch and even a librarian called Colin Hunt.

Yes, really.

Fortunately the real Colin bore few of the characteristics of the Fast Show character of the same name.

There was also a hard-drinking night news reporter called Ken Gibson who was quite possibly the first journalist in the country to hear of the Lockerbie jet disaster – and dismissed it.

Part of Gibbo's evening routine was to call the police press office every hour and the coastguard station at Hall Road every other hour, to enquire: "Hello Chix, what do you know now that you didn't know two hours ago?"

Fortunately a switched on reporter called Tony Storey was sat alongside him to hear the words: "Really? No, no, it's alright. That's too far north for us to cover."

"What's that Ken?" enquired Tony, to which he received the astonishing reply: "A sodding jumbo's just gone for a burton in jockland."

Tony immediately scrambled a team of writers to head north

while Ken got to his feet and murmured: "Spiral Staircase if you need me…" then headed over the road for the first of his evening tipples.

Brian Reade also worked at the Daily Post then. In 1987 the future award-winning Mirror feature writer and author was a charismatic downtable news sub, who used to croon passable versions of Frank Sinatra classics throughout his shift, and a genuinely decent version of Officer Krupke from West Side Story.

He was conservative and withdrawn by comparison to his peers.

And that was just the Daily Post. Separated by a wall of cupboards was the Echo and its myriad of daytime staff.

I quickly learned that while the Post and Echo shared an office, the rivalry between the 20,000-selling broadsheet morning paper and the 200,000-shifting tabloid evening paper was intense.

I did land one early 'exclusive', though, thanks to my Southport Visiter affiliations.

Every six weeks I would get my hair cut at a trendy salon on Lord Street. The same girl had been cutting my hair for a few visits and during the usual barber shop chit-chat, "No, I haven't been on holiday yet. Yes, the weather's a bit grim isn't it?" And "Yes, that new Channel Four show Brookside is very good isn't it?" Carol asked, "So where do you work?"

I gave my role just a little top spin: "Oh, I write about football."

She countered with a penetrating return: "Oh that's interesting, because my husband plays football."

"Oh yeah?" I replied, with a gentle lob. "Does he play for Southport, because I've written about them?"

She smashed a forehand winner right through my defences.

"No. He plays for Everton."

It's impossible to fall out of a barber's chair with a shawl wrapped around you. But I almost did.

Carol's surname was Bracewell. And she was the hairdresser responsible for the coolest style change in football at that time, when Paul Bracewell's floppy fringe and regulation side part was replaced in the summer of 1985 by an American GI-style shaved back and sides flat top.

Bracewell had been one of the heroes of the 1984/85 season. Mention 'that pass' and any Evertonian will know what you're talking about, the glorious volleyed, crossfield exocet exactly into Trevor Steven's path for a third goal against Sunderland in 1985.

But that summer he returned to training with a new hairstyle, and his already significant standing in the Everton 'cool' stakes was elevated a couple of notches higher.

Carol became my regular hairdresser and it was during one of our six-weekly chats that she told me Paul was "popping over to San Francisco for a few days."

Bracewell hadn't played for 18 months as a result of a mystery ankle problem which no English experts could fathom, so Everton had decided to send their midfielder to a world expert in the field in the USA.

And Carol had kindly desposited the information into my lap.

I'm sure I would have landed a full-time job on the Daily

Post sports desk without delivering that story…but it didn't do my standing any harm.

And on April 7, 1987 I received 12 pages of A4 paper through the letterbox, which began: 'Dear David, I am pleased to offer you the position of sports sub-editor/writer on the Daily Post, effective from April 8, 1987 subject to our receipt of satisfactory references.

'You will receive an annual basic salary of £9,209 plus the opportunity of earning Productivity Bonus with a fallback figure of £624 per annum.

'Your first six months will be of a probationary nature, successful completion of which will result in your appointment being confirmed.'

It ended, 'Finally, I would like to wish you a long, happy and successful career with this company and although I shall not be here to witness it (the editor offering me the job, Jim Mansell, was joining the Daily Star) I know you will make a significant contribution to the Daily Post.'

I don't know quite how significant my contribution was to the Daily Post – it didn't fold until December 19, 2013 after all – but I know I was one huge Derek Mountfield-sized stride closer to landing my dream job.

Six days after that letter dropping through the letter box of my Birkdale flat I was sat proudly alongside Phil McNulty in the Goodison press box, as Everton demolished West Ham 4-0 to move within touching distance of their ninth league title.

Peter Reid curled in a stunning left-footed finish from 20 yards and quipped afterwards: "I thought I'd show Kevin

Sheedy and Liam Brady (both on the pitch that day) what a left foot was all about."

A week later I was in the South Stand at Villa Park, part of a small travelling army of around 10,000 Evertonians as Kevin Sheedy showed Peter Reid exactly what he could do, regularly, with his left foot. He crashed in the only goal of the game from 20 yards to put Everton on the brink of their second league title in three seasons.

That title was duly clinched at Carrow Road on Bank Holiday Monday. The following Saturday, Luton Town made a concerted, but fruitless, attempt to spoil the title celebrations at Goodison Park, with me watching on from the Gwladys Street (no fake cockney accent needed this time). Then I persuaded Len to let me loose on the nannies for the final, meaningless, match of the season on a Monday night against Tottenham.

'Nannies' was one of those curious journalistic terms which you still hear occasionally amongst older hacks.

It's cockney rhyming slang. So clearly I was perfect for the job. Nannies is short for Nanny goats. Which rhymes with 'quotes.' Obviously. And it was my job to gather the post-match quotes while Phil was filing his match report on the final whistle.

Nowadays Premier League post-match reaction is heavily formalised. Managers speak to TV, they speak to radio, and then they attend a post-match press conference packed with journalists.

Rules were less stringent in 1987. Howard Kendall popped up to the press room at the top of three flights of stairs at

Goodison Park to deliver his assessment, but Spurs boss David Pleat had understandably gone missing.

With an FA Cup final against Coventry City just five days later the Spurs boss had 'rested' TEN of his cup final starting XI, Chris Hughton the only player considered robust enough to be risked in both matches.

This was the pre-squad rotation era and managers who didn't select a full strength starting XI for league games would be punished by the FA.

This was also the era of a curious journalistic system, known as the local mafia.

As far as I know it only existed in sports journalism circles. Many of the regional national newspapermen joined forces – in the era of intense circulation wars – to protect their jobs. With a sense of self-preservation verging on the paranoid, if one reporter got wind of a story they would usually inform their rivals, to ensure that they were never 'scooped'.

Sports editors were usually complicit. Their newspapers would rarely enjoy an exclusive. But equally they could go to press at night safe in the knowledge that they weren't going to have to rip up the back page and start again when the first editions landed because a rival had a different story.

At that time the Daily Post was not part of the Mersey mafia.

So when I became aware that some of the nationals had spoken to David Pleat about his team selection I had to go hunting.

Access to the inner sanctums of football stadia was altogether more liberal in the 1980s.

Reporters could loiter outside dressing rooms waiting to quiz footballers as they emerged, and they were allowed to wander freely along the players' tunnel, which is where I spotted David Pleat as he emerged from one of the side rooms off the Goodison tunnel.

He was walking quickly and purposefully towards the Tottenham dressing room so I pounced. "Excuse me Mr Pleat could I have a quick word?"

Without breaking strike the Spurs boss said: "Yes."

Breathlessly I carried on: "Are you concerned about possible FA punishment for the team you selected tonight?"

"No," replied Mr Pleat, before he disappeared inside the Spurs dressing room, the door closing soundlessly behind him.

Well, it was a reaction. A little light on depth and insight admittedly. But a story nonetheless.

Despite the lack of depth to my first quotes piece I soon graduated to fully blown match reports, on top of my subbing shifts looking after the Daily Post sports pages.

The two years I spent at the Daily Post were enjoyable, entertaining and enormously educational. But 3pm-1am shifts play havoc with your social life when you're 25, so when the opportunity came to move on to the Echo I jumped.

This time I received a significantly shorter letter of appointment, maybe underlining my new paper's more tabloid approach.

A letter dated March 31,1989 confirmed:

'I am writing to confirm your appointment as a sports sub-editor with the Liverpool Echo. The appointment will take effect from May 1. Yours sincerely Brian Hill.'

Len Capeling gave me a couple of books as a leaving gift. I

am told it was an act of generosity which had no precedent during his sports editorship so I was genuinely touched.

But even more importantly, I was another step closer to the dream job.

## Chapter Six

# DISTANT ECHOES

MY job description in my first role at the Echo was 'sports sub editor' – which meant I had to sub-edit other writers' copy.

Which was fine. But all I really wanted to do was write.

So I sub-edited other writers' copy – but I also volunteered to write features about synchronised swimming, produced stories about local snooker stars and pestered the Echo's esteemed boxing writer, Syd Dye, for opportunities to sit ringside with him whenever possible.

I love boxing. The noble art has been my second favourite sport ever since I sat glued to my television set as a child watching the greatest sportsman ever to walk this planet, the peerless Muhammad Ali.

He never visited Goodison Park, like the actor who played another celebrated heavyweight, Rocky Balboa, did many years later, but he did clown about with a group of Evertonians in Hyde Park on the morning of the 1966 FA Cup final, ahead of his own showdown with Henry Cooper. So, like Sylvester Stallone, he was clearly an honorary Evertonian.

I only ever got to see him in action through a TV screen.

But that was sufficient to forge an unbending fascination with the sport he represented and promoted.

The Greatest had hung up his gloves four years earlier when I sat ringside at the famous Liverpool Stadium for the only time, reporting on a Liverpool heavyweight hope for the Bootle Times.

The charismatic Noel Quarless topped the bill that night, but was stopped by Horace Notice in an eliminator for the British heavyweight title, watched by Notice's stablemate Frank Bruno.

I only later discovered that was the last professional boxing show to be staged at the Stadium before it tragically became an NCP car park.

As a result, when Syd allowed me to sit ringside for the West Lancs and Cheshire ABA semi-finals in 1989 it was at the atmospheric Everton Park Sports Centre.

It was an electrifying experience.

But it was also brutal. Sefton ABC middleweight John Jones, a classy and consistent performer, turned from one rugged clinch, coughed and spat out a pink, glistening, quivering piece of flesh onto the ring apron. I was convinced it could have been a piece of his lung. Of course he continued to box.

The flesh remained there, just in front of my blood-spattered note book, for the remainder of the evening, constantly reminding me that while two dedicated amateurs were producing what passed for entertainment for almost a thousand paying punters, they were also putting their health and lives on the line.

It was a lesson which never left me.

Much as I thrill to the bravery and marvel at the technical aspects of top class boxing, there's always the nagging fear that by celebrating the sport in print I'm encouraging the possibility of a young man or woman taking it up and suffering serious injury. Or worse.

One such near-tragedy involved a man I still call a friend. Carl 'Wildcat' Wright was returning from an unsuccessful British title challenge at the Sheffield Arena in 1997 when he slipped into a coma with a blood clot on the brain.

Fortunately he was with his trainer Chris Moorcroft, and just as fortunately he was near to Liverpool Hospital with its exceptional neuro centre.

They saved his life.

But for years afterwards Carl had no feeling down the right side of his body, suffered from short-term memory loss and could not be left alone.

At the time of the near tragedy Carl's wife, Nicola, was seven weeks pregnant.

Five years later, during a fight for compensation with the British Boxing Board of Control, he said: "I used to love the game but I have nothing to do with it now. I haven't got the heart for it any more."

But it wasn't long after that that I started to see him at boxing shows again. And he still regularly texts to ask for views on upcoming title fights.

Boxing is a crack level addiction.

It's a grim balance that wordsmiths more erudite than myself can't come to terms with.

The magnificent Hugh McIlvanney tried, over four conflicted pages of his McIlvanney On Boxing book. Here's just a brief excerpt in which he discussed a ring tragedy which did end in a fatality.

'Anyone who imagines that Johnny Owen was under any kind of duress when he went into the ring for the world bantamweight championship match with Lupe Pintor of Mexico that led to Owen's death in that same autumn of 1980 simply did not know the boy. He was, as it happens, an extreme example of someone who desperately wanted to box. His personality was a small cloud of reticence until he entered the ambience of boxing, in a gym or an arena. Once there, he was transformed from a 24-year-old virgin whose utterances tended to come in muffled monosyllables into a confident, skilled practitioner of a rough but exciting trade. It may be – as I suggested in the hours after seeing him disastrously injured at the Olympic Auditorium in Los Angeles – that Johnny Owen's tragedy was to find himself articulate in such a dangerous language. But the people who say he should have been denied access to that language run the risk of playing God.

'Maybe I should not be drawn to it, but I am, and I acknowledge no hypocrisy in deciding in 1980 that I could be at graveside in Merthyr Tydfil when Johnny Owen was buried and at the ringside in New Orleans a fortnight later when Roberto Duran met Sugar Ray Leonard. Our society will have to become a lot more saintly before the abolition of boxing qualifies as an urgent priority. And until it does I'll feel entitled to write the kind of pieces that follow.'

If you feel the need, seek out the entire chapter. It's as close as you're ever going to get to a justification of boxing.

For a handful, boxing can offer wealth and success.

That same year my notebook wasn't bloodied, but the gallant Paul Hodkinson's eyes were when Syd allowed me to cover Hoko's world title challenge to Marcos Villasana in Manchester.

That was in an era when a world title challenge from a Merseyside boxer was rare. John Conteh had been Liverpool's last – and only – world champion in 1977.

But I was fortunate enough to work through a golden era for Merseyside boxing.

Hoko lost that challenge to Villasana but then became a world champion on a glorious night in Belfast a year later.

He was followed by Shea Neary, Colin Dunne, David Burke, Peter Culshaw, Derry Mathews, Tony Bellew, Robin Reid, Paul Butler, and even two members from the same family, Liam and Callum Smith, as Mersey boxers to sport W-something initials on their belts.

Carl's brother Paul, captured the Central Area title. There were also countless British, European and Commonwealth champions.

And, virtually to a man, the boxers I dealt with throughout that 30-year spell were helpful, courteous, communicative and utterly dedicated individuals who appreciated the value of publicity.

You might raise an eyebrow at that, especially if you witnessed Tony Bellew lurch at rival Nathan Cleverley during a televised press conference, venomously spitting the words "you fucking rat" at him, or threatening to climb out of a boxing ring to brawl with David Haye at ringside.

But you need to know boxing and boxers to understand the curious dynamic which accompanies this most primeval of sports.

Tony is a clever man. And, as he showed in the Hollywood movie Creed, he's also an excellent actor.

A lifelong Blue, I bumped into him outside Wembley in 2012 and introduced him to my wife and children, and after several minutes of urbane conversation he moved on to chat charmingly with other fans on Wembley Way.

My wife declared incredulously: "That lovely, engaging, friendly man is the fighter who screams at people on TV?"

He was. But Tony is much, much cuter than people believe. And boxing is also a very complex sport.

The need to sell a fight – and generate the income to feed your family – is almost as important as the work a fighter produces inside a ring.

And Tony was as good at selling fights as he was at ending them.

Boxing is tough, grim, brutal and occasionally rewarding. It fosters fitness, respect, discipline and camaraderie. And it attracts dedicated, driven individuals.

It is also a sport which has produced some of the finest sports writing ever generated.

Check out that McIlvanney On Boxing, the short stories of F.X. Toole, Joyce Carol Oates – and the magnificent Norman Mailer.

I re-read Mailer's report of Benny Paret's tragic death often, and am consistently in awe of its quality.

Mailer was ringside for that Paret contest with Emile Griffith, and while he didn't snatch up a phone and bark out his report within seconds of that fight finishing, as McIlvanney did with many of his masterpieces, it is still a work of art.

Look at this excerpt…

'And Paret? Paret died on his feet. As he took those eighteen punches something happened to everyone who was in psychic range of the event. Some part of his death reached out to us. One felt it hover in the air. He was still standing in the ropes, trapped as he had been before, he gave some little half-smile of regret, as if he were saying, 'I didn't know I was going to die just yet,' and then, his head leaning back but still erect, his death came to breathe about him. He began to pass away. As he passed, so his limbs descended beneath him, and he sank slowly to the floor. He went down more slowly than any fighter had ever gone down, he went down like a large ship which turns on end and slides second by second into its grave. As he went down, the sound of Griffith's punches echoed in the mind like a heavy axe in the distance chopping into a wet log.'

Poignant. Chilling. Devastatingly sad. And utterly brilliant.

Only a handful of writers are gifted with such a rare talent – but that didn't stop me from offering my own views on some awe-inspiring spectacles.

One of the most stunning was the night Andy Holligan clashed with local rival Shea Neary for the WBU light-welter-weight championship of the world.

The 800 capacity Everton Park couldn't possibly hope to accommodate the volume of fight fans who wanted to watch.

And in early March 1998 a football stadium was an unlikely

option. So promoters John and Stephen Hyland, and their business partner Neil Munro, decided to erect a marquee on Stanley Park to accommodate 5,000 spectators.

Their vision was rewarded with a five rounds, two minutes and 42 seconds classic, watched by many players from Everton and Liverpool.

My report that night may not have the imagery, the metaphors or the poignant poetry of Mailer, but it WAS filed within minutes of me leaving the portable dressing rooms having spoken to each boxer.

Here's a chunk of it.

'In an age when bombast, hype and self-promotion are the watchwords in professional boxing, Shea Neary remained refreshingly humble after his sixth round stoppage of Andy Holligan. 'I'm a nobody. I'm nothing,' he muttered. 'Yet five and a half thousand people turned up to watch me.'

'It was the only thing Neary got wrong all night. He is a somebody – a WBU champion of the world for one.

'But to retain his light-welterweight title the former soldier, from Kensington, had to resist the most compelling challenge of his career from his one-time hero.

'Andy Holligan produced a heroic performance which left a grimly attritional contest in the balance right up until the moment when Neary delivered two meaty, cleaving hooks at the close of the sixth round.

'Just seconds earlier, Holligan had looked on the verge of victory – and that was the way an awesome boxing match had swung for the most compelling 17-and-a-half minutes of sport this city has seen for decades.

'The most fitting tribute that ringside observers could pay is that the contest lived up to pre-fight expectation.

'The 'super-tent' in Stanley Park was close to capacity – more than 5,000 fans witnessing a local dust-up which will have international reverberations.

'After six pulsating rounds of boxing, Neary finally prevailed.

'Neary launched a murderous fusillade of hooks at Holligan and, finally, inevitably, the challenger sank to one knee. He smiled grimly and tapped his gloves together, acknowledging the quality of the shots, but he refused to end his challenge there.

'He dragged himself to his feet at the count of nine – and demanded that he be allowed to continue.

'Referee Darryl Ribbink, an excellent WBU official, complied with the request, but there was no respite. Neary swarmed over the stricken challenger to finally end a compulsive contest.

'Ringside judge Glenn Feldman, from Connecticut, turned from his stool as the referee draped his arms around Holligan's shoulders and drawled: 'That was the best fight I have ever seen.'

'It was no American hyperbole.'

Glenn has officiated in some of boxing's biggest fights since then, having offered his verdict on fighters like Deontay Wilder, Tyson Fury, Floyd Mayweather and Manny Pacquiao – and he still keeps in touch.

He even became a long distance Liverpool FC fan as a result of that trip to Merseyside.

But boxing is like that. It's an easy world in which to make contacts, friends and lifelong acquaintances.

So was football. Initially.

My big football break came thanks to a lanky, pacy Tranmere striker called Chris Malkin – a young man who had swapped his career in a bank for the chance to play professional football.

Just four days before Everton were setting the seal on their title campaign, with that victory over monosyllabic manager David Pleat's Tottenham, Tranmere were preserving their Football League status with a dramatic victory over Exeter City.

That started the countdown on Johnny King's famous 'rocket to the moon'.

Tranmere embarked upon a run of form so impressive that they won one of the two Fourth Division slots available for the Football League's centenary celebrations at Wembley in April 1988. Then they stole the show at Wembley, beating FA Cup winners Wimbledon, a Newcastle team featuring Paul Gascoigne and were only beaten on penalties by eventual winners Nottingham Forest.

I received a shocking insight into the machinations of some elements of the tabloid press that afternoon, when a reporter from the Daily Sport 'interviewed' Rovers coach Ronnie Moore.

People who recall that softcore porn publication will know that the only nod towards 'Sport' was in its title.

So to questions like "So what division are you in?" Ronnie politely replied: "Division Four, you've done your homework haven't you?"

"What was it like playing against Gascoigne?" Ronnie: "I didn't, I'm the coach?"

And "What sex toys do you prefer?" Alright, that last one was made up – like most of the Sport's stories – but it shouldn't really have surprised me. Neither should Rovers' success.

That was the first of several trips to Wembley made by the upwardly mobile Rovers, culminating in a famous victory over Phil Neal's Bolton Wanderers in 1991 which secured promotion to the second tier of English football.

Chrissy Malkin was the matchwinner, steering in a shot from 12 yards in a moment so intensely celebrated that Rovers winger Johnny Morrissey insists he temporarily passed out on the pitch.

The goal earned promotion to what is now known as the Championship.

And it gave the Echo a dilemma.

Previously, Tranmere had been covered by local sports agencies, but now we had to decide if their status as a club in the second tier of English football warranted a full-time writer, following them home and away.

I resolved the dilemma by agreeing to fill two roles – continuing as a sports sub-editor in the mornings, but interviewing players, the loquacious Johnny King and writing in the afternoons. And following Tranmere home and away.

That spell between 1991 and 1993 honed whatever characteristics I later brought to my role as Everton correspondent.

Johnny King had created a wonderfully attractive team who played with three centre-backs, two out and out wingers and full-backs who supported and often overlapped them.

There were experienced senior pros in the squad, men like John Aldridge, Eric Nixon, Neil McNab and Mark Hughes.

In fact Aldridge's arrival at Prenton Park had more than a bit to do with my old sports editor, Len Capeling.

In his weekly column – the ones written from his desk rather than his hospital bed – he had constantly campaigned for an English club to bring Aldridge back from Real Sociedad and constantly suggested what a good fit Tranmere Rovers would be.

If Len didn't actually act as an unpaid agent, he certainly planted the seed in Peter Johnson's mind, a seed which germinated and ultimately bloomed.

But as the Echo's first full-time Tranmere correspondent I naturally gravitated towards and was embraced by the youngsters in the squad – Kenny Irons, Ged Brannan, Tony Thomas and Johnny Morrissey, whose brother-in-law I later learned was my strike partner for Leisure Sport! Small world, football.

After an unexpected 2-0 win at Brighton, relegated from the top flight the previous season, on the opening day of the 1991/92 season, Rovers went to Halifax Town in the League Cup. They won a seven-goal thriller, Aldridge adding to the two goals he scored on the south coast with a hat-trick.

Aldo was still an international class striker and Tranmere's transfer swoop was a truly inspired piece of business.

Whatever words I filed for the match report, regardless of how withering the assessment, it was always the one paragraph Man of the Match which caused most comment.

After that Halifax victory, Ironsy, Ged and Tank (Tony Thomas' entirely appropriate nickname) emerged from the players' lounge near the dressing rooms holding pints of lager. And they insisted on me joining them.

By joining them, that involved sharing a post-match pint as well as views on the match. They'd clearly spotted the new boy on the block and decided to see if a little post-match subliminal suggestion – and a couple of beers – would work.

Didn't they know I was a young journalist with a point to prove and an unbreakable code of journalistic ethics?

Clearly not. So did their post-match analysis influence me? The Man of the Match in the following day's Echo read: 'Striker John Aldridge caught the eye (caught the eye? He scored a hat-trick!) with an impressive display of finishing, as did Jim Steel for his unselfish approach play before being forced to retire with double vision at half-time. But the young man who earned the vote was KENNY IRONS for a commanding display of the midfield arts capped by a spectacular strike.'

Of course Kenny deserved the MOM that night. Hat-tricks can be over-rated at times, you know. I ignored the claims of another Aldo hat-trick after a 5-2 demolition of West Ham and gave the MOM to Johnny Morrissey instead. Aldo forgave me but warned that his wife Joan was going to kill me next time I called to do his column.

As a result of my affinity with the younger members of the squad I was invited to the players' Christmas party at Liverpool's now demolished Club Continental.

It was fancy dress, obviously.

Which led to a weird incident in the gents.

I loped in dressed as the Pink Panther, which caused initial difficulties because cocking my leg wasn't going to cut it. I had to disrobe almost completely before peeing. Pat Nevin was stood alongside me, dressed as a cat. Not a pink one. Just a regular, family pet cat. But being a bright sort Pat had hired a fancy dress containing a zip which allowed him to answer the call of nature without removing his costume.

He was still dressed from head to toe as a cat and I only knew it was Rovers' winger because I'd been party to the pre-club pub crawl when Pat had to remove his cat's head to take a sip of his drink.

As we stood, shoulder to feline shoulder, a Rovers fan wandered in, looked across and muttered. "Alright Dave. Having a good time? Alright Pat. Great costume."

Pat turned to me, perplexed, and declared: "How did he know? Have I got an instantly recognisable penis?"

I was lost for words.

Just a few years after cheering Pat Nevin on from the Gwladys Street I was stood next to him at a nightclub, in the daytime, discussing his manhood. Could life get any better?

Well, actually it could.

## Chapter Seven

# **FEELING BLUE**

MY first match as the Everton correspondent of the Liverpool Echo was on February 20, 1993.

Actually, in hindsight I don't think I was ever formally appointed. I stepped into the role vacated by the newly appointed sports editor Ken Rogers – and by the end of that season it was clear no-one was going to take it away from me.

I started by doubling up as the Tranmere AND Everton writer, which for the two-and-a-half months which remained of the 1992/93 season proved eminently practical.

Everton entertained Oldham on Saturday February 27. Tranmere conveniently arranged to host Newcastle the next day.

Tranmere went to Bristol City on Saturday, March 6. The Blues faced Coventry City – on the way home – the next day.

Then Tranmere travelled to Brentford on Tuesday, March 9 in west London. Everton's fixture the following night? Chelsea, just six miles along the Great West Road!

It was almost as if my doubling up act had been pre-ordained.

I was replaced as Rovers' correspondent at the end of the season when Tranmere missed out on joining Everton in the top flight in a heartbreaking play-off semi-final defeat by Swindon.

Everton underlined their capricious inconsistency with a run of fixtures which saw them end the season losing 5-3 at home to Queens Park Rangers, fail to score in three matches which ended 0-0, 0-0, and 0-2, then won 5-2 at Manchester City in the first Premier League match to see four goalkeepers used.

Covering Everton was going to be anything but predictable.

That run of fixtures kicked off the first of an unbroken run of seven years of watching the Blues. Home, away and abroad.

It became an addiction.

I was a single man when I started as Blues correspondent. I was married, with children, when I finally missed a match in 2000.

And even then it was a wrench, even if it was an insignificant home match with Derby County which broke the sequence.

Melanie, the soon to be Mrs Prentice, and myself had been invited to Radio Merseyside sports editor Ian Kennedy's wedding in Anglesey (a BBC sports editor getting married on a Saturday? In the football season? Bob Azurdia would have turned in his grave).

Melanie not unreasonably asked: "Do you really need to be at a home match against Derby County?"

The honest answer was, I didn't.

So I stood aside. Reluctantly.

I later heard that Everton had disappointingly drawn 2-2. But more importantly we had a great weekend. A bat flew around the dining room of the lovely traditional old hotel we stayed in, as baffled waiters tried to work out how to catch it.

The most visually stunning thunder storm lit up the North Wales skyline. And Ian and Debbie tied the knot in a beautiful ceremony.

A month later I stood aside again. This time for the long trip to Ipswich. The umbilical cord had been well and truly broken. But on February 20, 1993 I was a sports writing rookie thrilled with excitement.

The match itself was significant for a number of football reasons.

While I was starting an unbroken run of 339 matches covering the Blues (and that total didn't include pre-season friendlies, which I never missed either), Neville Southall was missing his first match for six years, a run of merely 212 successive matches.

Even more astonishingly, Villa's Earl Barrett lobbed a rare goal over Nev's understudy Jason Kearton.

I later got to know both Nev and Earl well. Both are very different personalities, but both are lovely, sincere individuals.

My father-in-law discovered as much when he sat for an afternoon at Goodison Park once, chatting to Earl.

"What a lovely man," he declared afterwards "but what a strange name?"

"Yeah, you don't hear of too many Earls, do you?" I shrugged. To which Poppy's face fell in dismay.

"Earl? Earl, you say? I've been calling him bloody Pearl all afternoon!"

Earl, such was the gentleman he was, had declined to correct him. Everton lost that match 2-1 and tumbled to 18th in the then 22-team Premier League table.

They were different days.

In Howard Kendall's programme notes for the next home match against Oldham he reflected: 'I think Sansom would be disappointed with the way the Villa goals came.'

It was a throwaway paragraph at the end of a full page of sincere observations.

Nowadays club media officers and spin doctors would ensure such honest criticism would never appear.

But Howard was right.

Kenny Sansom had been the best left-back in the country for much of his 19-year career. But his seven-match Everton swansong saw him enjoying one last payday.

Howard was always willing to take a chance on a player, though.

He was also very superstitious. The first home match I covered saw Everton recklessly toss away a 2-0 lead to Joe Royle's Oldham with a Neil Adams brace in the 87th and 88th minutes leaving Joe jovial and Howard convinced I was a jinx. Two games and just one measly point to report on.

Tony Cottee convinced him I wasn't a Jonah when he cracked a matchwinner past Blackburn's Bobby Mimms the following Tuesday.

Howard was only half-joking when he said to me in the tunnel afterwards: "You can come again now, son."

I was on a roll. Wins against Coventry and Nottingham Forest followed, either side of a narrow defeat at Chelsea, where Billy Kenny scored the only goal of his unfulfilled Everton career.

I was revelling in it. I was being paid for delivering my opinions on the team I loved.

And I was about to enjoy my first pre-season tour...

BALSTHAL is a picturesque Swiss village just 50 kilometres north of the capital, Bern. It boasts a pretty village centre which wouldn't have looked out of place on the cover of a chocolate box.

And in 1993 it boasted a train station, one hotel, two pubs. And a brothel disguised as a Chinese restaurant.

That curious conglomeration was the destination for my first pre-season tour with the Toffees.

Everton's recce probably hadn't looked too deeply into the operations at the 'restaurant' with the red lantern hanging outside. I'd always believed the 'red light' to be a dated cliche. So, too, did Peter Beagrie, when he went out exploring one evening.

His plaintive cry as he bounced into the Balsthal Hotel dining room will live with me forever.

"Gaffer! Gaffer! That restaurant down the road is a bloody knocking shop!"

Quite how he'd stumbled upon such interesting information remained unsaid.

Maybe he'd popped in for an Egg Foo Yung then followed that old journalistic watchword and 'made his excuses and left'.

Warned by their intrepid explorer the playing staff studiously avoided the venue for the rest of the week.

After all, they had a new season to prepare for.

And there were a couple of new faces in the first-team squad trying to catch Howard Kendall's eye and claim a place of their own.

I'd been used to Johnny King's garrulous and mixed metaphor-laden press conferences. He once likened Dave Higgins to a sheepdog shepherding strikers where they didn't want to go, compared Ian Muir and Chris Malkin to schoolchildren playing around the maypole, Jim Steel, and once described a patched up John Aldridge riding into battle as like El Cid, the dead warrior, his corpse strapped to his horse for one last cavalry charge.

But Howard was an altogether cuter operator with the media, particularly the local press. He had enjoyed a warm and mutually beneficial relationship with my predecessor, Ken Rogers, and as our plane climbed out of Manchester Airport, Howard leaned across the aisle to me and said: "Should have told you this before we took off son. We've got a striker on trial with us in Switzerland. A lad called Jack De Gier. We'll be having a look at him in the first match."

It was little touches like that which made Howard so popular with newspapermen.

During the halcyon days for him and Everton of the mid-1980s he would routinely delay his Friday press briefing until Kenny Dalglish had already spoken to the national hacks, then enquire: "Right, what line has he given you? Really? Let's see what I can give you which will knock that off the back pages tomorrow."

He was promoting his beloved Blues – as he did throughout his life – and also looking after the local press pack. Shrewd.

And then he also saved little nuggets for the local paper, like a new striker enjoying a trial.

A little digging when we landed (well, a phone call to my colleague, Ric George, who knew European football inside out) revealed that Jack's nickname was The Vulture, which was also the nickname bestowed upon the legendary Real Madrid striker Emilio Butragueno.

Could it possibly…? Could he…? Would history repeat…?

In a word. No.

The Vulture swooped to crash in a 20-yard volley against Swiss minnows Grenchen then hit the inside of a post for Tony Cottee to score another.

But the next day's Echo was unimpressed.

'All permed hair and perspiration, De Gier showed plenty of determination but his touch was lacking and he did not look like the answer to Everton's search for a new target-man.'

Yes, I was now offering sweeping statements on the eligibility of players to play for my beloved Everton.

Another tour trialist, the neat and tidy midfielder Shaun Brooks, also failed to catch Kendall's eye.

But Howard was casting the net far and wide to juggle his very limited resources to try and improve Everton's striking options.

Just six years after being crowned champions, Everton were, if not skint, operating on a tight budget. The absence of European football, dwindling gates in the pre-Premier League era and the money spent on players who couldn't cut it at Goodison had all taken its toll.

An indication of the financial juggling Howard was having

to conjure came when he called me into his Bellefield office the week before the 1993/94 season began and told me that Mo Johnston, a forward he had spent £1.5m on just two years previously, had been placed on the transfer list – for nothing.

MoJo was being offered a free transfer, effectively to try and free up more money on the club's wage bill.

Maurice's salary was considerable, as I discovered when I first spoke to him one evening in Formby's Grapes Hotel.

Maurice was sat with his father-in-law at the bar and far from the hell-raising, hard drinking, party animal reputation he had been saddled with, he was quiet, entertaining, self deprecating company.

Mind you, I never did see him out without the chaperone of his wife's dad. Maybe Mrs MoJo had found the way to tame him?

On this particular evening, Maurice held court. He was entertaining and he told us about the hard bargain he'd driven when he moved from Rangers in 1991 – and probably the reason why Howard had felt the need to move him on.

"I asked for the earth, I really did," he declared. "And they gave it to me. Everything I wanted they agreed to."

"So why are Everton so broke now?" I enquired.

"No idea," he smiled. And raised a glass.

But if he'd pushed Everton hard for every penny he could get, he was also generous with it. Or tried to be.

That same pre-season Everton played a friendly in Edinburgh against Hearts, and when I told Mo I'd booked a bed and breakfast for myself and my girlfriend who was making the trip with me, he was appalled.

"Bed and breakfast? In Edinburgh? Why?" he demurred.

"Because it's cheap," I said.

"Forget that," he replied. "The Balmoral is the best hotel in Edinburgh and the manager is a personal friend of mine. Say I sent you and he'll look after you."

It wasn't a throw away offer. Every time I saw him Mo reminded me, "Don't forget, say I sent you and he'll look after you."

So I did. And the manager had absolutely no idea what I was talking about.

We stayed there anyway. And the hotel WAS excellent.

And besides, it was surely the thought that counts?

Ironically Edinburgh became Johnston's next permanent destination, when Hearts agreed to take him on a free transfer from Everton. I wonder if the Balmoral manager ever asked him about the couple who turned up at their reception desk dropping his name?

The only striking arrival was a short-term loan for a big, powerful-looking striker from Southend called Brett Angell. Howard effectively made up his mind about him after 24 minutes of a 5-1 home humiliation by Mike Walker's Norwich City in September, a match which saw Toxteth's Efan Ekoku show off a stunning display of the striking arts as he rattled four goals, while Brett spent some of his time after stepping off the bench scrabbling around on his hands and knees in the Gwladys Street penalty area. Apparently the on-loan centre-forward wore contact lenses and one had been knocked out.

Whether that influenced Howard's ultimate decision not to make the loan permanent I never discovered.

But the financial juggling act he was trying to carry off reared its head – fatally – in December.

And absolutely no-one saw it coming.

The Blues had been understandably toothless for much of the first half of the campaign, scoring just 19 goals in 17 games when Southampton arrived at Goodison Park on December 4.

Tony Cottee scored the only goal of an uneventful afternoon to take Everton into the mid-table mediocrity of 11th place.

Then, to coin a phrase, it all went off.

Howard had already climbed the three flights of stairs to the Goodison press room to deliver his post-match verdict, as had The Saints boss Ian Branfoot.

The game was such a dull affair that questions were in short supply.

"I take it you gentlemen have not been impressed today?" said Howard. "Well don't worry about me. I'll be alright."

No-one gave the statement a second thought, until half an hour later. The Sunday newspaper boys were busy filing their reports, the national pack were stood in a circle discussing their lines, when the Daily Mail's Colin Wood spotted Howard coming back up the stairs again. He clearly had more information to impart.

"Let's talk outside, Howard, the Sundays don't need to hear this," joked Woody.

"I'm afraid they do," said Howard. Then delivered the bombshell.

He had resigned.

The most successful manager in Everton's history had cut short his second coming, and the reason was incredible.

The previous Tuesday Everton had been knocked out of the League Cup by Manchester United at Goodison Park, but Howard had tried to put a gloss on the evening by asking Alex Ferguson about the prospect of signing striker Dion Dublin.

Fergie wasn't letting the player leave cheaply, but he was prepared to do business.

Sadly the Blues board wasn't.

Maybe chastened by the money lost on the Johnston deal, they refused to back their manager's judgement.

Having been prepared to offer £3.5m for Duncan Ferguson earlier in the summer, they refused to hand over the £1.5m it would have taken to land Dublin.

And that left Howard in an untenable position.

That incident has still never been satisfactorily explained. Some say Blues board members had seen Dion Dublin playing in a reserve match and had witnessed a player who had recently recovered from a broken leg limping, hence their reluctance to sanction the deal.

Colin Harvey recently claimed in a podcast that his mate jumped because he was about to be pushed.

Whatever the reasoning, Everton were managerless.

Ken called in his years of reporting on the Blues to land an exclusive chat with Howard, who even posed for a picture from his Formby home looking suitably disconsolate.

Even on the day he'd left, Howard was still looking after the local paper.

I produced a comment piece lambasting the board for failing to back their boss, then mopped up the player reaction which was equally critical.

Tony Cottee, then a weekly columnist for the Echo, told me: "We would like to know what's going on? We have lost our manager and apparently Jimmy Gabriel has taken over, but no-one has bothered to tell us."

His information was accurate, even if the manner in which it had, or hadn't, been delivered was shoddy.

Jimmy Gabriel, the coach who had taken over for one match in 1990 when Colin Harvey had been sacked, and oversaw a 3-0 victory over QPR, was back in temporary charge.

It was a traumatic second spell.

It seems the old adage about 'never going back' applied to caretaker managers, too.

Jimmy later described his spell at the helm as like being handed the controls for Battlestar Galactica.

He couldn't get it off the ground, let alone into hyperspace.

Everton failed to score in their next six matches, losing five of them. And when Tony Cottee and Stuart Barlow finally ended the goal drought with goals at Stamford Bridge, Chelsea scored four to leave a team which had been comfortably in mid-table on December 4, on the brink of the relegation zone on January 4.

A new manager was desperately needed – and that 5-1 home hiding by Norwich City in September had clearly resonated with the Blues board. They turned to Mike Walker to try and revive the team's fortunes.

## Chapter Eight

# THE GREAT ESCAPE

THERE'S a neat football phrase which says 'he's having himself'.

It's a comment which suggests that the individual on the end of the barb is little self-consumed, pompous, narcissistic even.

It quickly became clear that Mike Walker was 'having himself.'

The former Norwich and now new Everton manager was expensively tailored, meticulously groomed, he even had the initials MW painted on the prime spot in the Bellefield car park – which caused him a little consternation when Mark Ward insisted on parking there.

But despite his inflated opinion of his abilities, or maybe as a consequence of, Mike was happy to continue with the morning media arrangement Ken had hatched during Howard's tenure, of the Echo turning up at Bellefield every morning before training for a 10-minute chat with the manager.

Mind you, chat suggests it was a two-way intercourse.

Mostly I'd ask one question and then Mike would talk at me for the remaining nine-and-three-quarter minutes.

Seeing a manager so frequently created an opportunity to develop lasting relationships. You start to see situations from their perspective, understand why they take the decisions they take – and try to reflect that in your copy. I forged several close relationships during my time as the Echo's Everton correspondent. Joe Royle and Walter Smith came to my wedding and I still speak to David Moyes today.

It's not an outdated concept.

In 2020 Wayne Rooney revealed: "With England, after Gareth Southgate took over, one of our first conversations was about the media. I said football writers should stay in the same hotel as the players to build more trust and create fairer reporting about the camp. I used my speech at the Football Writers' dinner to talk about trust and at the World Cup in Russia I was delighted to see Gareth make England more open to the media, with positive results."

Sadly, Mike Walker was less interested in creating any rapport. He's one of the few Everton managers who never offered his private phone number.

Maybe he simply wasn't there long enough for me to win his trust. Or perhaps my attempts at winning him over were clumsy.

When Everton were linked with signing the Brazilian striker Muller in the summer of 1994, my colleague, Ric George, was appalled.

In a time before the internet, when information on foreign players was so sketchy that then Southampton boss Graeme Souness once picked a man who claimed to be George Weah's cousin for 53 minutes of a Premier League match – he wasn't;

Ali Dia was football's most famous phoney – Ric was aware that Muller had some off-field skeletons lurking in his closet.

I tentatively tried to broach the subject with the new Everton manager, in the spirit of a concerned supporter rather than a journalist, and was shot down in flames.

"Mr Prentice, I am not in the habit of buying bad footballers for Everton Football Club," he declared.

I gave up. Although Walker's bold claim was later challenged when he signed Brett Angell, swapped Tony Cottee for David Burrows, and gave West Ham a cash top-up as part of a frankly baffling deal.

But Walker's 'reign' if we can give his nine-month spell as Blues boss such a grand title, started well.

The 6-2 demolition of Swindon Town, however, has to be put into some perspective. The team soon to be relegated after conceding a record 100 goals, was actually the better side at Goodison Park for long periods and even drew level at 2-2 despite playing half the match with 10 men, my former Southport and District league rival Andy Mutch having been sent off just two minutes into the second half.

Everton were knocked out of the FA Cup four days later by second-tier Bolton, managed a couple of home wins against Chelsea and Oldham, then collapsed as spectacularly as Mike Walker's reputation.

Everton lost five of their next six matches, the exception a grim goalless draw at Aston Villa. I say lost, Everton were actually excoriated 3-0 at Norwich and humiliated 5-1 at Sheffield Wednesday.

In hindsight, Tony Cottee's beautifully-rifled winner at West

Ham a month before the end of the season is one of the most important forgotten goals in Everton's history.

That kept Everton's head briefly above the relegation dead zone, but after defeats at QPR and Leeds and a stultifying goalless draw at home to Coventry the Blues were back in it again.

We were up shit creek. But we still had a paddle, didn't we?

We did, but it was slipping out of our grasp.

It was a horribly traumatic time.

Those who tell you football is 'only' a game clearly haven't lived through a relegation battle.

Everton had spent just four years of their 116-year history at that point outside the top tier of English football, and by 1994 had enjoyed 40 unbroken years of top-flight football.

But the prospect of losing that cherished status was close to breaking people.

We fielded scores of calls at the Echo that week from distressed supporters who just wanted some comfort, some confirmation that the unthinkable couldn't really happen, some words of hope.

We couldn't give them any.

Everton had to beat Wimbledon on the final day of the 1993/94 season – the Crazy Gang who revelled in rubbing the traditional big guns' noses in it, as Liverpool had discovered at Wembley a few years earlier – and still hope that results elsewhere went in their favour.

An unsavoury example of the heightened anxiety levels was presented at the Lord Daresbury Hotel the night before the match, when the Wimbledon team bus was burned out.

It was, presumably, meant as a stark message to the Wimbledon players. Don't play with fire or you'll get burnt.

Except this was Wimbledon, sixth in the table, on a run of seven wins from nine and promised a week on the ale in Las Vegas by owner Sam Hammam if they ended the campaign with a win.

They didn't do intimidation.

Swindon were already down, but Ipswich, Oldham, Southampton, Sheffield United and Everton all had a chance of joining them.

Oldham took the lead at Norwich, Sheffield United led 2-1 at Chelsea, Ipswich somehow held firm at runners-up Blackburn and Matthew Le Tissier did what Matthew Le Tissier does, scoring a sublime free-kick to draw Southampton level at West Ham.

None of this seemed even remotely relevant when The Dons took a 2-0 lead on a surreal afternoon at Goodison.

It really was a dreadful, ecstatic, awful and ultimately sensational afternoon.

The Stanley Park End was in the process of being rebuilt, so one end of Goodison was a building site, devoid of fans with only scores of supporters hanging precariously from the trees in nearby Stanley Park visible from that end of the ground.

They saw the incredible tension which enveloped that afternoon like a heavy blanket manifest itself in the mind of Anders Limpar. He ridiculously stuck out a hand to paw a corner away from Robbie Earle – who was stood a good six yards away.

There was still hope. The great Neville Southall was in goal and he got two hands to Dean Holdsworth's decently-struck penalty. But the half-screams of joy caught in the throats of the supporters who uttered them as the ball squirmed into the corner of the Gwladys Street net.

There was just one scream of anguish from a solitary female supporter when Gary Ablett hooked an absurd own goal into his own net a few minutes later. But it was chilling.

Dave Watson jumped into Paul Rideout trying to win one aerial ball, he jumped into David Unsworth trying to win the second ball, and Andy Clarke's awkward volley which was probably going wide anyway, bounced off the lunging Gary Ablett and span crazily into the net.

Want to know what utter, wretched desolation feels like?

Evertonians felt it in that moment.

But then Anders redeemed himself. Cynically, fraudulently and immorally. But he redeemed himself.

Limpar tumbled theatrically over Peter Fear's challenge (there is usually more contact on a busy train) and Robbie Hart pointed to the spot.

Redemption! Then I had a grim, dawning realisation.

Graham Stuart had been a near neighbour for a few months.

And he had confided with me over a pint several weeks earlier: "Guess who's on penalties now?"

"Not TC again?" I asked. Tony Cottee had missed two already that season.

"No, me," he said. "I can picture it now. I'll need to score a penalty to keep us up and my arse will be going."

That very same conversation raced through my mind when Mr Hart pointed to the penalty spot and chaos reigned.

Wimbledon had kicked the ball down the pitch in disgust

and it appeared at one stage like Neville Southall was going to take the penalty.

He strode down the pitch with the ball held out, as if he was offering to take it but waiting to see if anybody else fancied the responsibility of keeping 40 years of top-flight football intact.

'Diamond' fancied it.

He strode purposefully back to the halfway line, took the ball from Nev and headed back to the Park End penalty area.

There was a smattering of applause from some supporters who recognised the courage of a player putting his balls on the line, then there was a tense, nerve-shredding silence heavy with anxiety.

I was sick with worry for him. I needn't have been.

Hans Segers dived to his left, Diamond's penalty arrowed sweetly, decisively and perfectly into the other corner.

And the roar was primeval.

Diamond had neglected to mention to me during our Grapes conversation that his only other previous penalty kick had flown over a Stamford Bridge crossbar.

This one was perfect and gave Everton a platform.

What subsequently happened was plucked straight from the pages of a comic book.

Dean Holdsworth missed one sitter from six yards, fluffed an only slightly more difficult chance minutes later, Segers made a decent stop from Diamond, who then smuggled one off the line from Holdsworth – with his arm, claimed the Dons striker.

Then Barry Horne happened.

The man who Mike Walker insisted on calling, to Barry's

intense irritation, 'Horny', scored a goal which elicited an almost orgasmic reaction amongst the Goodison crowd.

Barry had scored a goal on his Everton debut 18 months earlier and told supporters at that time "don't expect too many more."

He had fulfilled that prediction by scoring precisely no more until he picked up a bouncing ball midway inside the Wimbledon half, pushed it forward off his thigh, then unleashed an absolute thunder-bastard of a strike.

A beautiful, season-saving, relegation-sparing thunder-bastard of a shot.

No other phrase does it justice. Even thunder-bastard underestimates the venom and the vicious swerve in Barry's exocet.

Hans Segers didn't stand an earthly.

And while Goodison exploded into paroxysms of joy, the thoughtful and the calculating Barry simply put his head down and jogged back to the halfway line.

He knew a winner was still needed.

And it came in unexpected circumstances.

With nine minutes of the season remaining Diamond tried to play a one-two with Tony Cottee on the edge of the Wimbledon penalty area. The ball bounced back to him off a defender and he lunged at it.

It was half shot, half block tackle, and Hans Segers horribly misjudged it. It spun crazily past him and the celebrations for Barry's goal were magnified by another 100 per cent.

It was incandescent ecstasy mixed in with profound relief mixed up with extreme elation.

And I was at work.

I'd been dictating copy down a phone line to copytakers at the Echo back in Old Hall Street all afternoon, where a team of subs were designing what may well have been a historic Football Echo.

Roy Wright was what used to be known in the profession as a 'good operator'.

In the days before quotes became known as nannies and printers were banged out of buildings when they retired, one of the greatest compliments you could receive from another journalist was that you were a 'good operator'.

Roy fitted that description perfectly.

He had two Football Echo front pages designed, plated up and ready to hit the streets.

Each featured the biggest point size I think I've ever seen used, before or since, on a newspaper page – to highlight one word.

Up until 4.25pm a page dominated by the word DOWN was sitting tragically on the bed, ready to go to print.

At 4.40pm it had been dragged off and replaced by the page dominated by the word SAFE.

When I emerged from Goodison Park more than an hour after the final whistle, having grabbed Diamond in the tunnel, hugged him and bizarrely asked him to sign my programme (the erratic, barely recognisable scribble underlines his state of excitement) that front page was being brandished by supporters like some sort of victory flag.

The decision to ask Diamond for a signature underlines my own state of mind. I have no idea why I wanted his signature on the programme.

But it wasn't a day for thinking straight.

Barely 45 minutes earlier I had been grasping a telephone receiver waiting to file half-a-dozen paragraphs of front page copy to the desk, but couldn't because I still didn't know Everton were safe.

Everton didn't just have to win, they also needed other results to go for them.

I knew Blackburn hadn't broken Ipswich down, Oldham were losing at Norwich but that still left another place to be filled and last we'd heard Dave Bassett's Blades were 2-1 up at Chelsea and therefore safe.

Then my colleague Phil McNulty screamed at me: "It's okay. Sheffield United have lost!"

After they led Chelsea 2-1 at half-time they'd slipped off our radar.

This was pre-Sky Sports Centre and internet days. We relied on radio stations and phone calls.

But Phil had heard confirmation from a radio feed.

I barked out seven pars of copy.

"There were unbelievable scenes at Goodison Park as Everton saved their Premiership skins by pulling back a 2-0 deficit to beat Wimbledon.

"The afternoon started disastrously for the Blues conceding two goals in the opening 20 minutes.

"The first, a penalty for handball against Anders Limpar, came after just three minutes. Dean Holdsworth scored despite Neville Southall getting his hand to the ball. The second was an own goal by Gary Ablett.

"Anders Limpar atoned for his earlier error by winning a

24th-minute penalty which Graham Stuart boldly converted to put the Blues back in the match.

"Everton struggled at the start of the second half until Barry Horne brought the house down with a superb 25-yard goal.

"The winner came nine minutes from time when Graham Stuart fired past Segers from 20 yards.

"The pitch was invaded by thousands of fans at the final whistle."

Okay, it wasn't Watergate. The Pulitzer Prize would have to wait because I was in a state of high, emotional excitement.

I then battled into Goodison Road, fought my way through hordes of cavorting supporters and headed off to the Childwall Fiveways to meet my then girlfriend to drink as many as was necessary to calm my jangling nerves. Which was plenty.

Last day relegation deciders are the most stressful football matches imaginable. Don't believe me? When Everton found themselves in the same position four years later the venerable Brian Labone couldn't watch.

A man who had played in a World Cup quarter-final, an FA Cup final and a man who had captained his team to championship glory had to leave Goodison Park and anxiously pace the streets as Everton scrambled the point against Coventry which preserved Premier League safety.

Relegation battles are hellish. And Everton had a few more to endure.

## Chapter Nine

# THE ORIGINAL SPEEDO MICK

THE 1994/95 season was the last Everton campaign which can accurately be labelled as 'successful'.

It ended with Joe Royle's Dogs of War triumphantly parading the FA Cup around Wembley Stadium on a memorable May afternoon, as Evertonians looked forward to a 42nd consecutive season of top-flight football. Yet Mike Walker's meek mutts could quite easily have earned the epithet of having been responsible for the most wretched season in the club's history.

Just 73 days after that dramatic and lucky escape against Wimbledon, Everton faced Bournemouth in a pre-season friendly – with exactly the same squad of players that hadn't just flirted with relegation, they had raised their skirts and assumed the position.

Vinny Samways arrived from Tottenham shortly before the season started, a bid to sign Muller got as far as the Brazilian striker arriving at Goodison Park – until he realised he'd have to pay tax on his already considerable wages, while Daniel Amokachi landed from FC Bruges a fortnight after the big kick-off.

So new faces were thin on the ground but football fans are eternally optimistic. And a month's rigorous pre-season training, buttressed by coaching and defensive drills from Mike Walker and his trusty lieutenant Dave Williams, would surely elicit an improvement...wouldn't it?

No.

I've written about that pre-season many times because, in hindsight, I still shake my head in bewilderment at what I witnessed.

It was only my second pre-season tour, so I was still unsure as to what was the norm. Subsequent excursions proved that what went on in Sweden, Germany and Italy was anything but normal.

Tony Cottee had been on many pre-season trips and his engaging 1995 autobiography 'Claret and Blues' offered a little insight into what he made of it all.

'Mike Walker was a firm believer in the continental approach to football, but I still couldn't understand why Everton arranged THREE pre-season tours abroad that summer,' he wrote.

'We spent nine days in Germany, seven in Sweden and three in Italy doing the wrong things, eating the wrong things and drinking the wrong things. It seems crazy to me.'

All true. But for a wide-eyed young hack enjoying trips to countries he'd never visited before, it was an eye-opening experience.

Everton kicked off their preparations with a short flight to Copenhagen – a lively experience in itself with notoriously bad-flier Paul Rideout mercilessly taunted and ribbed by his team-mates at every hint of gentle turbulence – then enjoyed a picturesque catamaran crossing to Helsingborg on the south coast of Sweden.

Well, most of the party did.

A couple of notable absentees soon became apparent when the team checked into the hotel.

As the players milled around reception, Mike Walker barked: "Right lads. On the training ground in 10 minutes for a loosener. Jimmy, Les, get the kit ready. Jimmy? Les? Where the hell are Jim…"

The realisation dawned that long-serving kit man Jimmy Martin and physio Les Helm had been left to unload the kit skips unaided at Helsingborg – and left behind.

Red-faced Les, a physio never afraid of injuring a player's pride – or his manager's – stormed into reception 45 minutes later to snarl: "There's a taxi outside. I'm not paying."

The manager paid for it, literally and metaphorically as the week wore on. That was just a foretaste of things to come.

Ian Snodin injured his ankle on the first day of training and begged to be sent home.

"No chance," said Walker. "You're staying here for team spirit."

"But I'll only get bored boss and be a nuisance," complained Snods.

"You're staying Snods, that's the end of it."

Walker surely regretted the decision when Snodin's ideas of injecting a little life into the tour became quickly apparent.

Late-night drinking sessions, pizza deliveries, midnight dips in the hotel swimming pool…Snodin did indeed become a nuisance to stoic room-mate Brett Angell. And to the travelling media.

I was sharing a room with my morning paper colleague Vic Gibson, and we'd told Snods he was welcome to join us for a glass of Bacardi or two that Vic had picked up from Duty Free should he ever get bored.

Snods had clearly got very bored. Early one evening the hotel room phone rang and Vic picked it up – but the caller clearly had difficulty making himself understood.

Was it a Swedish member of staff? Unlikely because they all spoke excellent English. Was it a bad line from back home?

Neither. It was an Everton footballer from a couple of doors down, evidently well refreshed, who was hosting a "bit of a party in our room" – and had remembered that the travelling press had a bottle of Bacardi going spare.

I took the receiver from Vic and negotiated a compromise. We'd happily bring the Bacardi along, provided we could join the 'party'.

A surreal scene awaited us in Snods' room. Brett Angell was suffering from a virus and was tucked up in bed looking like death warmed up, while a couple of bemused-looking local girls were sat on the other bed wondering what had happened to the party they'd been promised.

"Look Snods, we need some coke to go with the Bacardi," I reasoned.

Then Snods had a lightbulb moment. "Yesh, we can get shome from reception," he declared, his trademark Yorkshire burr abandoning him for the moment, and led the way, followed by Vic and then myself.

We trooped down the stairs and along the corridor, school crocodile style, until we hit reception, when I suddenly hit the wall like a soldier after shots had rung out.

Mike Walker was sat in reception enjoying a coffee with Anders Limpar and it took him precisely four nanoseconds to assess that his injured defender's stumbling gait wasn't down to his bad ankle.

"Snodin, you're a disgrace!" he roared. Ian's comeback was, in the circumstances, quite admirable.

"No gaffer," he replied. "You're a disgrace," his words suddenly attaining the clarity and crispness of a man who has dramatically sobered up. "The lads are bored. We're going stir crazy in here. We want a night out."

Walker, naively, complied.

Maybe he'd fallen for Snods' reasoning, perhaps he felt a little team bonding was in order, or maybe he just wanted to show off his tan under disco strobe lights.

Because Sweden in the summer of 1994 was in the grip of a heatwave, which was bad news for footballers training, but great news for their new manager who loved nothing better than soaking up the sun in high cut orange swimming trunks.

Now there is no dispute that Mike Walker liked high cut swimwear, way before Speedo Mick made them semi-acceptable, but there is some dispute as to the colour he sported. I'm convinced they were orange. Snods believes they were pink. Maybe Mike boasted more than one pair?

Regardless of the colour of his trunks, the manager's face was a deep, bronzed hue. Because he loved to sunbathe. During morning press conferences on his hotel room balcony I had to sit with my back to the sun so he could catch the full rays on his face, while he sprawled poolside after training, then topped up his tan in the evening on the hotel patio.

It was not behaviour guaranteed to earn respect amongst a group of footballers.

Goalkeeper Neville Southall, meanwhile, not a man to ever concern himself with the benefits of a tan, almost caught an unexpected bronzey in the most unusual of places.

Before a clash with a team of Swedish lower league minnows, Southall, irritated that his strip wasn't ready in time for his lengthy warm-up, threatened to walk out as he was if a kit didn't materialise instantly.

It didn't – and Southall was always a man of his word. Cue a hugely decorated Welsh international goalkeeper striding out in front of startled Swedish spectators wearing nothing more than boots and shin pads, a pleading kit-man chasing behind.

Southall himself was left behind when the players departed on a coach for the big night out Snods had astonishingly engineered – Big Nev didn't do partying or alcohol.

The rest of the squad did, though, spectacularly.

The team bus returned to the hotel several hours later minus a back window and 70 per cent of the party who set out.

They all returned from various Swedish outposts…eventually.

My stop-off point en route to the hotel involved a house party, with Ian Snodin and assistant manager Dave Williams.

The image of Williams practising imaginary drunken golf swings in a back garden as the sun rose on another glorious Swedish day will stay with me forever.

So will the memories of that tour. But Sweden was only the start.

Soon after returning from Scandinavia, the Toffees were off on their travels again, this time to Germany.

The team hotel was in a small, sleepy town called Wiefelstede – alongside a huge cornfield which might or might not have been responsible for the enormous amount of houseflies which infested every room.

A striker by trade, Tony Cottee spent most of his downtime with a fly swatter at the ready, assassinating insects and piling up mini-mountains of dead bugs.

But flies weren't the biggest complaint amongst the players.

A friendly match had been arranged against St Pauli in Hamburg – a four-hour coach journey away – which meant no opportunity for a pre-match meal.

The motorway service station which the team bus idled outside for half an hour en route didn't have the kind of refuelling required for top flight footballers – which meant that on only my second pre-season tour I was given an unusual pre-match task.

I was asked to surreptitiously ferry huge bratwurst sausages from a pitch side stall to a couple of decorated international footballers, without the manager's knowledge, of course.

Everton won 2-1.

"It's Dog and Duck United on tour," Neville Southall and Andy Hinchcliffe memorably quipped.

But if that tour was unusual, it was nothing compared to the Italian job which followed.

The Blues flew to Aosta, a frontier town in northern Italy, for a three-team tournament with a difference. Torino and Lazio were the opposition – and the difference was that the matches lasted just 45 minutes.

That was fine for the sides playing back to back matches, but one unfortunate team had to sit out for the best part of an hour while the other teams slugged it out.

Predictably that was Everton.

The Blues comfortably disposed of Torino 2-0 – then had to watch while Lazio and Torino fought it out, before dragging their rapidly stiffening limbs out to face the light blues.

They lost 4-0.

As if to make up for the lack of organisation of the tournament, the organisers tried to make up for it by arranging a night out for the management and press…which is how I ended up in a car being driven around the twisting, winding roads of northern Italy alongside Mike Walker and his assistant, Dave Williams, to an outdoor disco.

The management duo were certainly livelier on the dancefloor than their players had been on the football pitch just a couple of hours earlier.

It wasn't all drunken revelry, though. The Daily Post's Nick Hilton was my travelling colleague in Germany, and one evening he arranged a quiet pizza with Joe Parkinson and Gary Rowett, and asked if I would like to join them.

Both were young footballers who had signed from Wigan and Cambridge respectively in March, and both were trying to come to terms with life at a football club where the expectations, pressure and demands were utterly different to what they'd experienced in their brief careers so far.

"I knew absolutely everyone at Wigan," said Joe, "but here I don't even know all of the staff at the training ground."

Both were striving valiantly to make the switch from an environment where they had been the stars, big fishes in small ponds, to a huge football club which was now the focus of national rather than local attention.

Parky, predictably, had been christened Pie-man by his new team-mates because he hailed from Wigan, but Gary, cruelly, had been nicknamed 'Village', which was short for Village Idiot – a nickname bestowed presumably because he'd been a little slow on the uptake on his first few days at the club.

Both were endearing and candid company. And while Joe enjoyed a playing career which was on the brink of being recognised with international honours when a knee injury ended it, Gary went on to enjoy a solid career outside the top flight as a player and then an excellent career as a manager.

He was clearly anything but a Village Idiot. But dressing room banter is notoriously fierce in football, and those that don't handle it don't survive.

Those two innocent young footballers didn't just survive, they flourished.

The nicknames in that particular dressing room were weird and wonderful. Some were more obvious. Andy Hinchcliffe had a prominent chin, so was either called 'Chin', or welcomed into a room by bad Bruce Forsyth impersonations.

Anders Limpar was known as LS, which was short for Little Shit. Not because he was unpopular, he was actually an engaging and entertaining member of the squad, but because that's how his previous boss George Graham had referred to him.

Barry Horne was briefly known as Ted, after the pilot, Ted Stryker, in the film comedy Airplane (I never did get to the bottom of that one), Matt Jackson was 'Floppy' because he was so laid back and Gary Ablett 'Ninja', because he apparently resembled a Ninja warrior.

I took it as a sign of acceptance amongst the players that I was also saddled with nicknames.

Neville Southall, usually the creator of the cruellest, let me off lightly when he christened me TJ, after the William Shatner character TJ Hooker, because I had a quiff, while after I'd piled on a few pounds one summer I turned up at Bellefield one pre-season and was called Gazza.

Of course the real Gazza landed at Goodison several years later but before then I still had relegation battles, FA Cup wins and fights between team-mates to observe.

## Chapter Ten

# BLACK AND BLUES

FOOTBALL dressing room banter was, and still is no doubt, famously fierce. And in 1994 it wasn't just restricted to dressing rooms.

It also extended to hotel bars – and it could sometimes lead to punches being thrown.

Mike Walker was proving that the finish to the 1993/94 season he had overseen was no one-off, as the Blues made the worst start to a season in living memory in 1994/95.

Perhaps as a result of that perplexing pre-season, the Blues had drawn three, lost six and won precisely none of their first nine matches of the campaign – and then faced back-to-back matches on the south coast.

After a League Cup second round second leg at Portsmouth on a Wednesday night, the following Saturday they were due to play just along the coast at Southampton.

As a result the Blues had decided to stay in the area. And I'd managed to persuade my desk colleagues it was a good idea to stay with them.

I'd be in the right place to hoover up player interviews, I'd be able to contact the manager to check on injuries – and my role as the local hack who travelled everywhere with the team would be reinforced.

This was the pre-internet era, remember. Readers under the age of 30 may find it difficult to accept that any information we collected had to be picked up first hand, by speaking to a manager or a player, a club secretary or a board member, and club press officers wouldn't exist for a few years yet.

But it was also an age when football clubs didn't hide their players away behind closed doors. If you wanted to stay in the same hotel as a football team, you just booked a room.

So I was booked into the same hotel as the Everton team in Bournemouth after their League Cup hopes had been extinguished by an 88th-minute Paul Hall goal at Portsmouth.

After finding themselves 3-0 down in a Goodison Park first leg, the Blues had rallied to trail second-tier Pompey 3-2, then Dave Watson had headed a typically heroic opening goal in the second leg.

Extra-time was beckoning when, in the 88th minute, Ian Snodin was beaten by Paul Hall, a winger who made chain lightning look sluggish, to score a dramatic and decisive equaliser.

Everton went out 4-3 on aggregate, so the mood was already tense back at the team hotel.

Some players headed out into Bournemouth to try and find a late-night watering hole to drown their sorrows. Some went straight to bed, while Duncan Ferguson sat on a couch with his ankle packed in ice – and I attempted to break the ice with the Blues' new loan signing.

It soon became clear he was more taciturn Tartan than jocular Jock.

"Do you think you'll be looking to stay on after your three-month loan?" I enquired.

"I wouldnae thought so," he replied.

Then fellow loanee Iain Durrant got wind I was a reporter and quickly guillotined the conversation.

So I joined Ian Snodin and David Burrows, who were playfully bickering at the bar. Well it was playful, at first.

Snods had been baiting Burrows about his Liverpool links.

"I turned down Dalglish to sign for Everton," he crowed.

"Good decision that turned out to be," laughed Burrows.

"Certainly was," Snods hit back. "I won a title medal in my first season."

"I've got one of them, too," bickered Burrows. "And an FA Cup winners' medal."

Then as the beers flowed and the 'banter' became more and more pointed, the barbs became more cut throat until Burrows raised the stakes.

"We're out of the League Cup because of you," he snapped. "That lad went past you like you weren't there."

I cringed. This was getting personal.

But Snods was untroubled. "You're right. I was poor. Should have done much better."

Just as the crisis point looked to have passed, Burrows enquired with a tone of mock amazement: "You were in an England squad weren't you?"

"How did YOU get into an England squad?"

Snodin had been called up by Bobby Robson in 1989, but

an appallingly-timed hamstring injury effectively ended any hopes he might have had of an England cap.

And that was it. That was the kindling which ignited Krakatoa. The spark which lit the blue touch paper.

Snods leaped at Burrows, fists flying, his team-mate tried to fend him off and Duncan's pal, long-time Evertonian Tommy Griffin, had to jump in to separate them.

Tommy was a big man but it took all of his strength to hold back Snods who was flailing and snarling like a Tasmanian Devil.

A grim incident was given some comic lightness as Burrows' thick Brummie accent plaintively rang out through the melee: "I thought you were my mate?"

Snodin probably was.

But I'd heard of these volcanic eruptions before. When Snods was sent off against Charlton towards the end of the title-winning 1986/87 season, he tried to break down the visitors' dressing room door afterwards to get at the rival he held responsible for his red card. Then 10 minutes later he strolled out fully dressed and showered to deliver the most calm, collected and ice-cold interview.

Minutes after that Burrows outburst he was controlled, collected and cool once again.

That evening at Portsmouth was the last of the 201 appearances Snodin made for Everton while Burrows was back in the starting line-up for the trip to Southampton a few days later.

But Snods returned to the club permanently in the noughties, when the absence of on-field pressures meant that his engaging personality, his easy-going charm with supporters and his obvious passion for the club proved perfect qualities to become a club ambassador.

Back in 1994, without him in the side, Everton lost at Southampton, just as they lost at home to Coventry – when, of course, Dion Dublin scored – then lost again at Crystal Palace.

The Blues were rock bottom of the table with three points from 11 games – and it wasn't just on the pitch that things were unravelling.

The Z-Cars theme – Fritz Spiegl's evocative reworking of a traditional Liverpool folk song – had been accompanying the players on to the pitch at Goodison Park since 1962.

Until 32 years later and the first day of that 1994/95 season.

In an ill-conceived and ill-advised experiment, new chairman Peter Johnson thought he'd try to lift the Goodison atmosphere by playing a soaring, moody, classical piece of music. He chose the soundtrack to 2001 A Space Odyssey.

It was surely the decision only a man who had once owned a season ticket at Anfield could have made.

Z-Cars is as much a part of the Goodison Park fabric as the Gwladys Street End, St Luke's Church and Archibald Leitch's criss cross stand design.

Stanley Kubrick, the director of the 1968 sci-fi classic, had actually commissioned a score for his movie from Hollywood composer Alex North, the man who had composed the score for Spartacus.

But he neglected to tell North he had abandoned his work post-production in favour of the piece PJ liked so much – and the cuckolded composer only found out when he attended the film's premiere.

He probably looked a little like the Evertonians did as the players ran out against Aston Villa on the opening day.

The new regime realised the experiment had failed, so replaced it at the next match…with a version of Bad Moon Rising, a reworked version of the Creedence Clearwater Revival classic, penned by Swedish supporters who had helped organise that summer's pre-season tour.

It proved even more unpopular than Richard Strauss's classical composition and Z-Cars was reinstated, where it has happily remained ever since.

But Everton's status as a top flight football club in 1994 looked even less secure than Z-Cars.

After a home draw with Arsenal, Walker's men actually managed to achieve their first victory of the season – a 1-0 win over West Ham which was as streaky and as fortuitous as it was slender – and then ground out the grimmest of goalless draws at Norwich City.

Mike Walker believed the back-to-back clean sheets indicated his team had finally turned the corner.

They hadn't. The only lessons that Peter Johnson and his right-hand man Cliff Finch took from the Carrow Road bore was that both teams on show that night had effectively been created by the same man.

The about-to-be ex-manager of Everton Football Club.

## Chapter Eleven

# NO ORDINARY JOE

MIKE Walker was sacked on November 8, 1994, just three days after the Carrow Road draw and 72 hours into a two-week international break.

Peter Johnson already knew the identity of his successor, a man familiar to every Evertonian.

But while I knew the name, Joe Royle, I'd never spoken to the man personally.

Over the course of the next two-and-a-half years that situation changed dramatically.

I am a sports journalist and in 1994 I was the Everton correspondent of the Liverpool Echo, so it was my job to report everything I could unearth about Everton Football Club.

And Joe Royle made that job so much easier for me.

I was at home one evening shortly after he had been appointed when the telephone rang. "Hi Dave, it's Joe Royle here. I just wanted to make you aware that we've agreed a fee of £1.1million with Coventry for the transfer of David Burrows. The deal should go through tomorrow."

A little bemused, I muttered a word or two of thanks and put the receiver down.

Bollocks. A transfer deal being announced at the perfect time for the national newspapers. I'd be reading about it in the morning and getting my backside kicked for missing it. At least Joe had given me the chance to prepare my excuses.

These were the days when the Echo published four editions a day, the first leaving the printing presses at 11.30am, so I arrived at Old Hall Street at 7.30am, as usual, to scan the morning papers and see what I could follow up.

And there was no mention of David Burrows' move anywhere. Joe had dropped a transfer story right into my lap.

My delighted sports editor was able to take a transfer exclusive into morning conference and I set off for Bellefield with a spring in my step.

As was the routine under Joe, and then Howard and then Walter, and last of all David, I was ushered upstairs by Bellefield secretary Mary, crossed the dining room where a handful of players were eating breakfast and entered the little office that had been used by a succession of Everton managers since Harry Catterick.

The glass-topped table with the football pitch underneath the see-through surface had been replaced during Mike Walker's era by a more traditional wooden desk, but otherwise the scene was as it had been since Bellefield's construction.

But Joe's demeanour was altogether more cordial than Catterick's had ever been with the media.

"Hello son. Cup of tea? What can I do for you?"

I started: "Well first of all I need to say thank you. I thought you were ringing around all the press guys last night when you told me about Burrows. I didn't realise you were only telling the Echo."

Joe waved my thanks away. "Forget it son. I've got a catch-phrase 'support your local sheriff.' That's all I was doing."

Joe supported me throughout his tenure. And I supported him. And in doing so I felt in no way compromised.

When Everton were knocked out of the League Cup by York City in 1996 I used an easy metaphor about Everton's perfor-mance and the historic York street called The Shambles. I used words like 'shame' and 'the most appalling Everton capitula-tion in living memory.' And Joe accepted the analysis.

Yes, I worked for a local newspaper, read by fans who wanted to read good things about the football team they supported, but I criticised whenever I felt that the circumstances were justified.

The thing is, for more than two years words of criticism were rarely necessary.

If the Wimbledon match had been deemed The Great Escape, the 1994/95 season was its more improbable, unlikely, unbelievable sequel. It ended with the sight of an Everton cap-tain lifting the last piece of silverware to be paraded by the Blues, the FA Cup. That was followed by a sixth-place finish in Joe's first – and only – full season as Blues boss. And there was an unbeaten run in Merseyside derbies which stretched to fully nine matches, spanned nearly five years, encompassed Joe's entire reign as Blues boss and started with his first match as Everton manager, the first Merseyside derby of the season.

That was a wildly improbable night.

Everton were bottom of the Premier League, Liverpool were fourth.

Liverpool had scored 32 league goals, Everton nine.

The Reds had lost only three league games all season, Everton had won just one.

But Everton had an inspirational new manager in the dugout, and a centre-forward who was about to forge an unbreakable bond with the Goodison fanbase.

When Duncan Ferguson muttered that "I wouldnae thought so" to me in the Bournemouth hotel bar a couple of months previously, I think he genuinely believed it. His Everton arrangement was a three-month loan which suited both parties – he escaped the Glasgow goldfish bowl where he was awaiting a police charge for headbutting Raith Rovers' Jock McStay, and Everton acquired the kind of number nine their supporters considered their birthright.

Except we hadn't seen any swashbuckling exploits from Big Dunc or any feats of derring do. Until now. In true super-hero fashion he was saving it all up for when it really mattered, for 48 hours after he'd failed a police breathalyser after, according to Duncan himself, having "been on the lash Thursday, Friday and Saturday."

Duncan scored his first Everton goal, at the seventh attempt, and he did it against Liverpool, down at the Gwladys Street End, having leaped almost as high as the Street End crossbar to score a towering header.

It was his aerial presence which also created the second goal for Paul Rideout, and he left the pitch that night to the newly-created 'Duncan Ferguson' chant, with scores of young Evertonians hanging off him like some latter day Pied Piper.

I truly think that was the night he found a second home, discovered people who adored him and unearthed a place where he felt appreciated. And in Joe's words "became a legend before he'd become a player."

Almost three decades later he's still there. He just doesn't talk about it very often – and in 1994 he didn't like to talk about it at all.

I'd asked many times if Duncan wanted to say a few words for the Echo but he always declined. I thought I'd cracked it when he expressed an interest in watching the "wee boxer Paul Weir" challenging for the world light-flyweight title against Baby Jake Matlala at the Everton Park, and I secured a couple of tickets for him from the promoter.

He appeared genuinely grateful – but then didn't turn up at the show.

On one occasion Tommy Griff, the Bournemouth bar interventionist who had forged a lasting friendship with Duncan, suggested to me that his mate might, finally be in the mood to talk to the Echo. So I asked again – and I was stunned when on Friday, January 13, 1995, he said: "Aye. Come and see me Monday. We'll do it then."

I should have noted the date.

The next day Ferguson was harshly sent off at Highbury for the faintest of shoves on John Jensen.

I still went through the charade of asking Duncan to fulfil his promise on Monday morning as he strolled across the Bellefield car park, but the chance had gone. Forever.

This was the season that Blackburn won the Premier League with their SAS strike force of Shearer and Sutton. But in their own RAF forward line, Rideout and Ferguson, an Everton team which couldn't buy a win earlier in the season won three in a row with either Rideout or Ferguson scoring in all three.

It was an astonishing transformation, effected with exactly the same squad of players Mike Walker had bequeathed.

But Joe had made some significant switches.

Andy Hinchcliffe had started five matches all season and none since October 8, but he was immediately recalled and asked by his new boss: "Why aren't you in the England squad?"

He soon would be.

John Ebbrell had started three matches all season and none since August. He was immediately drafted back in, alongside Barry Horne who had bizarrely been asked by Mike Walker to start the home defeat by Coventry as a right wing-back.

Anders Limpar had started four matches all season, none since September, and was brought back into the fold and told he was "a genius" with talents on a par with "Michel Platini."

It wasn't just local journalists that Joe had a way of making feel good about themselves.

But not everyone was enjoying life under the new Blues boss.

My mate Diamond couldn't get a look in as the RAF ruled the airways up top and Parkinson, Horne and Ebbrell held a vice-like grip on the midfield slots.

Graham wasn't picked to start a match by Joe until February 1, and even then his appearances were sporadic, which is why he occasionally sought solace by "going on the lash." And like his team-mate, Big Dunc, one such session actually prefaced the turning point in his Everton career.

To chip a football deftly and delicately over an England goal-keeper's head from 20 yards takes precision, technique and a sure eye.

Graham had all three qualities on the afternoon of Saturday, April 1, 1995, which was a spectacular recovery because barely 39 hours earlier his balance had been weeble-like.

Diamond had been in the Grapes Hotel in Formby, well refreshed, along with his close pal Peter Beagrie, myself and the landlord Colin.

The tale is in no way a slur on Diamond's professionalism.

He had been bombed. He hadn't started a match for almost six weeks, since February 18 when he had scored the final goal of an FA Cup rout of Norwich, and hadn't even featured in the squad for Joe's last two matches.

So having received no hint that Joe had suddenly thawed in his appreciation of his talents, he decided to ease his frustration with a blow out.

We started in Formby, headed to the Kingsway in Southport where we bumped into Vinny Samways, also bombed by Joe, then ran into Peter Beagrie, then weaving his wing wizardry with Manchester City.

Thursday night in Southport was clearly a popular night for disaffected footballers.

When the bars in Southport closed we headed back to Formby, where Colin offered to open up the bar for a few private nightcaps.

Eight years older than Graham, and with nothing like a professional footballer's constitution, I bowed out at around 4am. Graham was still going strong, while Beagers was enjoying 40 winks in a comfortable leather armchair in the corner.

The following afternoon the phone invaded my pounding head.

"You'll never guess what's happened," said Graham. "He's only gone and named me in the squad. I'll have to go to bed and try and sleep this off. See you tomorrow."

Peter had no such luxury. He had to get a taxi home, then on to Manchester City's training ground where he boarded the team bus for the long drive to Crystal Palace.

The recuperative powers of a night in your own bed were clearly more restorative than a six-hour coach journey and a hotel room.

Graham wasn't just in the Blues squad, he was named in the starting line-up. And he justified his manager's eventual faith when he dinked that delightful chip over Tim Flowers to halve the lead champions elect Blackburn had taken at Goodison Park.

Down at the Palace, Peter was hauled off at half-time.

Diamond's display was enough to earn him a starting place in the following week's FA Cup semi-final. He produced one of his best performances to date at Elland Road, scored and was rarely out of Joe's starting line-up from that moment on.

Of course not all players respond well to an alcoholic pick-me-up.

Brett Angell enjoyed his first – and last – Everton appearance of Royle's reign at Loftus Road.

It was a cruelly curtailed appearance, in a match which

ultimately proved significant in keeping Everton in the top division, Andy Hinchcliffe curving a magnificent last-minute free-kick which earned a come-from-behind victory against QPR.

It was a clash Angell will probably remember vividly.

Whether he will recall what happened afterwards is less likely. Angell hadn't kicked a ball in the first team since September 1994 but he was finally given the opportunity to impress the new boss when Ferguson was injured for the trip to Loftus Road.

Big Dunc may not have been involved, but because Neville Southall was hosting a testimonial dinner in west London at the Swallow International Hotel later that night, he also made the trip south.

Angell did not enjoy a happy return to first-team football.

His control was rusty, his second touch usually a tackle, and when referee Kelvin Morton spoke to him after Angell had already been booked the Everton fans chanted: "Off! Off! Off!"

Joe Royle replaced him at half-time with Daniel Amokachi.

It was a humane hook, and Ferguson, watching the match from a hospitality box, tried to lift his crestfallen team-mate's spirits with alcohol. Lashings of alcohol.

It worked. Briefly. Until the Everton players had to congregate, several hours later, in a packed reception room at the Swallow International.

It was hot. It was claustrophobic. And Daily Post crime reporter and lifelong Blue Richard Elias, who had accompanied me to the function, turned and whispered in my ear: "I think Brett Angell has just been sick in that plantpot."

Richard needn't have been so discreet.

Angell's inflating cheeks quickly made it clear that his earlier chunder wasn't an isolated incident.

The big striker flailed helplessly looking for an exit, so his team-mates did what all team-mates would do – highlighted his discomfort, pointed and mocked loudly. I can still hear the anguished shout of one female guest screaming: "You're all mean! Help him out!"

Brett needed no help.

Showing a turn of pace and nimble footwork which had eluded him earlier in the day, he wheeled and plunged through a nearby firedoor. And never returned.

It was his last act I witnessed as an Everton player.

He joined Sunderland a week later, turning from fallen Angell, to an Angell of the North in one swoop.

Joe Royle later revealed the conversation he had enjoyed with Sunderland boss Malcolm Crosby.

"Hi Joe, it's Malcolm here. I'm interested in signing Brett Angell."

To which Joe, with his trademark deadpan humour. replied: "Sorry, Malcolm. There must be a fault on the line. I'm sure I just heard you say you're interested in signing Brett Angell."

Crosby retorted: "That's right. I don't really fancy him but we're desperate."

Angell wasn't the answer to Crosby's desperation. He failed to score for Sunderland, but a return to the Stockport stamping ground where he had first forged his reputation as a goalscoring centre-forward saw the goals finally flow again.

He plundered 60 goals in 157 appearances between 1996

and 2000 and then scored goals for Notts County, Preston, Walsall, Rushden and Diamonds and Port Vale, before playing his last league football, ironically, back at Queens Park Rangers.

Once again he failed to find the net at Loftus Road.

Some grounds are just plain unlucky for some players.

## Chapter Twelve

# THE FA CUP IN MY LAP

JOE always described keeping Everton in the Premier League as his most significant achievement as Everton manager.

It was. But no-one glories in avoiding failure. It was the spectacular gilding to the 1994/95 season for which Joe is most fondly, and rightly, remembered.

In 1995 the FA Cup still enjoyed much of the prestige, lustre and glory which had started to erode when semi-finals were staged at Wembley in 1991, and was fatally holed when holders Manchester United decided not to enter in 1999 in order to pursue world domination in Brazil. They failed.

Everton, however, enjoyed a glorious finale to a season which had at one stage looked like breaking their supporters' hearts.

In January Joe Royle had advised his chairman to have a wager on his team to win the FA Cup because they were going to be playing "cup tie football."

PJ followed the advice, but even he couldn't have envisaged the kind of cup run Everton enjoyed.

Everton's progress gathered momentum like a juggernaut with the handbrake off rolling downhill, slowly, imperceptibly at first but then accelerating into an unstoppable battering ram.

Derby were beaten 1-0, the most notable aspect other than Andy Hinchcliffe's late winner being the performance of the Rams' centre-half Craig Short, which caught Joe Royle's eye.

Then at Bristol City in the fourth round Everton survived an uncomfortable afternoon and looked happy to have earned a replay, until right-back Matt Jackson connected with the kind of volley he probably only ever dreamed about.

News of the World columnist Mystic Meg tipped Everton to win the FA Cup after that and the omens continued to add up. Having beaten the Rams and the Robins, Everton hammered the Canaries, edged past the Magpies and were thrilled to draw a team which sported a cockerel on their badge in the semi-final.

Tottenham Hotspur were that season's media darlings. They boasted box office stars (or should that be theatrical talent?) like Jurgen Klinsmann, Teddy Sheringham, Darren Anderton and Nick Barmby with the son of Everton's ex-manager in goal, Ian Walker.

If Walker was desperate to score a point for his dad, there was no doubt that many of the national media men also craved a Manchester United-Tottenham cup final.

One columnist even wrote: "I've looked into my crystal ball and never have I been so certain that we'll be watching a dream cup final of Spurs and Manchester United this season."

Unfortunately the writer of that column, the Daily Mail's Neil Harman, was in attendance at Elland Road that day, and just as unfortunately for him the Elland Road press box was an enclosed affair in 1995, reporters watching the match behind smoked glass.

That meant most crowd noise was muffled and asides uttered inside the press box were crystal clear.

Actually asides suggests that there was some attempt at concealing the words being spoken. There was no concealment as Royle's Everton produced one of the greatest performances any Everton team had ever turned in to utterly ravage Tottenham.

The final score was 4-1, and Tottenham's one – the only goal Everton had conceded on their cup run – came from the penalty spot when Klinsmann did what he did so effectively and fell like a puppet who'd had his strings cut when Dave Watson moved within half a yard of him.

My mate Diamond was inspired, Matt Jackson crashed a near-post header from one of Hinchcliffe's undefendable corner kicks, Joe Parkinson produced a divine drag back as Everton went into show-pony mode – and then there was the greatest substitution Joe Royle never made, Daniel Amokachi entering the field of play while Paul Rideout received treatment and scoring the first two goals of his Everton career.

After Amo's burst the Mersey press corps let their London counterparts know what they thought of the display.

I'll spare the writer's blushes because he's actually far more erudite in print, but he couldn't help himself as he shouted down the press bench: "Hey Neil, how's your fucking crystal ball looking now?"

It was a theme continued in the post-match press conference by a clearly delighted Royle.

"Sorry about the dream final, lads," he smirked. "But bollocks to you, and that's with a double-L."

It was an articulation of the Dogs of War, backs to the wall, us against the world spirit Joe had drilled into a squad of players who barely six months earlier had been feeling sorry for themselves.

"No need for that," muttered some of the irked analysts from the capital. But Royle was very cutely fostering a siege mentality which carried all the way through to the final.

United very nearly failed to fulfil their half of the dream final bargain when they trailed twice to Crystal Palace in their semi-final, needing a replay to eventually reach Wembley. But they were still 4/7 on favourites with the bookies to beat the Blues.

The final contained nothing like the drama or the free-flowing football of both semi-finals but that hardly mattered.

People only ever remember the winners in cup finals – and the trophy had blue and white ribbons tied to it at five o'clock that Saturday afternoon.

Yes, the FA Cup final was still played on a Saturday afternoon kicking off at 3pm in 1995, which meant that Evertonians could enjoy a legendary evening out in London town.

This time, though, I didn't sleep in a Sherpa Van parked up in the middle of Clapham Common.

I was working, if watching a football team you love win a trophy can really be considered as work.

But those same emotions which had caused that involuntary shudder down my spine in 1984 hadn't left me.

As I was dictating my six paragraphs of copy back to Old Hall Street, Dave Watson was climbing the 39 steps to lift the most recognisable piece of silverware in football into the skies. And I started to fill up.

I swallowed and tried again. But my voice was cracking with emotion and my eyes were filling.

In my defence I'd seen this group of players every single working day for the past two years, I'd travelled with them, drank with them and joked with them. I'd set quizzes for the coach journeys on pre-season tours and shared knockabout banter with them.

And I was as happy for them as I was for myself. The copy-taker who had listened to my emotion-choked words had also been happy to tell everyone interested back at Old Hall Street that "I'd lost it" and was "blubbing like a baby."

It isn't just journalists who exaggerate.

After finally completing my dictation I headed for the players' tunnel, where press were still allowed to mingle with players, and Andy Hinchcliffe made a beeline for me as he came out of the dressing room, bouncing like Tigger after a pint of Pepsi.

"Isn't this great? Isn't this incredible?" he beamed like a child experiencing his first Christmas morning.

Andy and Barry Horne were two of the more thoughtful, more cerebral members of that dressing room. But even they had given up on trying to rationalise the moment and given in to the uncontained glee that winning the FA Cup can bring.

Paul Rideout conducted a more considered interview for me, expressing his regret that Neville Southall had decided to spurn the post-match banquet to drive straight home, while

Duncan Ferguson tugged eagerly at his arm to pull him away and start the celebrations.

Neville himself reiterated his decision: "If you spent every day with them you'd want to go home as well," he only half-joked, then pushed his gloves into my hand.

"Put them in the paper," he said. "Auction them or something. But just get some money for Claire House or something for them."

So the Echo had an unexpected piece of extra content on Monday morning. And one delighted reader who pledged a sizeable donation to the Claire House Appeal collected a unique item of memorabilia. Or two.

Neville's altruism, which he displays frequently today via the social medium of Twitter, was very much in evidence in 1995, too.

I rang Neville every Thursday evening to gather his thoughts for a weekly column in the Football Echo. We paid him the princely sum of £70 a week, but he would let the cash build up until the end of the season – and then order me to donate it to a local charity. Anonymously.

I drove back to Merseyside after the match and opened a bottle of champagne when I got home. I'd grown up a little in the 11 years which had passed since Everton's last FA Cup win.

But there was one wonderful postscript to that FA Cup afternoon.

David Unsworth had recently moved into a house around the corner from me in Formby and when I got off the train at Freshfield Station one tea-time, his car sidled up alongside me and the window slid smoothly down.

"Hello mate, want a lift? Jump in. Just move that to one side when you get in," he said. And there, nestling on the passenger seat, almost iridescent in its sparkling beauty, was THE FA Cup.

I was speechless.

"Each of the players is allowed to have it for one night to get pictures taken with their family," he explained. "It's my turn tonight."

So Unsy drove me home with me proudly clutching the FA Cup in my lap.

Not many jobs have a perk like that…

## Chapter Thirteen

# THE ROYLE FLUSH

JOE Royle doubled his trophy haul in his very next match after the FA Cup final, Vinny Samways' cross-cum-shot beating champions Blackburn at Wembley in the Charity Shield curtain raiser to the new campaign.

But in many respects Joe's first and only full season as Everton manager was a frustration.

The summer signing of Andrei Kanchelskis had been a thrilling one. This was a player with absurd acceleration, a laser guided shot and a strong core which enabled him to run with the ball and resist the attentions of even the most dogged of defenders.

But after a month-long saga to complete his signing from Manchester United, he then sustained a shoulder injury after 14 minutes of only his third match and wasn't seen in an Everton shirt again until October 14.

When he finally did settle down he justified every iota of excitement which had been expressed prior to his arrival.

No player scored more league goals in a season for Everton until Romelu Lukaku arrived, exactly 20 years later, and his first two Everton goals came in a wonderful win at Anfield when Joe took his Anfield counterpart Roy Evans by surprise and started with both his talented wingers, Anders Limpar on the left and Kanchelskis on the right.

That was one of several stand-out Premier League performances that season that included a Boxing Day demolition of Middlesbrough, a five-goal stroll at Hillsborough and the last time Everton won at Arsenal – but the Blues couldn't add consistency to their undoubted ability.

And as a result, a place in Europe was denied on the last day of the season when Joe Parkinson crashed a late matchwinner against Aston Villa, but even later goals by David Platt and Dennis Bergkamp saw Arsenal retrieve a deficit against Bolton and the Gunners enter the following season's UEFA Cup.

And while the FA Cup had provided the highlight of Everton's 1994/95 season, the following season all three cup competitions offered desperate disappointment.

After easing past KR Reykjavik in the Cup Winners Cup, the Feyenoord of Henrik Larsson, George Boateng and a future Blues boss called Ronald Koeman won with a single goal scored over two legs, while any kind of run in the domestic cup competitions was ended by first Millwall and then Port Vale.

In a bid to while away a dull moment or two on the short-lived European excursions, Andy Hinchcliffe bet me that I couldn't insert phrases of his choice into my match reports.

I enthusiastically agreed, which is why the following sentence appeared about the frankly quite slick and lush playing surface in Reykjavik. 'Everton's jangling nerves were soothed slightly when Andy Hinchcliffe was knocked to the barren tundra of the Laugardalsvollur Stadium after linking smartly with Ablett, and Unsworth stepped up to calmly send Finbogasson the wrong way from the penalty spot."

In truth, getting the spelling of the Reykjavik arena right was more challenging than inserting the words 'barren tundra' into a report, which is why our 'game' was quickly abandoned.

But it indicated the level of intimacy I enjoyed with many of the Blues players, and if not a dressing room mole, Neville Southall certainly became a confidante during our weekly Thursday night conversations.

The routine would largely be the same. Neville would feign exasperation at me calling, tell me he could only spare five minutes, then 55 minutes later when I asked what the splashing noise was in the background, he'd say: "I'm on the bog TJ" or "I'm in the bath."

Neither were mental images I cherished.

But our conversations were always revealing.

After Everton terrorised Newcastle 2-0 on the opening day of the 1996/97 season, then let a 2-0 lead slip at Old Trafford to only draw 2-2, Neville revealed that Joe Royle had been furious.

"He said that if we're going to win the league we can't afford to drop points like that," he revealed.

Everton winning the league? Joe never voiced those ambitions publicly, or even privately to me at Bellefield, but it underlined the incredible change Everton had undergone in his tenure.

And it wasn't just Joe talking up Everton's title credentials that season. On December 16, Nicky Barmby nosed an 87th-minute winner at Derby County to edge Everton up to seventh in the Premier League table, eight points behind leaders Arsenal and level on points with eventual, runaway, champions Manchester United.

The match was screened live on Sky's Monday Night Football and Richard Keys asked afterwards whether Everton should be considered "dark horses for the title." Sky loved a drama, even then. But the significant point was that nobody laughed.

There were precious few laughs around Goodison Park for the next three months though and just 102 days later the man who had overseen so much progress at Everton and delivered the last trophy still to be paraded by an Everton manager was gone.

It still bewilders me.

Joe has had his say on what happened that transfer deadline day, when he was 'mutually consented', in his autobiography. Peter Johnson has largely kept his counsel but here's my take on what went on in those fraught 14 weeks.

The very next match after that Baseball Ground smash and grab – a goalless Goodison draw with Leeds – the enormously influential Andy Hinchcliffe tore his cruciate knee ligament. The next game after that, at Middlesbrough, Joe Parkinson sustained a knee injury which would end his career.

The influence both players exerted on that side could not be under-estimated.

In that Derby County match report I wrote: 'Joe Parkinson sounds like a name from a Charles Buchan annual but there's far more polish to his game than he's given credit for. His tackling possessed its usual bull terrier bite, but the passing was also authoritative and the shimmies and sidesteps neatly deceptive. After an outstanding first half, Parkinson's second half contribution was merely steady until he raced forward to join a promising late raid. The ball dropped for his left foot, a violent volley crashed against the crossbar and Barmby reacted quickest to meet the arc of the ball's descent to butt it past Hoult.'

Everton were about to lose that midfield generalship for good.

On the same bleak mid-winter afternoon Dave Watson limped off after 15 minutes, and his replacement Graham Allen was also forced off an hour later.

Joe was running out of bodies.

Diamond gave Everton the lead against Wimbledon but the aerially-efficient Dons were not a team you wanted to face with a makeshift defence of Marc Hottiger, Earl Barrett, David Unsworth and Gary Speed. Wimbledon won 3-1.

That prefaced a run of six successive league defeats, a sequence broken only by the welcome relief of a 3-0 FA Cup win over Swindon, a game in which a promising young defender called Richard Dunne made his debut.

Andrei Kanchelskis scored the first goal that afternoon from the penalty spot but there were signs that his patchy form up until then hadn't entirely been down to second season syndrome.

Earlier in the season Everton had suffered another cup upset, this time at York City in the League Cup, and so small was the press box at York's old Bootham Crescent ground that some of the press contingent were asked to sit on a school gym-style bench along the pitchside.

It was a wonderful vantage point to witness some of the instructions and messages being relayed across the pitch. So when Barry Horne exhorted Kanchelskis at a throw-in to track back more enthusiastically, that universal hand gesture so beloved of drivers when another driver has cut you up, which the winger delivered to his angry team-mate, was clearly visible.

"I wanted to rip his head off," Barry later confided. He didn't, but cracks were clearly starting to show in the team spirit which had proved so influential in the squad which had landed the FA Cup barely 18 months earlier.

If that Swindon Town success had provided some much-needed relief, it also earned a home fourth round draw against Bradford City.

And that was a spirit-crushing nadir for Joe.

It was also an afternoon when I think I was as depressed and distraught as I'd ever felt inside Goodison Park – and there's plenty of competition for that title.

Bradford won 3-2 and one of the goals proved symbolic, Kanchelskis robbed by an ageing Chris Waddle fully 40 yards out, who then promptly chipped the 38-year-old Neville Southall who struggled to get off the ground.

It was Kanchelskis' last act as an Everton player, while for Neville it was the beginning of the end of a glorious Goodison career. And as Goodison can do at times of crisis, the fans kicked off.

Some shouted into the press box. The usual demands. "Print the truth", "Not good enough" and "Do your job."

So I wandered disconsolately into the press room and did what I'd never done before in there. There was always a bottle of scotch and a bottle of gin mounted on pub-style optics on the wall. Press steward Ray and a couple of the more hardened national hacks were usually the only users but I collected a glass and poured myself a scotch, a large one, just as Vic Gibson sidled alongside me and said: "Some of the reporters have lost it out there. They're shouting back at the fans and agreeing with them."

Joe later blamed the Echo for a campaign against him but that wasn't the case. There was never a policy decision. While my colleague Phil McNulty was undoubtedly fiercely critical, I was spectacularly supportive.

We each had opposing views on what was happening at Everton and our sports editor was happy to showcase both points of view. That afternoon our views were diametrically opposed.

Phil bounced in, spotted the glass in my hand and said: "You'll be needing that."

Saddened, I enquired: "What line are you taking for Monday?"

Usually we'd discuss our themes so we didn't have two similar-sounding pieces in the same edition, but Phil made his plans patently clear.

"You write your piece and I'll write mine," he said.

So I did. I wrote the most passionate defence of Joe Royle I could muster.

Ironically it began: 'Royle must go.'

My Everton supporting editor, John Griffith quipped, "Nice intro. Not sure about the rest, though."

The 'rest' went: 'Easy isn't it? Now attempt a more difficult statement, like what you do once you've sacked the man who has presided over two years of topsy turvy Evertonia? Give a Goodison wannabe – Peter Reid say – two years in charge? And if he only wins one FA Cup before hitting a turbulent patch, boot him out as well? That kind of stability worked well for Manchester United didn't it?

'Saturday's shame, and that is the only word which can be used for yet another Cup defeat to a supposedly inferior side, turned Goodison whispers into screams. Screams of frustration at players. Screams of anguish at another Cup embarrassment. And screams of anger at manager Joe Royle. Everton are a club in crisis, no-one can deny that now.

'Mitigating circumstances could be put forward for some of the five successive Premiership defeats. They cannot for a catastrophic cup capitulation to a poor First Division team – and that's all Bradford amount to.

'But adopting the knee-jerk reaction of axing the manager would surely not improve matters. Not yet anyway. Peter Johnson is a supremely ambitious man. He appointed Joe Royle and has backed him with big money, but he will want a return for his investment.

'Patience, however, is the rarest commodity in modern football. Martin Edwards showed it when giving Alex Ferguson seven years to restore Manchester United to their current position.

'Football pressures have increased even in that short time,

though. Royle is likely to receive only 15 matches, from now until the end of the season, to prove his value.

'For what it's worth, I think Royle has already done that in his first two years at Goodison.'

I was a long way out.

Joe just had eight more matches of his managerial tenure to run. He won two, drew two and lost four, including the very next match at Newcastle when his reaction to the Cup defeat was tangible. He dropped Neville Southall for the first time in 15 years and axed record signing Nick Barmby.

By this stage Joe had also axed the press from attending Bellefield. Such was our relationship I was still allowed entry, but barred from asking questions of any depth or substance.

It was a curious few weeks. Joe would give me a squad news update, but then refuse to be quoted in the Echo. So we'd discuss Coronation Street, the bright young leader of the opposition party and what was happening elsewhere in the Premier League.

Joe couldn't buy any luck. Duncan Ferguson and Gary Speed gave the Blues a 2-0 lead at Southampton, but then two goals in two minutes, including an own goal by Craig Short, saw the game finish 2-2.

The following week Everton lost by the only goal at the scene of one of Joe's greatest triumphs, Elland Road, and in the Leeds goalmouth that day was Nigel Martyn.

David Moyes rated the former England keeper as the best signing he ever made at Goodison Park when he snapped him up SIX years later.

But Everton could and should have had the goalkeeper on

their books NINE months earlier than that 1997 clash at Elland Road.

Martyn actually arrived at Peter Johnson's Park Food Hampers headquarters on the Wirral in the summer of 1996, after Everton had agreed a fee with Crystal Palace to sign him.

But Joe had been forced to rush his wife, Janet, to Southport eye hospital the same day and Peter Johnson's right-hand man, Cliff Finch, was unable to persuade Martyn to delay his departure for Leeds, who also wanted to talk to the goalkeeper.

He signed for George Graham the very next day.

That afternoon at Elland Road, Martyn showed Everton just what they had missed.

A national newspaper match report read: 'Martyn had already produced an exemplary performance that included a textbook block on Michael Branch as the youngster had a free run at the goal, when he confounded Royle and Everton with a save of outstanding quality in injury time.

'Gary Speed was no more than six yards out when Paul Rideout's cross from the right reached him and there was little wrong with his header. The ball shot quick and low to Martyn's right but the keeper fell and stretched in a flash, his arm clawing it away to Speed's astonishment. Everton had been denied a point they deserved and dearly need.'

A bid to sign another goalkeeper had foundered just a month earlier.

Mark Schwarzer had been in the Bradford goal that fateful FA Cup afternoon, but Johnson refused to pay the £1.2million Middlesbrough were prepared to offer and another excellent goalkeeper went begging.

When Schwarzer made an outstanding debut for Boro in a League Cup semi-final against Stockport, PJ actually called Joe and joked: "He's really rather good this goalkeeper, isn't he? Why didn't we sign him?"

For once, Joe was speechless.

Joe finally got the win he needed when Dave Watson scored 11 minutes from the end of a home game with Derby, but a week later champions elect Manchester United won at Goodison Park.

And that was Joe's final matchday as Everton manager for 20 years...when he proudly stood alongside David Unsworth in the Goodison dug-out against Norwich City.

No-one saw that last day coming. Not even Joe.

The latest transfer calamity overseen by Peter Johnson had been and gone. Joe thought Everton had agreed a fee of £1.2m with Brann Bergen for their Norwegian international striker Tore Andre Flo, with defender Claus Eftevaag added to the deal for £300,000 as a transfer makeweight.

Peter was less enthusiastic. Maybe he'd already made up his mind about Joe.

I'd been invited to Goodison Park on the morning of Thursday, March 27 for the announcement of Everton's participation in that summer's pre-season Umbro Tournament.

Everton, Ajax, Chelsea and Newcastle were the teams unveiled, and the press release, contained appropriately enough inside a sombre black folder, contained statements from Peter Johnson CHAIRMAN and Joe Royle MANAGER.

Neither hinted at any forthcoming trouble.

Neither did Joe's demeanour. He spoke with his usual charm

and humour, then as he left the Goodison lounge he winked at me.

Neither of us knew he was a dead manager walking.

Joe then drove across to Peter's Park Food offices where the chairman caught him utterly unawares.

"Hello, Joe, Desmond tells me you've come over to resign," was the chairman's opening gambit.

Peter had just had lunch with Blues director Sir Desmond Pitcher, but Joe hadn't spoken to Pitcher for weeks and he certainly had no thoughts of resigning. Maybe it was PJ's ploy to force the issue.

If so, it was effective. An hour later Joe stepped out into the Wirral sunshine as the ex-manager of Everton Football Club and an unsigned Press Release chattered through the Fax Machine at Old Hall Street which read: 'Everton Football Club announced today the resignation of manager Joe Royle.

'Mr Royle commented: 'I have been disappointed by recent results and our current league position. Having spoken to the Chairman it has been agreed that we part company by mutual consent.'

'The club added that a further announcement concerning the managerial position will be made shortly.'

I'd had an inkling that something was amiss before the fax arrived.

The Daily Post's boxing correspondent, Walter Brennan, also a nurse at the Ashworth high security hospital, had recently sat down with Joe's right-hand man Willie Donachie to work on a mental health initiative.

Walter had called Willie barely minutes after Joe had deliv-

**Wembley bound:** Watford Gap services on the M1 before the 1984 FA Cup final

**wede reams:**
n awkward york tation for Swedish re-season riendly in 994. On our there vas as uch fun ff the pitch s on it

**Having a laugh:** Before long I got to know heroes like Neville Southall and new stars like David Unsworth really well

**Lows and highs:** Within a few years of becoming the Echo's Everton correspondent I had covered a dramatic escape from relegation in 1994 and a remarkable FA Cup triumph a year later

**Royle reign:** I got on really well with Joe Royle so was disappointed to see him leave hours after this press conference to announce a pre-season tournament in 1997. The vacant hotseat was eventually filled by legend Howard Kendall...for the third time

**Forward thinking:** Walter Smith was another manager I hit it off with and he had an eye for a striker who could make an impact, bringing back Duncan Ferguson and signing Kevin Campbell

**A fond farewell:** David Moyes only had the good fortune to work with the genius of Wayne Rooney for a short while but when the Scot left, many, including me, were sad to see him go

**This is the life:** I had an up and down relationship with former Everton chairman Pete Johnson but this was one of the better times, on his yacht in Saint-Tropez

**Pen pal:** Penalty king David Unsworth became a good friend, as did Joe Parkinson

**Fully engaged:** It was great to interview characters like Slaven Bilić

**Know the score:** My name was up in lights as a reminder to readers

**Can I have a moment?:** Catching a few words with 'theatre impresario' Bill Kenwrig

**bit of a player:** Taking up the opportunity to lay with and against greats like Colin Harvey, eter Beardsley, David Johnson and others at oodison or Bellefield is one of the perks of he job

**Terrific trio:**
Wife Melanie
with Daniel
and Scarlett

**Westminster bubble:** Melanie at
the pub she used to work in with
her mum, Barbara, and a picture
of the great Dixie Dean

**In his name:** Melanie holds the Dixie Dean
Memorial Award in the company of legends Brian
Labone and Dave Hickson

**Raising a glass:**
I joined Melanie at
the opening of
the Dixie Dean Hotel

**Big occasion:** Melanie and Daniel in 2016 at Wembley for the FA Cup semi-final against Manchester United

**Guests of honour:** Melanie, Daniel and Scarlett on the pitch at the Emirates

**All together now:** A collection of Dixie Dean's relatives

**Treading the boards:** My stomach was in knots as I appeared on stage with the likes of Roger Kenyon, Martin Dobson, John Bailey and George Telfer in an Everton-themed pantomime at the Royal Court Theatre

**Premium seat:** Melanie and I sitting behind Gareth Southgate, Marcel Brands, Bill Kenwright and Farhad Moshiri at Goodison

**London trips:** It was an honour to accompany the remarkable David France to Buckingham Palace to receive his OBE – and in 2012 I had the thrill of covering the Olympics in our capital city

**Top of hi game:** Melanie and I chatting with Car Ancelotti a manag who belongs in the to bracket Europea coaches

ered the shock news to his assistant and Walter, in turn, had called me.

Initially I was sceptical. It had only been a couple of hours since Joe was announcing a pre-season tournament for four months hence.

But then Joe called me and confirmed both our worst fears.

The 'further announcement' hinted at in the fax was still far from imminent, because if Peter's decision to part company with Joe was an off-the-cuff decision, he had no idea who was going to be caretaker manager for the seven matches which remained of the season.

An incident on the Bellefield entrance steps made his mind up and this time I was the third person to find out.

I drove to Bellefield, as usual, the following morning where Everton's first official press officer Alan Myers was waiting, smiling and shaking his head.

Neville Southall had arrived, as usual, in his Volvo Estate and parked, as usual, just to the right of the entrance door just seconds earlier, where Myers was chatting with chairman Peter Johnson.

Johnson told Alan: "I really can't make my mind up about the caretaker-manager. Dave Watson has such respect amongst the players but Neville Southall is such a strong personality and knows the club inside out. I really can't decide."

Neville made up his mind for him, as he closed his car door.

"Morning Mr Chairman," he declared. "Morning Myers... you fat cunt," then strode into Bellefield without a backwards glance.

Unused to Neville's, shall we say, acerbic humour, Johnson winced and declared: "I think we'll go with Waggy."

One of Watson's first acts as temporary manager was to call a halt to Paul Rideout's impending move to Huan Dao Vanguards, which resulted in a strange phone call to my home one evening.

Carolyn Rideout, Paul's wife, was the caller – in tears – exhorting me to do what I could to prevent her husband's deal from collapsing.

The deal did go through, with no help from me, but only after her hubby had produced a superb display as a makeshift central midfielder in a victory over Spurs which ensured Everton would not be dragged into a relegation battle, then headed to Manchester Airport as a pillion passenger on the back of a motorbike to catch his flight to China.

I'd never spoken to Mrs Rideout before and haven't since.

Strange days indeed…

## Chapter Fourteen

# HOWARD'S WAY...3

I'D like to gloss over 1997/98.

I wish it never happened. It was one of the most troubling, traumatic seasons in the club's recent history.

But it did happen. So we need to at least pay it lip service.

In his search for a new boss Peter Johnson courted Bobby Robson. He interviewed Andy Gray. I was even encouraged by an agent to set up a meeting between Johnson and former Dutch World Cup finalist Wim van Hanegem.

Robson stayed on at Barcelona, in a general manager's position, Andy Gray stayed with Sky and PJ never took to a boss who had won the Dutch league and cup with Feyenoord because he was wearing jeans when they met...

It almost seemed like an act of desperation when, having been searching since March 28 for a manager to replace Joe Royle, Peter Johnson waited until the end of June to ask a manager who he knew would accept the job in a heartbeat.

Howard Kendall returned, from Sheffield United, for a third stint as Blues boss, with Adrian Heath and Viv Busby alongside him.

We should have guessed something was amiss when Howard, usually the most sartorially elegant of managers, turned up for his introductory press conference in a gaudy lime green shirt and a two-tone spotted tie.

Something had changed. In many respects, especially his willingness to work closely with the Echo, this was the same old Howard. But that magic touch which had been evident in the 1980s wasn't quite the same – especially in the transfer market.

Slaven Bilic had effectively been gifted to him, a defender who cost a near world record fee for a defender of £4.5m, signed by the chairman when the club did not have a manager.

Howard never really fancied the Croat.

But the scale of that transfer meant that Howard had to try and juggle his resources elsewhere.

He swapped David Unsworth for Danny Williamson, a deal which West Ham undoubtedly got the better of, and took a chance on young might-have-beens like Gareth Farrelly, John Oster and Tony Thomas. All three never really were at Goodison.

I knew Tony from my Tranmere reporting days and he gave me an insight into some of Howard's team bonding methods.

The train-hard play-hard ethic which had served him so well a decade ago was still in evidence but not every footballer was on board with the methods.

Andy Hinchcliffe and Gary Speed were from the 'my body is a temple' school of thinking, and were uncomfortable at being told to join in with team bonding sessions – especially on a pre-season trip to Guernsey.

Tony later revealed: "I was new to the club and wanted to make a good impression, and I didn't know if it was some kind of test to see if I succumbed to temptation."

He didn't. But plenty did.

The pre-season results seemed to underline the wild inconsistency Evertonians would endure that season.

Glasgow Rangers were beaten 3-2 at Goodison Park, then four days later Tranmere beat the Blues 3-0 at Prenton Park.

Gary Speed scored a winner against Ajax, then Chelsea won 3-1 at Goodison the very next day.

Everton were sporting a paler, washed out version of their traditional Royal Blue strip that season – and it seemed wholly appropriate.

Even that most august of institutions, the Everton captaincy, seemed to be handed around like some kind of pass the parcel game, SIX different players wearing the armband that campaign (Watson, Speed, Barmby, Ferguson, Bilic and Hutchison, quiz fans).

Howard had decided to swap the captaincy from Dave Watson to Gary Speed barely an hour before the opening day of the season.

Waggy accepted the decision with his usual equanimity. "Let's just say his timing could have been better," he shrugged when I asked him about it.

Howard's reasoning was that he knew he would always get 100 per cent leadership from Watson, but giving Speed the armband might coax different qualities from an already excellent midfielder.

He was probably right, but the manner of the switch seemed

to hint at off-the-cuff thinking rather than a considered strategy.

That giddying inconsistency never manifested itself more than in the space of three October days.

On a Wednesday night at Coventry City, Everton tumbled out of the League Cup with, as I wrote in the following night's Echo, 'one of the most wretched, deplorable and thoroughly abysmal Everton displays I can remember.'

The passing of time hasn't changed my opinion.

Howard clearly agreed because he marched purposefully out onto the pitch after the final whistle had blown on a 4-1 annihilation to deliver a public dressing down to his under-performing players. It's probably best if I repeat the report from that night verbatim. It still makes for unsettling reading.

'Skipper Gary Speed turned to applaud the travelling fans. Most of his team-mates began to trudge towards the tunnel, only to be ushered towards the centre circle by a purposeful Kendall. Instructions were given, presumably for everyone to applaud the supporters, the substituted Duncan Ferguson joined the huddle, and then the players began to move towards the penalty area at the home supporters' end. Coaches Adrian Heath and Viv Busby joined the unusual gathering and the players then appeared to be told to start lapping the pitch.

'Craig Short's reaction was so angry he had to be restrained by Slaven Bilic. Speed also began to remonstrate angrily, gesticulating with his arms, and most of the squad turned to walk off. The clearly concerned teenagers, Michael Ball and Danny Cadamarteri were left wondering what they should do, until they too decided to leave the pitch.'

I subsequently learned that Craig Short had called the manager a "cowboy" – and Howard was overheard telling a director: "I've just told the press I ordered a warm-down. I don't think a single one of them believed me."

The next day Howard offered an equally implausible explanation to me for that night's Echo.

"I wanted the team to warm down, but Adrian Heath brought it to my attention that there were some people on the pitch and there was some question about the safety of the players," he suggested.

Then he moved onto firmer ground.

"When players do not perform to a certain level and, in fact, perform to the totally unacceptable level that we saw at Coventry then I do feel their days are numbered. They let both themselves and the club down. It was totally unacceptable and to say I was disappointed is a major understatement."

Paul Gerrard, Slaven Bilic and Nick Barmby were the men who carried the can for that defeat in the very next match – a Merseyside derby.

As always seemed to be the case at that time, Liverpool were an upwardly mobile seventh, Everton a cause for concern at third from bottom.

Yet the outcome was so improbable that a cute tannoy operator decided to play the theme tune from the popular TV series Tales of the Unexpected at the final whistle.

Everton won 2-0. And they were convincing, comprehensive, comfortable winners.

It was a result so unexpected that Adrian Heath even believed in the power of fate.

In the aftermath of that Highfield Road low he had said to me: "Just our luck we've a derby match next."

But Everton were on the crest of a six-match unbeaten run in derbies, a run which had coincided with Phil McNulty and myself sitting alongside each other in the press box.

And I managed to convince Inchy that some mysterious forces were at work and we'd be fine, because Phil and I would be sat side by side. Except we weren't.

I arrived at Goodison Park and was alarmed to learn that the Press Box seating plan had split us up.

Clearly seating arrangements, lucky underpants or putting your left sock on before your right and muttering "Everton are magic, Liverpool are tragic" under your breath three times before breakfast on derby day doesn't really work.

Because Everton won anyway.

And when an excited Inchy collared me in the tunnel afterwards and said: "Hey Dave, you were right! You and Phil will have to sit together for the rest of the season," I didn't have the heart to tell him.

In a quirk of fixture fate Everton were sent back to Coventry in their next match and laid the ghosts of that League Cup exit to rest with a hard-fought goalless draw, then promptly lost five in a row.

They were deeply worrying times, but it was chairman Johnson who was carrying the can rather than Howard.

No-one wanted to point the finger at a beloved boss who had brought so much joy to so many supporters, preferring instead to castigate a chairman who had once owned an Anfield season ticket.

A November home defeat by Tottenham, the 751st and final match of Neville Southall's glorious Everton career, was an ignominious end to a storied spell but the chant from the Street End at the final whistle was "We want Johnson out!"

The days when I'd supped Guinness with the Everton chairman in Dublin had turned bitter.

At a stormy December AGM he finally chose to answer questions I'd posed of him in the Echo 15 days earlier: 'Does the club have money to spend?', 'Is the chairman committed to the club long term?' and 'Where has all the money gone?'

He answered them impressively, too, and then guillotined the meeting to take Lorraine out for dinner!

You had to admire his brass neck.

But if I wasn't speaking to PJ and Lorraine anything like as often as I had done, I was speaking to Gary Speed once a week.

In addition to my Echo duties I'd been producing large chunks of the Everton programme, including the captain's column – which is how I was able to coax Gary into an interview, of sorts, after he had refused to travel to West Ham in February and handed in a transfer request.

"You know why I want to go," he said. Except I didn't.

I'd guessed the manager's methods had jarred with his own football philosophy, but Speedo had never actually articulated that to me.

He simply said: "Write this. If I came out and said why I handed in a transfer request it would tarnish the good name of Everton Football Club, which is something I would never do. I have always been an Evertonian and even if I leave the club I will remain an Evertonian. But I do want to apologise to my team-mates who played so well at West Ham, and also to the supporters who spent so much hard-earned cash to back the team. I listened to the match on the radio and I could hear what they were chanting (about me). I realise I let them down but it is something I feel strongly about."

That encapsulated Gary Speed. Dignified, noble and unwilling even to criticise fans who were calling him a Judas and a traitor. But most of all, an Evertonian.

He took his reasons for leaving Everton to the grave, and even when John Richardson ultimately outlined those reasons in Speed's posthumous biography, 'Unspoken' Richo wrote: 'I can hear him now almost certainly remonstrating with me, that he didn't want this to become public knowledge.'

I don't want Gary's spirit remonstrating with me so I won't repeat those reasons here.

But with Gary getting his wish to move to Newcastle, Everton lurched closer and closer to what seemed like an inevitable relegation.

Transfer deadline day brought little in the way of succour.

Howard had signed the spiky little Scottish striker John Spencer from QPR for £1.5m but he laboured through his whole, admittedly short-lived, Everton career without scoring a single goal.

Then on transfer deadline day Howard told me to hang around the Bellefield entrance hall because he was hoping to get a transfer over the line in time to be announced in that evening's Echo.

I rang the office and word got back to my season-ticket-holding editor that a transfer announcement could be imminent.

Ten minutes before deadline Howard emerged from the canteen, beckoned me halfway up the stairs, and triumphantly declared: "We're good to go, lad. I'm bringing Peter Beagrie back from Bradford on loan until the end of the season."

Tumbleweed definitely didn't blow down the staircase at that moment but it felt like it was rolling down the phone line when John Griffith, that season-ticket-holding editor, had insisted on taking my call, to hear the 'good' news first.

Beagrie wasn't the player he had been. Even at his peak he was an inconsistent performer, memorably described by The Independent's Joe Lovejoy as 'the archetypal blue-assed fly winger.' But by 1998 his buzz had started to wear down. He started four matches and was hauled off early in three of them, including a harrowing 4-0 humiliation at champions Arsenal when he was replaced at half-time with The Gunners already two goals to the good.

By now the mood around the club was horribly tense.

Howard stood in a corridor just off Highbury's famous Marble Halls after that match and agreed to speak to myself and Paul Joyce.

Earlier in the week Everton's entire squad had been spotted at Haydock races and whether the trip had subconsciously lodged in his cerebral cortex, Howard started by saying: "We weren't at the races today."

Today Joycey is a football correspondent for The Times and one of the national pack's finest story gatherers, but back then he was a young and impressionable reporter.

He jumped in and naively quipped: "That's funny Howard. I've just written that."

Kendall's usually sunny countenance clouded.

"Fuck off, lad. That's out of order," he rapped. "You know that was a contractual obligation. We all had to make that trip whether we wanted to or not."

Regardless of the circumstances, it was a PR own goal, to go with the actual sixth-minute Slaven Bilic own goal which precipitated that Highbury horror show.

Everton collected just three points from the final five games of the season, the only apparent survival strategy being to hope that their relegation rivals also didn't win.

Except while Everton were losing at home to Sheffield Wednesday and being annihilated at Arsenal, Bolton were beating Aston Villa and Crystal Palace – and faced a final match of the season at a Chelsea team who had a European Cup Winners Cup final just three days later.

Everton played the same Coventry team who had humiliated them six months earlier, with Dion Dublin, the centre-forward who had inadvertently led to Howard's departure four years before that, leading their line.

The symbolism was heavy. The portents were Shakespearian.

And, well, you all know what happened next.

Dion Dublin did score. Obviously.

Everton were awarded a lucky penalty. And missed it.

But Gareth Farrelly finally came good from 20 yards and while Everton drew 1-1, Bolton lost to two late goals at a Chelsea side who rested only three players due to face Stuttgart in the following week's European final.

Rather than the scenes of celebration which had encompassed the stadium four years earlier against Wimbledon, this time the mood was angrier and more primeval. But again it was the chairman, not the manager, who bore the brunt.

The Goodison fans knew how much Howard Kendall cared about the football club he had described as being married to.

And within minutes of the final whistle the chant: "We want Johnson out!" boomed around the old arena again.

The emotion of that day was all too much for Howard. While we waited upstairs in the Goodison press room for the post-match conference a rumour filtered around that the manager was delayed because he was already half-cut.

He wasn't.

Don Hutchison, one of Howard's shrewder signings that season, explained exactly what had happened in an emotion-charged podcast he gave a year or so after Howard's tragically premature passing.

"The final whistle went and it was emotional," he said. "Howard Kendall was on the pitch. Adrian Heath was on the pitch. Viv Busby was on the pitch. Fans were on the pitch. But we weren't celebrating. It was just the fact of staying up. It was 'thank God that game's over and we've survived'. Everton should never ever be in that position ever again. We were in the dressing room and it felt wrong, but there were a few bottles of champagne and the music got turned up very loud.

"It's not right, but it is, because we've survived. It's not the right thing to do but it felt right at the time. I've looked around and everyone was taking tops off and getting in the showers and I couldn't see Howard. I saw Adrian and I saw Viv and I went 'where's the gaffer?' And Viv said 'He'll probably be in the boot room.'

"First left out of the home dressing room was the boot room. So I've knocked on the door. Nothing. So I've done the knock where you're being slightly respectful but open it at the same time, and as I've got an inch open it's pitch black. No lights on. So I opened it and I saw Howard, crying like a baby in the boot room. I've gone in, didn't turn the light on, just shut the door, sat with him and embraced him. I was quite okay but he let it all out. You could hear all the emotion coming out. He let it all out. You could feel his heartbeat, tears, in a pitch black room. Forget about football, we were just two human beings on that level. It will never ever leave me."

Evertonians didn't need to witness that scene to know how much Everton meant to Howard.

So while it was clear that a change needed to be made, waiting until the end of June before Howard was finally put out of his misery saw even more criticism head Peter Johnson's way. Some of it from myself.

Howard visited Peter Johnson at a holiday retreat in Lake Como – and still left as Everton manager.

He spent a full six-and-a-half weeks after that Coventry game on managerial death row, until, on June 24, the decision was finally announced that Everton's most successful ever manager had been sacked.

It was a grim end to a truly dreadful season.

## Chapter Fifteen

# BONDING IN SAINT-TROPEZ

THE photograph still hangs on my office wall at home.

I'm sat, bare-footed, wearing a brand new T-shirt with a gaudy pattern on the rear, smiling at a camera while Peter Johnson is pulling a face at me behind my back.

I'm holding a mobile phone in my right hand, sunglasses tossed loosely on the table in front of me.

And the photographer was Lorraine Rogers. It is the summer of 1998 and I'm sat on the deck of the Everton chairman's yacht in the Mediterranean.

I pursued a career in journalism to watch football matches on cold, winter's evenings at Stoke. To trudge through snow on a New Year's Day at Middlesbrough and have notebooks slowly turn to papier mache mush in rainstorms at St James' Park.

I never imagined leading the life of the super-rich, even for a day, because of journalism.

But it did come about because of sports journalism, or specifically those critical comments I'd been making about the Everton chairman in print, the "hurtful articles" referenced at the stormy AGM.

Lorraine had had the good idea to try and arrange a summit between myself and her partner, a sort of clear-the-air meeting.

And because I was in France covering the World Cup that summer – and Peter was watching England play Tunisia in Marseille – it made sense for us to get together in the south of France.

I'd just never expected it to be in the circumstances which ultimately materialised.

Howard still had a few days remaining as Blues boss when I spent a night on the yacht owned by the man who would sack him, moored in Saint-Tropez.

Howard would have appreciated the rendezvous.

We'd arranged to meet in an atmospheric bar in Marseille's Vieux Port but when I entered people were lounging around on the floor on mats and bean bags, like some Bacchanalian flop house. That was just the start of a strange 24 hours.

I found Peter and Lorraine, we exchanged stilted pleasantries, and then we decamped to a people carrier parked outside the bar.

"We'll pop back to the boat," said Peter. "We'll be more comfortable there."

Except I had no idea that the 'boat' was his multi-million pound yacht, and it was moored 'up the road' at Saint-Tropez.

The iconic French seaside town is 135 kilometres from Marseille, a two-hour drive.

So PJ decided to while away the journey by popping on a DVD of Everton's FA Cup semi-final defeat of Tottenham – there were screens in the front and back of the vehicle, obviously.

I pretty much knew that match off by heart but Peter tried to convince me that he really did have a big blue heart by ooh-ing and aahing throughout and interjecting with comments like "I love this moment", "Here's that dragback by Joe" and "Look at little Anders go!"

It all sounded a little forced, a little artificial, like when Lorraine rang me towards the end of a match at Nottingham Forest early the following season, and when I told her Duncan Ferguson had just scored, actually uttered the word: "Yippee!"

We arrived in Saint-Tropez and boarded the yacht but I had no overnight bag with me. So I had to pop into a nearby market for a clean T-shirt, toothbrush and undies.

Then we sat down on deck, enjoyed a few drinks and a meal and retired to bed.

The next morning I was up and about early, with just the crew pottering around for company, so I wandered up on deck. There, two boats down, I spotted the world class Italian striker Gianluca Vialli tending to his own boat.

So I did what any self respecting Scouser would do.

I shouted: "Alright Luca lad" waved, and when he waved back I took his picture.

I then rang Neville for his weekly column and said: "You're never going to guess where I am?"

His response was predictable.

"Fuck off TJ. Put him on then." So I did.

TJ passed the phone to PJ, and whether they discussed Neville's midriff-based put-down to Alan Myers which had cost him the caretaker manager's role I don't know, but they seemed to be getting on famously.

When he hung up we discussed the managerial situation at the club, we talked about the "hurtful articles" I'd written and we agreed to start afresh.

Then we headed out into the Med for lunch on the high seas.

I'd flown from England's training base at La Baule, near Nantes, to Marseille and was due to head back north later that day.

So when our time came to part, Peter simply asked his captain to change my flight reservation from Marseille to Cannes and popped me on an outboard launch which taxied me into Cannes harbour, while he waved me away from the deck.

That is undoubtedly the best way to arrive in Cannes and I have to admit I did feel just a little like James Bond – okay, the slightly wimpier Brosnan version rather than the chiselled Daniel Craig version – but a Bond nonetheless.

Back in La Baule, England's performances at the World Cup were clearly uppermost in everyone's mind, but some of the players involved were also keen to find out what was happening back home.

Steve MacManaman especially wanted to know what I'd heard about Howard's future. So did Preki, when I spoke to him at a USA press conference, and Thomas Myhre who was with the Norway squad.

The simple fact was, despite having spent a night discussing the matter with the man who would make that ultimate decision, he had clearly decided what needed to be done, but just couldn't decide when.

Another 10 days passed before the axe finally fell on June 24, 48 hours before England faced Colombia in Lens, which at least gave me some time to write comment, call players and speculate as to who the new manager may be.

I quickly learned who it wasn't going to be.

For the last week of England's involvement in the World Cup I'd travelled with the Leicester Mercury's Bill Anderson, who introduced me to one of the managers strongly linked with the now vacant post.

Martin O'Neill effectively interviewed me.

"I'm not sure I'd be interested in leaving Leicester," he said. "Besides, I've heard the chairman can be a bit odd. Isn't that the case?"

I couldn't disagree.

## Chapter Sixteen

# WALTER RALLIES

"YOU'LL be fine with Walter," Joe reassured me. "He's a good guy."

And not for the last time, Joe was absolutely spot on.

The arrival of a new manager was always a nervous time for the media, especially the locals. 'Would he still see the Echo every morning? Did he even know what the Echo was? Would he be as open and honest as his predecessor?'

The answer to all three questions where Walter Smith was concerned was a resounding 'yes'.

Paul Joyce had moved on from the official club newspaper The Evertonian to take over as the Daily Post's football correspondent shortly before Walter was appointed Everton manager and we both forged a lasting rapport with Walter which endures to this day.

Having operated in the football goldfish bowl which was Glasgow, the former Rangers boss was adept at putting up a stern screen, a public image which suggested aloof, authoritarian, prickly – or just a miserable old sod.

Nothing could have been further from the truth. Behind the

mask displayed to the public, Walter was engaging company, candid and loved a laugh.

I'd had several staid meetings with the new Blues boss before I was handed the opportunity of a proper ice-breaker, in unexpected circumstances.

As the most successful Glasgow Rangers manager in living memory, a man who had taken the Scottish giants to the brink of the 1993 European Cup final, Walter Smith was a sought-after boss in the summer of 1998.

And Peter Johnson had convinced him to turn down overtures from Sheffield Wednesday with the promise of what today would probably be referred to as a 'transfer war chest.'

So Walter went to war.

He bought future World Cup finalist Marco Materazzi for £2.5m, brought John Collins from Monaco on a modest fee but massive wages, added French midfielder Olivier Dacourt, a player who was as classy as he was spiky, for £4m and Alex Cleland from his old Ibrox club on a free.

Steve Simonsen was signed from Tranmere Rovers for a fee which was dressed up at the time as a world record £3.3m transfer for a goalkeeper. In truth Everton handed less than a million to Johnson's old club.

Then Ibrahima Bakayoko arrived in October for £3.8m.

It was a whopping spending spree, the likes of which Evertonians had rarely witnessed since the days of John Moores' Mersey Millionaires.

Except Everton were spending money they didn't really have. The Blues were living on the never never.

Alarm bells started to clang when my old pal David Unsworth called me on the eve of a pre-season friendly at Chester.

"Can you do me a favour, mate? I've screwed up. I need you to pass Walter Smith my number," he said.

Unsy certainly had messed up but the Everton chairman had been complicit in that screw up.

After a year at West Ham, Unsy learned that Walter Smith wanted to bring him back to Goodison Park.

It was a dream move for him, except PJ had pulled off what would become an increasingly effective disappearing trick at the time transfer negotiations were at their most delicate.

Walter wanted Unsworth, so did Aston Villa boss John Gregory, but Unsy's agent could only make contact with the Birmingham club's chairman Doug Ellis.

While Walter was constantly on the end of his mobile phone, Peter had gone to ground.

One July evening Unsy called me from Villa Park in a state of mild foment. Villa wanted him to sign there and then. But he didn't want to commit if Everton were definitely interested.

But while Walter was interested, PJ had buried his head in the sand, ostrich-style and couldn't be reached. He finally emerged, blinking innocently into the daylight, the following day when he learned that Unsy had actually put pen to paper on an Aston Villa contract.

"He's signed for Villa has he? Oh, what a shame. I think Walter quite fancied him, didn't he?"

Which is where my one and only involvement as a would-be transfer facilitator came in (well, until Rafael Benitez hijacked Everton's move for Mohamed Sissoko, but that's for later).

Following a pre-season friendly at Chester City which ended 1-1 and was significant only for the fact that John Spencer actually scored, I stood pitchside, waited until Walter had completed his radio interviews, and said: "Walter, can I give you a phone number?"

"No," he barked.

So I repeated, "Just look at the name on it please Walter, he's my pal and he's still desperate to come."

So Walter glanced at the piece of paper with Unsy's number written on it, and popped it in his jacket pocket without another word.

We later discussed the issue properly, and I quickly learned that the new Everton manager was already having reservations about his relationship with his new chairman, a man he'd christened "Jinky" after the legendary Celtic winger Jimmy Johnstone, a player who was capable of twisting and turning out of any situation.

John Gregory was also having reservations about David Unsworth's desire to move further north, and so decided that the easiest way to save face would be to traduce the reputation of the defender and his wife Jayne.

"Apparently it took David three-and-a-half hours to drive home to Merseyside last Friday following his first training session with us," said the Villa boss, with a level of creativity Enid Blyton would have admired.

Pouring lashings of home-made imagination onto an already imaginary storyline he added: "It obviously set him thinking, because the poor lad was clearly under the impression that Birmingham was somewhere on the outskirts of Bolton!

"When David eventually arrived home, his dinner was in the dustbin – or perhaps it was in the cat!"

None of which was true. David just wanted to play for Everton, not Aston Villa.

Having saved face, Gregory then agreed to allow his new signing to complete that move, but only if the Blues matched the £3m deal Villa had agreed with West Ham.

So PJ prevaricated some more.

More than a week later, with Unsy still training in the Midlands and actually appearing in one pre-season friendly, Gregory told local reporters: "This has been rumbling on for 10 days.

"With Everton not prepared to reach agreement so far, we've had no choice but to call him back. It would appear that Peter Johnson is trying to get the fee reduced."

PJ relented, eventually, found the £3m Villa wanted and Unsworth finally became an Everton defender again.

But alarm bells were starting to ring.

Soon they would be clanging.

Chapter Seventeen

# DUNCAN'S DEPARTURE

EVEN now the headline makes me wince just a little: 'Blundering, Inept and Crass - That's the verdict of Peter Johnson's reign as Everton Chairman' was strong even by national newspaper standards, let alone a local paper which always aims to be more supportive.

But the circumstances were exceptional.

It was the headline to my Football Echo comment piece written in the immediate aftermath of Duncan Ferguson's transfer to Newcastle United – a sale conducted without his manager's knowledge on the evening of Monday, November 23, 1998, just four months after Walter Smith's arrival as manager.

If Walter had been blissfully ignorant of the icon's exit, he wasn't alone.

I learned of Duncan's departure standing at the bar of the Cross House Hotel in Formby shortly before 11pm. Unsy was standing opposite me as we had a swift post-match pint when Mark Denney – one of those well connected fans who always seemed to know more about the inner workings of the club than many staff – called me.

"Where are you?" he snapped.

"Er, having a pint, I've filed my report," I replied defensively.

"Well Duncan's been sold. It's all going off here. I'm standing on Goodison Road and I can see him in a window upstairs. The fans aren't happy."

Sometimes tips like that ring true. More often than not they have less validity than a politician's promise.

So I asked Unsy: "What do you know about Duncan being sold?"

"Nothing," he said. "He never said a word when we saw him before the game."

Pre-match, Duncan, who was injured and not involved against Newcastle, would have been blissfully unaware of his impending move. So, too, was his manager.

Later that week Walter Smith told me an anecdote which, in hindsight, was hilarious. At the time, though, it was horribly unreal.

Content after a hard fought 1-0 win, Walter, his assistant Archie Knox and their respective wives Ethel and Janice were descending the stairs at Goodison when they bumped into Duncan coming back up.

The big man murmured: "I thought you might have stuck up for me gaffer."

Puzzled, Walter replied: "Stuck up for you, how?"

"With the move. I've been sold to Newcastle."

Walter, capable of incendiary explosions at the merest trifle, was admirably restrained.

"What are you talking about? Have you signed anything?" he asked.

"Well no, gaffer. But I've shaken hands on a financial package."

"Well, sign nothing. I need to speak to Jinky."

First, though, Walter needed to confer with his trusted aide.

He and Archie trooped down to the referees' room in the tunnel – long since vacated – followed by their wives, and started to discuss the shock news.

"What do we do about this then?" Walter asked.

Archie, for once, was stuck for an answer and Mrs Knox took the opportunity of the pause in the conversation to offer her own take on proceedings.

"Well, Walter. Ethel and I have been listening to the fans in the lounges tonight and if you have got £8million for Duncan Ferguson it sounds like a good deal."

Archie had rediscovered his tongue. And how.

"Janice. Shut the fuck up," he snapped. Ethel jumped in: "Archie, you can't talk to Janice like that." And the meeting was postponed.

It was Walter's turn to get angry the following morning.

The Echo's first edition had a deadline of 11.30am in 1998, which meant I had to have a story filed by ten past. And so I headed to Bellefield for my daily sit down with the Everton manager.

This wasn't back page news, it was front page.

And before I left Old Hall Street the acting editor, Tony Storey, told me he simply didn't believe that a record breaking transfer fee could be completed without the manager's knowledge.

The Echo's editorial policy, unless I could convince him otherwise, was that Walter Smith had been fully aware his centre-forward was being sold to Newcastle.

Tony had a background in business reporting, and probably genuinely believed that no credible business could operate in such a way. Either that or he was cutely pushing me to persuade Walter to go on the record.

Walter was his usual genial self when I walked in, until I told him that the Echo had reservations about his claims to have been unaware of Ferguson's sale.

His face darkened to the colour of deep purple as he snapped: "Don't you fucking move. You're sitting there until you hear him on the phone tell you I knew nothing about that transfer!" then proceeded to dial Peter Johnson's number.

He tried his mobile phone. His home. His office number. The number for his yacht.

Peter had gone to ground. Again. As every answer machine message kicked in, the phone was in mortal danger of being slammed through his office desk. I'd seen enough.

"Okay Walter. Calm down," I said. "I believe you, and I'll try and convince them in the office you knew nothing about it."

And eventually I did. But not helped by Lorraine, who had been in touch with the Echo, but hadn't asked for me.

She went directly to the news desk, where she informed them that Walter had been aware of the sale, but that Peter was nobly taking all the flak for the good of the club.

The news desk preferred my version of events.

Walter made it clear that unless a statement was issued by the club confirming he had been unaware of the sale, he would resign. He meant it. The chairman's position at the club had become untenable.

Cliff Finch, Peter's solid and sensible right-hand man, later explained: "Duncan Ferguson was a lovely guy, but it was the deal of the season.

"Peter Johnson and I were invited to his wedding and were the only people from the club to go. But the pressure was on from the cash side of the business.

"Financially we were in a pretty poor way, there was pressure from the bank and it was one of those things which, in Peter's defence, seemed like a good idea at the time."

Like selling Alan Ball in 1971 probably seemed like a good idea at the time to Harry Catterick.

The Catt sold Alan Ball because he believed his powers were on the wane. Peter had naively sanctioned Walter's summer spending spree because he believed European qualification, or better, would allow him to repay those transfer fees and more.

It was a model which saw Leeds United almost declared bankrupt, and a misguided 'strategy' which saw the bank threatening to foreclose on Everton unless money was injected into the club quickly. Like £8million.

The deal to receive that much-needed cash injection took place on the Monday evening at Goodison Park.

By a quirk of coincidence, myself and Joycie had already arranged to go for a meal with Walter and Archie on the Thursday of the same week.

In the circumstances we fully expected the dinner to be cancelled. Joycie broached the subject tentatively when we spoke later in the week.

"Of course we're still going out," said Walter. "I may not be manager of Everton at the time, but we'll still go out."

And we did.

To a chic restaurant on Liverpool's Smithdown Road called Left Bank.

It was a trendy place to eat out and clearly popular amongst the city's football fraternity. Reserve Liverpool keeper Tony Warner was dining when we arrived. A mortified Tony Grant was just leaving, concerned that his manager had seen him out socially on a Thursday night.

But despite the storm clouds which were hovering menacingly over the club, we had a great night.

We swapped anecdotes, jokes, drank lots of wine, ate good food and retired back to the Redbourne Hotel where Archie was staying to drink some more, this time good scotch whisky.

We had a very late night but I made it safely home, eventually, then the next morning arrived at our Old Hall Street offices and I proceeded to pen my 'Blundering, Inept and Crass...' article.

I was clearly wound up...

'Just when Evertonians felt they could endure no more punishment, along comes another sickening body blow. Already reeling, battered and dazed by four of the most blundering, inept and crass years of Chairmanship in the club's history, the Blues were subjected to one more – hopefully final – insult last week.

'Popular players sometimes have to be sold. That is a fact of footballing life. But the manner in which Duncan Ferguson was sold to Newcastle United was nothing short of a footballing scandal. The player did not want to leave – until he was offered £40,000 a week which softened the blow somewhat – and the manager would have blocked his sale until a replacement had been found. So Peter Johnson sold him behind the manager's back. The whole situation is simply beyond belief – and this a club which regularly stretches credibility to unparalleled levels.

'People make mistakes – especially in football – but generally they cough to them afterwards. Peter Johnson's ineptitude as Everton Chairman is matched only by his brass neck. Having presided over the most appalling public relations blunder of his four year tenure at Goodison Park (and he has hot competition for that tag), he has now attempted to lessen his part in the shameful situation of Duncan Ferguson's departure.

'We are in the happy position here at the Echo of being able to take soundings from all aspects of Goodison life – boardroom, manager's office, players, ex-players, backroom staff – and there is absolutely no shadow of a doubt that Walter Smith was unaware of the sale of his centre-forward and skipper. More to the point, he was unaware that his Chairman had even instigated moves to sell Duncan Ferguson.

'Having pulled off such an audacious, appalling piece of chicanery, the Chairman then attempted a furtive damage limitation exercise. No public statement, of course. No full and frank interview. Not even a terse sentence. Instead, somebody representing the Chairman made a telephone call to the Liverpool Post and Echo offices to inform anyone who would listen that Walter Smith had been party to the Ferguson sale and brave Peter had simply done the honourable thing by shouldering full blame. Not content with a situation where the manager could never trust the Chairman again, moves had then been started to smear the manager's name.

'This was the most damning moment of the entire week. And it is just one of the compelling reasons why Mr Johnson must sell his shares in Everton. The man has been a disaster for the club. The banner hauled humorously above The Kop said it all: 'Agent Johnson. Mission Accomplished.'

'Very nearly. This once great football club is now nearly on its knees, and before it finally keels over, the man responsible must go.'

The bon mots we'd once exchanged on deck in the Med had been long forgotten.

Clearly I'd been influenced by the stories I'd been told by Walter and Archie the previous night, but I'd also been growing equally disturbed at the manner in which the club I'd always supported was being run.

There had been the long and unnecessarily drawn out public execution of the much-loved Howard Kendall, the frankly bizarre mutual consenting of Joe Royle, the botched transfer deals for Nigel Martyn, Mark Schwarzer and Tore Andre Flo, the temporary replacement of Z-Cars, a ground move which never materialised…even season tickets with red covers.

And now this.

But if I was disturbed, the fanbase was appalled.

On Saturday I travelled down to Charlton for the first match AD – After Duncan.

We won 2-1 but there were banners out in force at The Valley, one of which stays with me to this day.

Simplicity is genius, they say, and this banner carried as much bluntness and simplicity as it did familiarity.

It read: Peter You Cunt.

His time was almost up.

Days later Peter did agree to step down as chairman and put his shares up for sale.

We spoke, briefly, at the press conference staged to announce his exit when he pointedly asked me to deliver the first question.

Several years later we had that wine-swilling exchange at the Moat House referred to in the introduction, then nothing.

One of my best friends – one of the crew who spent that night in the Sherpa Van in 1984 – later secured a high ranking role with Park Foods and unwisely mentioned his relationship with me to PJ.

"He just muttered something about 'having had a few problems with the local press'" said Chris.

Then years and years later PJ and I had a telephone conversation about trying to sell his shareholding with Tranmere Rovers.

It was friendly, genial. We could almost have been back in that Dublin pub again, and we ended with Peter saying that I must come over to the Wirral and have lunch with him one day.

I enthusiastically agreed. But we never did.

That bothers me.

Peter was ultimately a man who meant well for Everton Football Club. He just had a misguided and reckless way of trying to achieve it.

And he is still the last Everton chairman to enjoy the trappings of real success with that 1995 FA Cup win.

When a statue was unveiled to Rovers' legendary manager Johnny King in 2014, Peter was present at the ceremony. It was clear that he recognised my face, but he couldn't recall how he knew me. Either I hadn't played as significant a part in his life as I'd imagined, or a debilitating disease was clearly at work.

I felt a pang of real regret.

But I'm glad we'd at least had that phone conversation.

## Chapter Eighteen

# FIELD OF DREAMS

IN March 2011 I went back to a boarded up and deserted Bellefield.

It was a poignant visit.

Everton ended a 61-year association with their once state-of-the-art training complex on October 9, 2007, when they moved to their Finch Farm training facility.

It was the end of an era – not just for Everton.

Media demands on football clubs were growing more and more. Sky TV had been joined by other satellite TV channels and the internet had created a legion of online sports sites. Everton used the switch as an opportunity to finally end the Echo's daily visits.

While we still got to visit Finch Farm, it wasn't every day and it wasn't with anything like the intimacy we'd enjoyed at Bellefield.

It was symbolic of a changing media age, when every facet of a footballer's life was becoming 'newsworthy' and players were retreating behind mansion walls with security cameras.

A lengthy legal wrangle over planning meant that Bellefield

remained empty for four years before Everton were finally granted permission to sell the site to property developers Bellway Homes.

But happily they invited the Echo in for one last look around before the demolition experts put a wrecking ball through the site.

It was a wistful and poignant afternoon.

Weeds had sprouted in cracks in the car park.

The buildings were empty, the pitches overgrown, and the equipment which remained was damp and rusting. A site which for half-a-century and more had resonated to the sound of footballers' shouts, referees' whistles and shrieks of laughter from practical jokers, was eerily silent.

In Dougie Rose's old garage, the one used by Robbie, Jimmy and Bob to store their lawnmowers, I found an old damp and decaying notebook. On it was scrawled the message: 'Howard sacked. How's your luck baldy?'

The entry was dated June 24, 1998, the day that Howard Kendall was relieved of his duties as Everton manager for the final time.

It was an irreverent entry in an old groundsman's notebook which had lain there for almost a decade, left behind in the shell that was once the country's most prestigious training facility, and a place Howard had graced as a player and in three separate stints as a manager.

It was a place I had spent almost as much time at as I had the Echo offices in Old Hall Street.

Bellefield became part of my daily routine for more than a decade.

After an hour scanning the national newspapers in our Old Hall Street office I'd head down West Derby Road, past the Grafton on the right, along into Tuebrook and the site of the old Coconut Grove, turn right on to Queen's Drive, past the Jolly Miller, then take a sharp left along Sandforth Road where Merseyside's best kept secret was hidden.

If you drove along Sandforth Road at any kind of speed you would have no idea that a training ground existed there. While your eyeline was distracted by the Bill Shankly Playing Fields on the left, a narrow pathway just about big enough for a car to pass through snaked in between two semi-detached houses on the right.

It was so narrow that team coaches had to park on the street whenever they left from Bellefield.

But once you got past the gates, and said hello to gateman Harry Scott, a real-life Tardis opened up.

The old 'C' team pitch, affectionately known as little Wembley was on the left, before the sports hall which boasted a full-sized artificial pitch inside, while on the right, the other side of the car park beyond the trees, was a full-sized training pitch.

Behind the two-storey main complex, with a gym at the rear and a dining room upstairs, was another full-sized pitch.

It was an exciting optical illusion.

But despite its size, Bellefield stood apart from other modern training grounds because of its intimacy. Its compact nature meant that each visit entailed interaction with everyone there.

I loved it, even on the days I'd be left leaning against that radiator in the hall for two or three hours at a time, waiting for a player to finish his injury treatment before talking to me.

On arrival I'd chat briefly with Harry. As I parked up I'd hear "Beer-Can!" shriek across one of the pitches (an in-joke with groundsman Robbie) then I'd check in first with Mary, and then later Sue Palmer, PAs to a succession of managers.

For the first decade or so I was invited up into the manager's office for tea, toast and a conversation.

Occasionally I'd be asked to step back outside, like when Duncan Ferguson knocked on Walter Smith's door and asked if he could have a private word – with the manager, not me – whilst trying to hide a badly bloodshot eye.

Fortunately for Ferguson that was only the injury he had sustained whilst apprehending two burglars at his Formby home.

The intruders weren't so lucky.

During the David Moyes era I'd usually arrive round about the same time as he'd completed his commute from Preston, so we'd chat in the hallway for five minutes.

Then while I waited, a succession of stellar names would troop past. Some would stop to chat. Some would nod. Others would ignore me completely.

But an oasis of tranquility it rarely was. And some of the noises emanated straight from the African jungle.

Graham Stuart later explained, for a feature I'd written about Bellefield, the source of some of those primeval noises, especially those that replicated something from Jurassic Park.

"Jimmy Martin, our kit man, had been there for years and was top class, but the abuse he used to get was fearsome," he smiled.

"He's got a parrot's nose, a right old beak. All the players used to squawk at him when he walked on the pitch. We would squawk at him everywhere. Out of windows, on the bus, wherever…or scream 'Who's a pretty boy then!'

"Jimmy would go nuts, spinning round, threatening people. He must have threatened more than 60 people while I was there alone. Gary Ablett had the best squawk I have ever heard in my life.

"But despite all the stick, deep down all the lads respected him deeply. You don't give the amount of stick and abuse to people like Jimmy without secretly loving him.

"He was part of the team. I actually roomed with him on an end-of-season trip to Marbella rather than room with one of the players. I regretted it afterwards, though. His snoring is a disgrace!"

Those jungle squawks were a frequent soundtrack to my early visits to Bellefield, along with the shrieks from players stirring their tea then putting the burning hot teaspoon on a team-mates' arm, Andy Hinchcliffe teasing Mary the cook about her flaming hair – "What are you rustling up today, Bonfire Bonce?" – and Neville Southall tormenting everybody.

It was a privileged insight.

I even got to play at Bellefield several times.

That was a tradition which started during Colin Harvey's spell as boss.

The team line-up from that first clash is on my office wall at home. There's a young blond-haired keeper called Walshy, Everton heroes like Dave Jones, Mick Lyons, Colin Harvey, Paul Power, the youth coach Graham Smith and Terry Darracott. Of course we lost, 3-1, but there were contributory circumstances.

It might have been only a 'friendly' but professional sports-men don't do any form of football light-heartedly.

After being told to bring training shoes, no boots, we antici-pated a 'friendly' match on the artificial surface in the sports hall.

Suitably shod, we were then led outside by Paul Power towards the famous 'C' team pitch – boasting a surface like a snooker table – which had just been liberally watered by Mick Lyons.

Ex-pros didn't need their visitors to be sliding around like Todd Carty on Dancing On Ice to dish out a football lesson, which they promptly did. But I did manage to prod the one past Walshy, and Terry Darracott even got a photo of the moment for posterity. The fact I can recall it more than 30 years later underlines how excited I was.

Those clashes became annual affairs, but on one famous occasion we were invited back the following week – because we'd done the unthinkable and won!

That was during Howard's second spell. Echo crime reporter Paul Byrne rapped the winner past Peter Bonetti in a famous 3-2 triumph, and Howard growled: "Back here next week for the second leg!"

Just one face was changed in the Everton line-up for the re-match, a recently retired but still super-fit John Bailey – but the scoreline was dramatically different.

Everton declared at 7-0.

Enjoying such intimacy but still trying to write as objectively and accurately as possible might appear a difficult balance.

I still remember Paul Gerrard greeting me with: "Here he is.

Comes down and jokes with us all and then slaughters us in his paper."

But it wasn't difficult. And I didn't wantonly 'slaughter' players. I just didn't think Gerrard was all that good. I wrote like a privileged fan. If I enjoyed what I'd seen I'd report that. If I didn't, I'd be harder than most, because I cared deeply.

Football dressing rooms can be cruel environments and footballers are used to hearing home truths.

And besides, I'd often turn a blind eye to incidents which weren't relevant to the sports pages of the day.

Mobile phones in the 1990s were still only capable of making phone calls. So I just stood there open mouthed when Mickael Madar's Louis Vuitton toilet bag came flying past my nose out of the Bellefield entrance door one lunchtime, followed almost as quickly by the fraught French forward.

He then proceeded to kick it around the car park, ranting and raving in a form of French way beyond my 'A' level standard appreciation.

I never did discover what had wound him up that day, although in Walter's first pre-season I was made acutely aware of how I'd upset him.

It was Joycie who warned me, in our hotel in Holland.

The squad numbers for the new season had been revealed, and Mickael hadn't been given one, which led me to not unreasonably surmise in the Football Echo that he didn't have much of a future under the new Blues boss.

Mickael saw it differently, collaring Joycie, and demanding to know if he was "David Princess, the man who is writing these things about me!"

When Joycie caught up with me he advised: "I'd stay out of his way for the time being."

So I did, but it was impossible to stay out of the way of players for long at Bellefield.

On one Friday morning as I hovered at the top of the Bellefield staircase waiting to be ushered into the manager's office, groundsman Robbie was chatting to Daniel Amokachi and said: "Here you are, Dan. Prenno will drive it down for you."

Which is how I ended up behind the wheel of a World Cup star's eye wateringly expensive sports car for a trip to Southampton.

I didn't know Daniel. I knew nothing about cars. And I had a reputation – well earned – for collecting speeding tickets. But the Bellefield groundstaff had vouched for me and that seemed to be good enough for Dan, who was travelling on the team bus to the south coast but wanted his car at the team hotel so he could travel home independently after the match.

I don't know a lot about cars. But this was a Mercedes, it was flashy, it reeked expensive, and once I'd discovered how to release the handbrake (it was on the dashboard) it was a thrill to drive.

Peter Johnson's face was less impressed when I pottered up outside the team hotel on Friday tea-time. "What are you doing driving that? Do you know how much that's worth?" he enquired incredulously. He seemed about as impressed as Duncan Ferguson when I knocked on Daniel's hotel room door to hand over the car key and Dan's room-mate answered.

Bizarrely, Daniel didn't even get to drive the car home in the end.

He missed the match at Southampton with a virus and Joe Royle ordered him to travel home with the rest of the squad alongside the physio on the team coach.

I was due to travel back with Radio Merseyside's Ian Kennedy, so Andy Hinchcliffe was tasked with driving Dan's car home once we'd dropped off a female friend of Dan's somewhere near Oxford.

"Who is she?" Andy mouthed to me as we drove away from the team hotel.

"I have no idea," I mouthed back. Just as I had no idea why I was driving a footballer's enormously expensive car down to the south coast.

They were heart-warming times.

## Chapter Nineteen

# THE ITALIAN JOB

I REALLY wanted Walter to succeed.

He was a decent, dignified Everton manager and we'd forged a very close working relationship.

But for a worrying spell at the end of his first full season it looked like he, too, might have to go through the trauma of a last-day Great Escape.

The inspired acquisition of Kevin Joseph Campbell, or Super Kev as he should henceforth be known, avoided all that.

Signed on loan from Turkish side Trabzonspor – where he had suffered some quite bizarre racist abuse from club president Mehemet Ali Yilmaz – he proudly took the number nine shirt and promptly produced a scoring burst which had once been the preserve of centre-forwards like Dixie Dean and Tommy Lawton.

Super Kev clattered nine goals in five games, Everton won four of them, and the brooding spectre of relegation was banished. A team which had ground out a grim eight goalless draws throughout the season, SEVEN of them at Goodison Park, even put six past West Ham on one joyous afternoon.

That goalscoring glut meant that the mood at that summer's training camp in Tuscany, ahead of the 1999/2000 season, was light and optimistic.

After inheriting the previous season's pre-season arrangements Walter had insisted on taking the players to a resort and fitness spa familiar to him this time, one which had proved popular, and successful, for his Glasgow Rangers players.

It was called Il Ciocco. And obviously Joycey and I tagged along.

It was easy to see why it was so beloved.

Ciocco – Walter and Archie said the word best in their gravelly Glaswegian burr – was luxurious, well equipped and private, situated at the top of a steep Tuscan hillside.

A sentry post with a barrier guarded the bottom of the hill and prevented vehicles from accessing the vertiginous road up the hill, which was probably unnecessary. Only the foolhardy, or the very drunk as Joycey later discovered, would even consider attempting to ascend on foot.

It had luxurious rooms, a swimming pool and was a short coach ride up another steep hill to the training pitches.

As a result of Peter Johnson's feckless financial planning a number of faces signed the previous summer had already been sold and didn't travel with us, like Marco Materazzi, Olivier Dacourt and Ibrahima Bakayoko.

But there were a couple of new faces in the travelling squad: Richard Gough who had been signed on a free transfer from San Jose, and a journalist and author called Ian Stafford.

Gough was 37 and nearing the end of a distinguished playing career. But his fitness levels were still astonishing. Ian was thirty-something, at the peak of a fine journalistic career and with questionable fitness levels. But their presence added significantly to the light-hearted mood around the camp.

Ian had already written one book, 'Playground of the Gods', which had proven highly successful.

For nine months he lived out his sporting fantasies, playing sport with the world's greatest sportsmen in their own environments.

Having trained with Brazil's biggest football team, played squash against Jansher Khan, ran with long distance athletes in Kenya, rucked with the South Africa national rugby team in Johannesburg, come on as 12th man for the Australian cricket team and climbed into a boxing ring with Roy Jones junior, he decided to produce a sequel, which included him playing for Everton.

Of course, before he was even allowed to come on for the last 15 minutes of John Ebbrell's testimonial match against Manchester City in August, he had to endure a full pre-season training schedule. Which is how he ended up at Il Ciocco.

That might have been a dream assignment for Ian. But in truth his experience was only marginally better than mine and Joycey's. These really were halcyon days for local sports writers.

I'd chat to Walter in the morning for a back page story for that day's Echo, Paul would chat to him in the evening for the next day's Daily Post.

We'd then interview a player after training for a feature for the following day's inside pages, and spend the afternoon writing it up. The only 'pressure' was that sufficient footballers would be prepared to offer us their time to fill a week's worth of papers.

And that wasn't really an issue.

Mitch Ward and Don Hutchison had bought a portable roulette wheel at Manchester Airport which helped kill some time (and empty Joycey's pockets), Michael Ball had bought a chess set which other players indulged in, but usually the players were so bored they were happy to spend half-an-hour chatting about their hopes and ambitions for the forthcoming campaign.

As a result the evenings were our own. Not that there was a huge amount to do tucked away high in the Tuscan hills, miles from the nearest villaggio.

So when Joycey persuaded Walter and Archie towards the end of the camp that they needed to enjoy an evening out, along with the club's first full-time media officer Alan Myers, we all jumped at the chance.

Walter chose the restaurant, an outdoor affair specialising in Tuscan banquets, and it was a memorable meal.

Course after course of local delicacies were accompanied by bottles and bottles of good Italian wine.

And then the Grappa arrived.

Now I'd drunk Grappa before and lived to tell the tale. So I passed, and warned Joycey to do likewise.

But he is younger, and foolhardier than me, so he dived straight in and tried to match two seasoned Glaswegian drinkers glass for glass.

The outcome was inevitable.

I mentioned it was an outdoor restaurant, which was fortuitous because Paul was able to discreetly turn his head and deposit the contents of his stomach into a nearby rose bush.

We returned the following year and noted that the bush had positively flourished from the attention.

Paul's pre-emptive strike proved wise, because the restaurant owner then insisted on driving us personally back to Ciocco.

It was a magnanimous gesture, except that the restaurant owner's small vehicle was perfectly suited for the tiny, winding Tuscan roads and not for carrying five passengers in comfort.

It was like a scene from The Italian Job, except the Mini Cooper was replaced by an even smaller Fiat, which zoomed at breakneck speeds around the hairpin bends of north-western Italy. As Walter and Archie chatted amiably to our driver, Joycey and Alan shared jokes which were clearly hilarious and I muttered "We are the Self Preservation Society" to myself over and over again.

We got back intact, quickly.

But my self preservation mantra only remained intact for a little longer. Because Walter had a brainwave. The players had worked sufficiently hard all week, he reasoned, to have earned a night out at a disco. Open air again, obviously.

Now remember, Il Ciocco was remote, so this necessitated yet another long coach journey.

This was also Italy in July 1999, when air conditioning on coaches wasn't uniformly standard.

And barely 18 hours earlier I'd been eating, drinking and making merry.

So after several kilometres of the coach lurching left and right, with no air circulating, there was a real prospect of me following my journalistic colleague's lead of the previous night. With no bushes handy I left my seat and headed for the front of the coach.

I didn't get there.

Before I'd even got halfway I was pressing myself against the coach floor like a commando on night-manoeuvres. I thought I'd stumbled, fainted even. Maybe I had, although Unsy's later contrite admission that he'd given me a dig in the stomach as I walked past "for a laugh" probably didn't help.

Walter's concern was admirable.

"You've got two options son. Man mark Steve (the club physio, Steve Hardwick) and you'll be fine. Or you can become a legend, drink a load more beer and have another great night."

I opted for the less than legendary option. But sipping water, getting on Steve's nerves, while watching Ian Stafford getting cuffed around the head by his temporary team-mates didn't help my own banging brain cells.

Yes, Ian was being beaten up. And he was actually enjoying the experience.

He was playing a game in which a player stuck a coin to his forehead, and then had to slap the back of his own head to deposit it into a glass.

But while Michael Ball and Don Hutchison could uncannily pull off the feat every single time, Ian couldn't manage it once.

"It's because they're footballers. They've got good hand-eye coordination," I ventured.

It wasn't. It was because they were cheating. They had only pretended to press a coin into the unwitting Ian's forehead, but were only too happy to help out with a few extra slaps to the back of his head to "help out".

Ian was becoming more and more confused as to why the coin appeared to be miraculously welded to his forehead. Or maybe he was already concussed.

I needed my bed, and could live without seeing Ian sustain brain damage, so I begged for a taxi, which were in short supply in the middle of the Tuscan countryside.

Eventually Walter procured one for me, and also found me a willing chaperone in Richard Gough.

Goughy clearly had my best interests at heart. He was engaging company, got me back to the hotel, ferried me to my room and it was obviously merely coincidence that he'd "just heard about" a disco taking place in the basement of the hotel which he "might as well visit" – on his own – while he was there.

I think he had a good night.

So, too, did the squad he'd left behind. And I have no idea how it happened but Joycey somehow got separated from the travelling coach party back, only to loom out of the bushes at the base of the Il Ciocco hill as the coach idled to let the sentry post barrier rise.

Maybe he'd been playing coin-based games, too?

Regardless he had returned to Ciocco the same way he'd left, on board the team bus, just a little more dishevelled and disoriented.

It was an entertaining end to a solid – and successful – camp.

Everton played six pre-season matches that summer, winning four, drawing one and losing just once at Burnley.

And despite having a journalist replacing super Kevin Campbell for the last 15 minutes of John Ebbrell's Testimonial, one of those victories was against Manchester City.

Even with treble-winning European champions Manchester United due at Goodison on the opening day, optimism for the new campaign was high.

So the Blues could have done without an eve-of-season bombshell.

But that's just what they got.

The rapport I'd developed with Walter was so good that he beckoned me into his Bellefield office on the eve of the new season, sat me down and earnestly informed me: "I'm going to have to fall out with you, son."

I was surprised.

"Why's that?" I ventured. After all, I hadn't collapsed on any more of his team buses.

"Because Francis Jeffers has handed in a transfer request," he replied. "I want the fans to know but I don't want people to know how you found out."

Franny had burst into the first team at the end of the previous campaign and had looked a young striker of immense promise and ability. But he was also not a young man to hide his light under a bushel.

He had demanded a new contract commensurate with his talents which the club was reluctant to offer him.

So I had a back page exclusive and had to feign a fall-out with the Everton boss, which was all a little surreal.

But while I was getting the weirdest of cold shoulders from Walter, things were warming up on the pitch.

Everton turned up like sacrificial lambs to the slaughter when the treble winners arrived at Goodison on the opening day of the season and secured a morale-boosting draw.

And after waiting until Halloween to score their first Premier League goal at Goodison Park the previous campaign, in 1999-2000 the free-scoring Toffees scored four in back-to-back home games against Southampton and Wimbledon – in August!

Despite the financial mess which existed behind the scenes, Walter even managed to bring in a few new faces.

The transfer activity at Goodison in the second half of 1999 was frenetic. As the club tried to keep the banks at bay, Craig Short, John Oster, Tony Grant, Gareth Farrelly, Thomas Myhre, John O'Kane, Michael Branch and Terry Phelan all joined the aforementioned Dacourt, Materazzi and Bakoyoko in leaving the club.

And Slaven Bilic was released.

But arriving at Goodison were two starkly contrasting new faces.

Even though he'd signed from the charismatic Portuguese giants Benfica, Welsh midfielder Mark Pembridge was a practical, prosaic and professional addition to the squad - memorably and ironically nicknamed the Merthyr Maradona by some website wags.

Another addition, from PSV Eindhoven, was anything but prosaic, the colourful and impressively coiffured Portuguese utility player Abel Xavier.

For a long time Abel, perhaps the only footballer whose surname starts with the letter X, was the first name on my mobile phone contacts list.

There was a logic involved. I entered names as I called people. Alan rather than Myers. Bally instead of Michael Ball.

(Actually that's not strictly true, Alan is listed as Myarse, which was the pet name handed him by Archie Knox. And it stuck. Although he's the exception which proves my mobile phone rule).

It's easier to remember. And as I didn't know Aaron Lennon, Abel came first…which later that summer became a bit of a nuisance for the Portuguese international.

I still hadn't learned how to put a lock on my Nokia (mobile phones were still in their infancy and technology is not my middle name). And one afternoon, traipsing round Chester Zoo with my then very young children, the phone rang.

Melanie (you'll meet her next chapter) rolled her eyes, I shrugged apologetically – then answered.

It was a foreign-sounding gentleman, angrily wanting to know why I'd called him.

"No, you've got that wrong," I snapped. "You've just called me."

"No. You have called me. Many times," he said.

"No I have not. You have definitely called me," I replied.

"Who is this?" he retorted irritably, before adding, "Davey…?"

"Abel?" I asked. Then the penny dropped.

I'd been walking around Chester Zoo all day, phone lock off, with him listening to my phone jostling around in my trouser pocket.

That wasn't, he later explained, the reason for his name change at the age of 37 to Faisal Xavier.

Abel Xavier had embraced Islam, revealing: "It's an emotional goodbye and I hope to participate in something very satisfying in a new stage of my life. In moments of grief, I have found comfort in Islam. Slowly, I learned a religion that professes peace, equality, freedom and hope. These are foundations with which I identify."

So I didn't feel quite so bad about disturbing him.

During his brief spell at Everton, Abel proved an endearing individual.

People usually noticed his elaborate, multi-coloured hairstyles, but it was his eyes which were his most unusual characteristic. They were an unusual pale hazel colour with a solid dark ring around the iris – and he fixed you with them while he was speaking, which was often. He was a very good communicator.

When Walter Smith came under increasing pressure in the bleak midwinter of 2001 it was Abel who led a player delegation to me, wanting to show support for the under-pressure boss.

Walter was uncomfortable with the gesture but it underlined Abel's genuinely good nature.

He was also supremely professional.

He invited me to an Albert Dock restaurant once when I was due to interview him, where he was 'enjoying' his post-training refuelling session.

The word 'enjoying' is in inverted commas because what was presented in front of Abel was a glass of sparkling water and a large plate of steaming white slop.

Nothing else. No accompaniment. Not even seasoning.

When I raised an eyebrow, Abel smiled and explained: "Twelve egg whites. Poached. All protein. No fat."

And presumably precious little taste, too.

Maybe I should have offered him a Grappa…

## Chapter Twenty

# GRAVE DAYS AND ALEX NARKS

WALTER Smith's three-and-a-half-year spell as Everton manager followed a cyclical trend.

He'd spend shed-loads of money on potentially exciting footballers, said players would look briefly promising, then he'd have to sell them again because of circumstances beyond his control.

His buy and sell situation reared its head again in 2000/01.

This time it wasn't a chairman urging him to spend money the club never had, it was a chairman urging him to spend money the club was about to have.

Bill Kenwright and Sir Philip Carter had stepped into the void left by Peter Johnson's hasty exit and Bill had swiftly negotiated a media deal with NTL worth £30million, the same deal that David Dein had just negotiated for Arsenal.

That was enough for a significant splurge on transfers.

The difference was that Arsenal's deal was with Granada, Everton's was with NTL, and while Granada are still with us now, NTL went bust in 2000 just three hours before the paperwork was due to be signed off with the Blues – which is why players like Steve Watson, Niclas Alexandersson, Alessandro Pistone, Gary Naysmith, Paul Gascoigne, Duncan Ferguson, Idan Tal, Alex Nyarko and Thomas Gravesen were all signed between June and October 2000.

And why, barely 12 months later, Francis Jeffers was sold to Arsenal, Michael Ball was encouraged to join Glasgow Rangers, Nick Barmby had already crossed the park to Anfield, and Alex Nyarko exited Everton almost as quickly as he'd arrived.

Actually there were other circumstances surrounding Nyarko's exit more than simply financial.

Thomas Gravesen is often cited as the most eccentric of Walter's many signings…and this was a manager who signed Paul Gascoigne.

But Nyarko certainly deserves inclusion in any hall of blame.

Gravesen was snapped up for a bargain £2.5m from Hamburg, and while his decision to turn up for training every day in a tiny dark blue Nissan Micra attracted most attention – it certainly looked incongruous parked up alongside Kevin Campbell's silver Bentley Turbo with customised wheels – players were quickly talking about the sublime talent the mercurial Dane was displaying on the training pitch.

He was also keen to impress – on and off the pitch. His sentiments were admirable, if his pronunciation less so, when he told Alan Myers that he had read all about the club's history and wanted to follow in the footsteps of legendary players like "the great Dean Dickenson".

Dixie Dean was the legend he was hoping to emulate.

But if Tommy was just eccentric, Alex Nyarko was simply baffling.

A Ghana international, he cost a hefty £4.5m from Lens – comfortably the club's most expensive signing that summer – and came with a reputation to match.

It was a lazy comparison, but because he was tall and rangy, operated in midfield and was signed from France, he was immediately saddled with a tag of 'the new Patrick Vieira'.

But initial comparisons weren't misguided. Really. Alex often appears now in teams of 'worst Everton XIs' but to begin with he looked like an inspired acquisition.

His pre-season performances whetted the appetite for the real thing, patrolling the Everton midfield like some kind of athletic Robocop, scoring twice at Exeter, once at Plymouth and back-heeling an audacious finish at Goodison Park against Manchester City.

When the real business began he looked just as impressive, scoring a fine solo goal at Tottenham and picking up an array of cautions for his spiky tackling.

Then something seemed to switch off.

Nyarko retreated into a shell. And when he was shown a yellow card in the closing minutes of a depressing 5-0 demolition at Manchester City in December, I was convinced he had collected the caution deliberately.

In my Monday match report I wrote: 'Would it be overly cynical to suggest Nyarko deliberately kicked the ball away four minutes from time to collect a booking which guarantees a ban over Christmas? If it is, his performance at Maine Road did nothing to dissuade the notion.'

No-one at the club challenged me over the assertion.

Nyarko didn't start again until New Year's Day, when he was

hauled off at half-time at Derby, then had to wait almost two months for his next start at Ipswich when he was promptly sent off for two stupid yellow card offences, ensuring another enforced break.

He looked like a player who wanted to be anywhere else but on a Premier League football pitch wearing a Royal Blue jersey and Evertonians had quickly come to the same conclusion.

One Evertonian especially.

Nyarko was strolling around the Highbury pitch on April 21, 2001, as Arsenal rattled four goals past Paul Gerrard, when Stephen Price had seen enough.

An exasperated Evertonian, he clambered over the pitchside advertising hoardings, made purposefully for Nyarko, took his shirt off and then angrily offered to swap shirts with the midfielder. Stephen's would arguably have been sweatier.

At the time it appeared an entertaining diversion to another miserable afternoon, but events took an even more amazing turn.

Firstly, Nyarko strode to the dugout and demanded to be substituted. Walter appeared reluctant but when Nyarko insisted, he introduced Idan Tal.

Then the substituted midfielder emerged unexpectedly in the interview area shortly after the final whistle.

After matches at Highbury, the press would usually wait in the tunnel area, speak to the respective managers and ask media officials from each club which players we would prefer to speak to.

But Alex got there before anybody, still agitated and upset, and delivered an incredible interview.

"This is the fourth or fifth time this has happened and that's it. I'm finished with football," he declared.

"This man has done the same thing before. He came and offered me a black T-shirt for my blue one and told me to f**k off.

"So today I have decided I am quitting football. I can't live my life like this. I can live without football and that is what I am going to do.

"I came to this club when I would have been better off joining another one but I have had no problems with anybody at Everton and I have full respect for everyone.

"I have been happy with the way I have played and I don't upset anybody, but this is too much."

I can still see the wide-eyed expression on the face of the Arsenal media officer as she stood, open-mouthed.

"Did he just say what I think he just said?" she asked.

He had. And there was more to come.

The world was different in 2001 and Walter was not prepared to show any support to his clearly troubled player.

"He showed a lack of strength," he rapped.

"Lots of questions come up – commitment, mentality. He gave up, which is not a great example to set."

When Walter was told that Alex had indicated an early retirement plan, he quipped: "I'll need time to think about that…about five seconds."

And that really was the last we saw of Alex Nyarko for a long, long time.

It took three years and a change of manager before Alex, who had signed a five-year contract with the club, finally returned.

Initially he moved to Claude Puel's AS Monaco on loan, then he enjoyed a full season at PSG, before he eventually returned to Goodison Park during David Moyes' tenure.

This time he agreed to sit down with me in a Cheshire hotel ahead of his return and have a less animated conversation than the last time we'd spoken.

He appeared relaxed, positive, chastened almost.

"I am happy to put the shirt on again," he said. "I came back and was telling chief executive Michael Dunford that I even wanted to see the guy (who had offered to swap shirts).

"I wanted to talk and if I had done something wrong I wanted to apologise.

"We are only human and I do not want to go to my grave before I say I'm sorry.

"I am here today and maybe tomorrow you will never see me again, so it is better to forgive.

"What will be will be, and God will decide my future."

It was all very Christian, which chimed with something Walter told me.

He believed that Nyarko had found God soon after signing for Everton, and that had affected his willingness to tackle and potentially harm opponents.

It was all Peter Knowles-ian, the talented Wolves midfielder who famously turned his back on football to become a Jehovah's Witness in 1969, citing exactly that concern about injuring his fellow man.

Was it a convenient excuse for Walter to trot out. Was it a genuine reason? Alex never expanded.

But his career never really recovered.

He made 14 uneventful appearances of his second coming, failed to score, picked up only one caution, then after unsuccessful trials with Southampton and Middlesbrough signed for Norwegian club IK Start in March 2005.

It was not a fresh start.

He was released after three months, joined a third tier Swiss side, Yverdon-Sport, where he lasted 18 months before retiring at the ripe old age of 33.

It was a slide which all dated back to that Highbury afternoon, Saturday, April 21, 2001.

I recall the date well. Because a week later I was getting married.

I was tying the knot with the granddaughter of the Goodison legend whose name Tommy Gravesen had tried so manfully to pronounce.

## Chapter Twenty-One

# **PERFECT MATCH**

LIKE all the best Liverpool love stories, this one started in a pub.

Before I swapped my scarf for a notebook there were a number of reasons why I chose to drink in The Westminster on Barlow Lane in Kirkdale on matchdays.

It was close to Goodison Park which meant you could be standing on the Gwladys Street End barely 10 minutes after draining your final pint.

The atmosphere was always bouncing.

You could knock on the back door and get a post-match drink on a Sunday, in those archaic days when the licensing regulations stipulated that pubs had to close between 3pm and 7pm on the Sabbath.

And Dixie Dean's granddaughter sometimes worked behind the bar.

She was stunningly beautiful. Still is.

Like every unattached Evertonian aged between 16 and 60 who drank in that hostelry I imagined a scenario where I'd somehow end up with this vision of Royal Blue loveliness.

But they were pretty much pipe dreams.

So busy was 'The Wessy' on matchdays it was impossible to even attempt to break the ice with a cheesy one-liner.

Which is where Melanie Ann Walker's grandad stepped in.

When I started working for the Echo we staged annual Sports Personality of the Year dinners, boozy, glitzy, lively affairs attended by numerous sports personalities, and club chairmen, where one of the awards presented would be the Dixie Dean Memorial Award.

As a result Dixie's daughter Barbara, her husband Mike and Dixie's granddaughter Melanie were regular attendees – and one year I was asked to host the table they were sitting on.

So I formulated a cunning table plan which included Melanie sat to my right, her friend to my left – and with my impossibly handsome colleague and table co-host Matt sitting as far away as possible on the other side of the table, looking after Melanie's mum.

It was foolproof, except this lovesick fool had smugly told Matt what he'd done, and he promptly sneaked back to the table to rearrange the place names so he was sitting next to Melanie and in position to try to capture her attention all night.

My intentions were only temporarily thwarted.

Matt was a Liverpool fan, so he wasn't present when David France staged one of his raucous Gwladys Street Hall of Fame dinners at the Adelphi Hotel, but Melanie was.

Our stars aligned that night. To cut a long and very complicated story short, we eventually moved in together to a house in Formby, not far from David Unsworth's.

It was modest by comparison, the Echo doesn't pay that well, but Unsy's proximity was significant.

After many months of idyllic cohabitation, and with my original wooing plans having been cruelly stymied, I hatched a meticulous proposal plan. It involved taking Melanie for a walk on Formby beach, dropping down on one knee on a sandy bank, popping the question and if Melanie said 'yes' digging up a plastic bag I'd recently deposited containing a bottle of champagne which I'd pop to pour into two champagne glasses.

And if she said no, well I could always come back and drown my sorrows.

At this time Unsy was the proud owner of a Porsche which was having some work done to it, and while it was on a ramp or wherever flash sports cars are taken to have work done, he'd been given a Bentley as a temporary 'run-around'.

After revealing my proposal proposition to him, he said: "Do you want to borrow the car?"

Do romantically-inclined journalists bury bottles of champers in the woods? So after I'd dragged Melanie all the way down Victoria Road, through the woods, back up Fisherman's Path, reached Proposal Hill, dropped down on one knee, received the answer I'd craved and then toasted our future union, we walked back across the level crossing, where idling in the sunshine was a big, blue Bentley.

"Look what's parked up there," said Melanie. "Isn't that a strange place to leave such a beautiful car?"

"It is," I agreed. "Do you want to go for a drive?" And pulled the key out of my pocket and popped the door open.

It was the perfect conclusion to a perfect afternoon.

We married in the church around the corner, Melanie wore a blue wedding dress, and Walter and Joe came to the evening do.

We married on a Sunday so I was even able to watch Bradford miss two penalties as Walter secured a much-needed victory the previous day.

Unsy, meanwhile, remained a near neighbour for several years.

We'd drink together, he came to Dublin to watch a Shea Neary fight with the lads, I was thrilled when he asked me to sit on his testimonial committee with Joe Parkinson, and he helped us physically when we moved in. I can still hear him exhorting "Come on, dig deep!" as he effortlessly picked up another huge crate and sprinted upstairs while I struggled into the hall carrying a potted plant.

More than 20 years later Melanie and I are still in the same house. Still married. Still happy. Barbara lives around the corner, and our children, Daniel and Scarlett, have been well and truly bitten by the Royal Blue bug.

And Unsy is still madly in love with Everton Football Club.

Some unions are simply made for each other.

And sometimes Everton can help you to live happily ever after.

## Chapter Twenty-Two

# ONE OF
# OUR OWN

COLIN Harvey was the first man who uttered the words 'Wayne Rooney' to me – and boy did I remember the name.

In the late 1990s part of my weekly ritual was to seek out Colin and Alan Harper at Bellefield every Monday morning for a quick resume of how the Under-19 and Under-17 teams had fared that weekend, then produce a short report.

This particular Monday morning Colin was as precise and perfunctory as usual.

"Lost 3-1 at Leicester, lad. Poor performance. Started badly but improved when we made a switch."

"Okay," I replied, scribbling shorthand notes into my pad. "Who scored the goal?"

"Rooney," was the reply.

"Rooney? I don't know that name," I enquired.

"You wouldn't lad, he's only 14."

My pen hovered over the pad. "Fourteen?" I replied incredulously. "And he's playing under-19 football?"

Then Colin uttered the words which have stayed with me forever.

Never a man to dispense praise cheaply, Colin's eyes almost went misty as he lowered his voice and said: "He's like a young Dalglish, only quicker across the ground and quicker of thought."

As my eyes obviously widened he added quickly: "And don't put that in your fucking paper!"

So I didn't. But I kept my eyes and ears open for talk of Wayne Rooney. Not that I needed to stay particularly alert. Soon everybody at Bellefield was talking about this young prodigy.

I broached the subject with Walter and he smiled and confided: "That kid is going to save me my job."

He was only half-joking.

Sadly even Wayne Rooney couldn't mature quickly enough to save Walter's job.

He was still seven months shy of his 17th birthday when a 34-year-old Paul Ince gleefully cavorted in front of the thousands of travelling Blues fans on Teesside after rapping in the third goal of a painfully one-sided FA Cup quarter-final humiliation at Middlesbrough.

Walter had gone by Tuesday the following week and a fiercely ambitious young firebrand from Preston North End called David Moyes was unveiled as his replacement.

There were only five months in it, but this was the first time I'd worked with an Everton manager who was younger than me.

But we hit it off – in as much as anyone can hit it off with David. His burning ambition to be a success as a football manager overshadowed almost every other facet of his life. He had little time for banter or small talk. He was serious, focused, overwhelmingly earnest, but also absolutely straight. Speaking journalistically he was the most honest manager I've ever dealt with.

Even Walter told me the occasional porkie. Like the day Nick Barmby crossed the Stanley Park divide.

I'd taken an anonymous call at the Echo offices from someone who claimed to work in Bill Kenwright's London office and he conspiratorially confided: "I've just heard Bill say 'Nick Barmby has broken my heart. He has just uttered the six words I thought I'd never hear from an Everton footballer – I want to play for Liverpool.'"

I always check out anonymous tip-offs, as outlandish as they may appear. George Weah was once spotted getting off a train at Lime Street Station (he hadn't). Duncan Ferguson had once been admitted to a hospital in Liverpool, failed a drugs test and the Echo knew and was deliberately withholding the information (he hadn't and we weren't). And a car had once been spotted at a local garage with the paint job 'Peter Beardsley of Leeds United drives Ford.' If it had it was a colossal waste of paint.

But something about that phrase rang true. It was just the way Bill would have reacted but I'd had one of our periodical fall-outs with the then deputy-chairman so I couldn't check it out with him.

I rang Walter and he was convincing. "No, he's not signing for Liverpool," he declared.

In light of his Duncan Ferguson experience I enquired: "But would you know if he was being sold?"

"Of course I'd fucking know Prentice, now leave me alone," he rapped.

He apologised the next day. After the morning papers had splashed news of Barmby's defection all over their back pages and I'd received a serious dressing down for not having had the story in the Echo first.

Apparently Walter had had Steve Watson sitting opposite him at the time I'd called and he was trying to keep his potential new signing in blissful ignorance that the club's best player was about to jump ship.

Feasible, I suppose.

David never tried to mislead me, regardless of the circumstances.

Early in his managerial tenure one of Franny Jeffers' friends called me to let me know that there was a very good chance his pal might be returning to the club.

David hadn't even met the player, but was planning to the very next day. He could have honestly said "No, I haven't ever met Franny Jeffers." He could have fudged the issue. He might have even deliberately misled me.

But he didn't. He told me exactly how premature and delicately poised the situation was, so I agreed to sit tight on publishing anything until a concrete deal had been agreed. And when it had, he told me.

But on March 16, 2002 David didn't know me from Adam. That was the day he took charge of an Everton team for the first time.

It was one of those uplifting Everton afternoons. Unsy crisply clattered one in after 32 seconds, Duncan Ferguson added a second, Tommy Gravesen stupidly got himself sent off before even half-an-hour had gone then Everton grimly defended their lead with 10 men, Steed Malbranque's 52nd-minute strike the only time their ramparts were breached.

A fortnight later Wayne Rooney scored two goals in an FA Youth Cup semi-final at Tottenham, the second of which became a mythical strike.

Already leading 1-0, from Rooney's first goal of the game, Everton were awarded a free-kick 35 yards from goal and the 16-year-old tyro decided to have a go. He slightly scuffed his shot into the defensive wall but the ball bounced back invitingly, so he took two steps forward and promptly crashed a rising howitzer of a shot into the White Hart Lane net.

It was the kind of goal comic book character Hot Shot Hamish might have hit. The only surprise was that the net remained attached to the stanchion.

Another fortnight later he was in a first-team squad which travelled down to Southampton for a Premier League match.

A young striker did make his full Everton debut that afternoon.

But Nick Chadwick was the youngster pushed into action while Rooney had to settle for sprinting up and down the touchline a few times.

He was away on international duty with England Under-16s when Everton were next in action and involved in an FA Youth Cup final three days after the final league match of the season at Arsenal.

So his opportunity to earn a place in the record books as Everton's youngest ever footballer, usurping my mate Joe

Royle, was denied him. But he would soon play a big part in the club's history.

That Youth Cup final against Aston Villa was the occasion he pulled up his shirt to reveal the 'Once A Blue, Always A Blue' message after scoring. It was an endearing moment.

Wayne was one of ours. He was born a blue, had grown up a blue, and would always be a blue. Apparently. Which is what made his ultimate departure so difficult to bear.

But in the summer of 2002 the excitement about his burgeoning potential had even spread abroad.

David Moyes' first pre-season tour was to the beautiful Austrian state of Styria.

Rooney was part of the travelling squad and despite Moyes' attempts to keep a lid on the growing excitement around his young starlet, word was out.

On this occasion the local media weren't invited to travel with the players, probably part of the security blanket Moyes was throwing over Rooney.

So the Daily Post's Andy Hunter and I made our way to Salzburg independently, where we were picked up by David's brother Kenny, quickly labelled 'Biff' by Duncan Ferguson because he was a dead ringer for Biff Tannen from the Back To The Future films.

Far from an over-bearing bully like Biff, Kenny was the polar opposite of his brother. If David could be a little dour, Kenny was charismatic. If David was serious Kenny was cheery and if David was overly-earnest Kenny made light of everything.

He brought a levity to the training camp which was appreciated certainly by Andy and I.

While in Styria, Everton had arranged a couple of low-key friendly matches against local Austrian teams.

The first was against SC Weiz, and ahead of the kick-off the man who looked after the tannoy announcements climbed down from his wooden box, sought out a member of the Merseyside press and asked, "What can you tell me about Wayne Rooney?"

I tried to be circumspect. I really did. But we were all insanely excited about the potential this young talent possessed, which is why I felt guiltily uncomfortable when Rooney scored the first goal of a hat-trick against the Austrian minnows and the six words which my CSE level German picked out from the tannoy announcement which followed were: "Wayne Rooney, das neue Alan Shearer!"

To be fair, his England record eventually outstripped Shearer's.

But he was still a 16-year-old man-child in 2002. The combination of that childishness and latent power and ability was outlined when I saw him mucking about with team-mate Kevin McLeod on the pitch long after the small crowd had dispersed.

Both youngsters stood in the centre circle, tossing footballs into the air and trying to punch them into the goal at the end of the pitch. Rooney could do it every single time, without the ball bouncing once.

Try it. If you can get the ball to bounce halfway without sustaining broken knuckles you're doing well.

That hat-trick wasn't Rooney's only matchball of the summer. He scored another treble at Hampden Park against

Queens Park as it soon became clear that regardless of Moyes' desire to shield the youngster, he simply couldn't ignore him for the opening match of his first full season as Blues boss against Tottenham.

He duly started, impressed in a quietly confident fashion and that 2-2 draw was the first time "Rooney, Rooney!" echoed around Goodison Park. It would soon become a familiar refrain.

Moyes did his best to assimilate the teenager slowly, introducing him from the subs bench as often as he started him, but every time he came on he would be accompanied by a frisson of excitement which he would usually justify.

He slammed one improbable effort narrowly over the crossbar at Anfield, ended one mazy, pacy run at Old Trafford with another near-miss. Then came Arsenal.

He'd already opened his Everton goalscoring account, striking twice at Wrexham in the League Cup on a night when the Welsh club's curmudgeonly manager Denis Smith tried to pour cold water over our growing excitement by sneering afterwards: "My mother could have scored them."

She couldn't. Unless Mrs Smith had secretly enjoyed a career as an international footballer.

Maybe Denis was trying to do David's job for him and keep the lid on the Rooney firework.

But the royal blue touchpaper had already been lit and it exploded on the last opportunity Rooney had to score a Premier League goal as a 16-year-old.

You've seen that goal many, many times. You know the circumstances. You don't need me to repeat it here. Although minutes later he almost added a second with an audacious chip which was just as technically magnificent and which dropped onto the roof of the Park End net.

That afternoon was one of those rare moments when no-one wanted to go home.

The crowd remained in their seats for at least 10 minutes after the final whistle, roaring "Rooney!!" and maybe trying to absorb the enormity of what they had just witnessed.

One of the greatest talents of his generation had just announced his arrival onto the Premier League stage.

Everton had had promising boy wonders crash and burn before. Martin Murray, Billy Kenny, Danny Cadamarteri, Michael Branch – and a few would go on to justify that anticipation, albeit briefly, like Mick Buckley, Gary Jones and Francis Jeffers. But the buzz and sense of anticipation around Rooney was palpable, and like nothing I'd ever witnessed around an Everton footballer.

He really was that good.

That Arsenal strike is rightly lauded for its audacity, technical expertise and dramatic denouement.

But a week later Rooney scored one which was even better.

Elland Road was an Everton bogey ground, in the league at any rate.

The Blues hadn't won there for more than half-a-century. But then Rooney jogged on with 15 minutes remaining and five minutes later slithered like a well greased eel past three Leeds challenges and clipped a shot back the way no defender was expecting for a riotously-received matchwinner.

He was rewriting history and we were lucky onlookers.

Rooney was handed a start in the next match, a League Cup tie at Newcastle, and while he didn't score on this occasion he was still on the pitch after 120 minutes of action to take part in a penalty shoot-out.

Everton hadn't won a penalty decider for more than 30 years, since the first ever European Cup shoot-out against Borussia Moenchengladbach.

They won this one and Rooney, obviously, converted his penalty.

A star had been born. He was ours. And the possibilities were endless.

Or so we thought.

## Chapter Twenty-Three

# A GENIUS DEPARTS

EVERTON enjoyed Wayne Rooney's genius for just two short years.

And it *was* genius.

Rooney might have gone on to become Manchester United's record goalscorer, his country's record marksman, a player who won every single club trophy available to him in a storied career, but there was always a feeling that at Old Trafford he had to be that little bit more disciplined than he had been at Everton, that little bit more coached.

Evertonians – and England fans at Euro 2004 – enjoyed watching a rapturous free spirit in full flow, a magnificent young maverick expressing himself freely and revelling in the experience.

He unleashed the unexpected. Frequently.

But during those carefree days there was always a fear that, given Everton's financial difficulties, they would struggle to keep hold of such a sought-after talent throughout his whole career. He was never going to be a Matt Le Tissier and remain at the club he supported for his entire playing span.

But there was a hope that we could keep hold of him for a little longer than just 48 paltry starts.

David Moyes, certainly, hoped he might be a Fernando Torres, a supremely talented young Spanish striker who had broken through with Atletico Madrid at a similar time and who ultimately made 214 La Liga appearances, scoring 84 goals, before he finally moved on, with Atletico supporters' blessings, to Liverpool.

David referenced Torres several times.

Evertonians, however, enjoyed Rooney for just 77 matches, 48 of them as a starter, and celebrated just 17 goals, none against Liverpool, before he left the club he loved.

The reasons were myriad.

But the controlling presence of his agent Paul Stretford had hovered over Rooney's Goodison future like a brooding portent of doom from an early age.

Rooney's interests had originally been looked after by Peter McIntosh, a good friend of the Echo and a solid Scouser, but in circumstances which eventually ended up the subject of a court case, the player subsequently came to be represented by a Mancunian former vacuum cleaner salesman.

And 'controlling' didn't even begin to describe the influence Paul Stretford exerted over the player and his family.

Paddy Shennan, a feature writer at the Echo, had spoken to Wayne's mum and dad many times during his rise to the Everton first team and when Wayne was called up to make his England debut at Upton Park against Australia, Paddy was invited onto the coach the family had hired to travel down to London.

It would have made for a lovely colour piece, given readers an insight into the pride the family had in young Wayne's achievements and offered a very different perspective to the football-focused report I would produce from the press box.

Except Stretford learned of the invite and promptly had Paddy turfed off the coach. He probably mused that he could have offered that seat to a national newspaper for a fee.

When Wayne won the Echo's Sports Personality of the Year award in 2004, and we went through the club, as usual, to ask the winner to turn up on the night to collect the award, Stretford belatedly learned of the decision.

He angrily dictated that Rooney would arrive at the start of the ceremony, collect the award, answer no questions, and then leave.

At least he was allowed to turn up.

It was no surprise, therefore, that after his stunning performances at the European Championships in the summer of 2004, Rooney started to be linked with a succession of suitors.

Newcastle made an offer but Manchester United was the club he ultimately chose to join, Stretford pocketing a reported £1 million as part of the deal and a further £500,000 on completion of the contract, believed to be the biggest payment ever received by an England-based agent.

And that move was how I ended up being called as a witness at the High Court of Justice Queen's Bench Division in a case between David Moyes and Wayne Rooney.

It wasn't what I'd had in mind when I aspired to become the Everton correspondent of the Liverpool Echo.

The first I knew of any problem was when David's lovely,

amiable PA, Sue Palmer, unexpectedly called me, at home, and said: "Hello Prenno, I've got the boss for you."

Now that was unusual.

I'd usually have to time my arrival at Bellefield to coincide with the conclusion of David's commute from Preston so I could catch him on his way into training. And on August 23 I'd done just that.

But this time he was chasing me.

"What have you put into tonight's paper?" he rapped.

Genuinely nonplussed, I attempted a quick resume of my evening's article, which included a summary of the clubs lining up to sign Rooney, mention of the lurid Sunday paper stories which had exposed Rooney's visit to a brothel and my belief that Rooney favoured a move to Manchester United.

"But why?" I enquired.

"Because Wayne's just come in and gone ballistic at me. He's accused me of leaking stories to you."

So I read out the story which had appeared in that night's Echo…and David's mood noticeably softened.

"Is that it? Wayne thinks I leaked that to you?" he said, which while not exactly a resounding endorsement of the quality of the story I'd filed that night, at least calmed him down a little.

And I thought no more of it – until three years later, when David asked me to hold back after a press briefing at Bellefield, assumed a very disarming demeanour with me and asked if I'd meet his solicitor, Eddie Parladorio.

Moyes was suing Rooney and the publishers of his first autobiography, 'Wayne Rooney: My Story So Far', for claims that he had told the Blues boss he wanted to quit the club after tabloids ran stories saying he had visited a prostitute. And apparently he'd 'leaked' that information to me.

As a result I had several meetings with Mr Parladorio, submitted several draft witness statements, the last of which ran to several hundred words and 14 separate paragraphs, and agreed that I would keep five days free from Tuesday, May 5, 2008 to appear in court.

It was all a little daunting to be honest.

Happily the case was eventually settled out of court (not happily for Rooney, though, as it cost him £500,000, a significant chunk of which went to David Moyes, who later suggested he would donate the money he received to the Everton Former Players' Foundation). It was all a little surreal.

Much of the information contained in the offending article I'd penned that day was already in the public domain.

I still don't know exactly what passages had caused him to "go ballistic."

Maybe it was the age-old reality of a lurid story which had already been published in a national tabloid, actually appearing in his trusted local paper, a paper read by his friends and family, which had upset Wayne Rooney so much.

It's a mindset which my editor Ali Machray articulated beautifully when former Brookside actress Jennifer Ellison once took him angrily to task over a story written about her which had appeared in the Liverpool Echo.

Ali, not unreasonably, pointed out that the same story had been published worldwide.

"It's even been in the pages of the New Delhi Herald," he argued plaintively.

To which Jennifer turned her angelic face towards him, opened a mouth in which butter wouldn't melt, parted her sugar sweet lips and barked: "Yes Alastair, but my nana doesn't buy the frigging New Delhi Herald."

## Chapter Twenty-Four

# TAKING
# THE PISS

IT wasn't just Wayne Rooney I upset that summer.

I managed to alienate the entire Everton first-team squad with one, admittedly, barbed article.

It was penned after the final match of the 2003/04 season and the headline 'Taking The P***' will probably give you some idea of the tone and content.

First, a bit of background.

After an inconsistent second full season as Blues boss, David Moyes had seen his side beat Tottenham at Goodison Park on Good Friday to mathematically achieve Premier League safety with six matches still remaining.

That win elevated them to 12th in the table, with just pride left to play for.

But pride came before a fall as those same players then took just two points from their last six matches to tumble to one place above the relegation zone, and on the final day of the season were embarrassed 5-1 at a Manchester City side who subsequently finished two points above them. Then they disappeared on their end-of-season jolly to Marbella.

What was even worse was that I kind of knew Everton were going to be beaten at Manchester City.

I'd been in the Bellefield hallway, as usual, earlier in the week and heard Thomas Gravesen moaning about the manager's inflexible attitude.

"We're going to get beaten on Saturday and the manager deserves it because of how hard he's pushing us," was the gist. There had been other grumbles too.

The new manager was an overly stern task master and he was training the players too hard.

There was some truth to the gripes. Everton had been knocked out of the FA Cup in 2003 by the team placed 92nd in the entire football pyramid, Shrewsbury Town.

But with the match played on an ankle-deep quagmire Moyes had trained his squad at a nearby school pitch on the morning of the match to acquaint his players with the conditions.

They were leg weary as a result.

And a few days after pulling back a three-goal deficit to draw level with Manchester United, but then suffer the crushing bodyblow of conceding a last-minute goal to lose 4-3, Moyes had the players in for extra training.

I tentatively tried to broach the subject of overwork with Moyes, and was slapped down spectacularly.

The players had gone out as a group to celebrate Kevin Campbell's birthday after that United game, four days before they were easily beaten 3-0 at Birmingham, a night match which preceded a 10-day break from football.

"Training too hard? Why didn't they wait until after the

Birmingham game to have their night out?" Moyes not unreasonably hit back.

I had sympathy with the young, new manager.

So when Everton were duly not just beaten but battered at City, I reacted spikily.

More spikily than usual.

I'd recently been promoted to chief sports writer of the Echo and I was probably trying to flex a little muscle, show that as well as providing insight and analysis from the training ground I could offer searing comment when necessary.

Accusing the players of 'taking the piss' was perhaps a little too hard-hitting, but there was no doubt in my mind it was justified.

Here's a chunk of it.

'By a happy coincidence the individuals this article is aimed at will be back in blighty just in time to read it.

'If they can be bothered. A large group of Everton's players, you see, returned home from Marbella yesterday, hopefully with a deep Mediterranean tan to disguise their red faces.

'They jetted out a week ago. Just 12 hours after becoming the squad of players responsible for the lowest points total in 115 years of football at Goodison Park, 14 players flew to Spain for what is politely termed an end-of-season wind down.

'It should be more accurately called a p*** up – because the p*** is exactly what those players were taking.

'I've nothing against professional footballers letting their hair down and enjoying themselves. Particularly when they have behaved professionally.

'But hands up how many Evertonians think that is the case

with many of the players whom their season ticket cash supports?

'There are some people closely connected to those players who didn't just fear Everton would lose at Manchester City, they knew it.

'And they knew it because those same players had let it be known they had no time for their manager.

'So what crime has David Moyes been guilty of that his players should decide to end their season one match – or should that be four games – early?

'Has he adopted a carefree attitude to training, letting the players come and go as they please?

'Was the energy drink those blue plastic Lucozade bottles carry switched for lager during a pre-season friendly?

'Is he tactically naive? All three are 'crimes' some Everton managers have been guilty of in the last 10 years.

'Not David Moyes. No. It appears his crimes have been threefold: He trains the players too hard; he never speaks to them outside of training sessions; he is unapproachable and bears grudges.

'Well boo hoo hoo. Pick your ball up and go home to count the 20 grand a week you're stealing from the fans who pay your wages.'

There was more. About another couple of hundred words in similar vein, but you get the drift.

I was wound up. I'd come across running stats – in the days when running stats weren't freely available – which proved that some players had put their flip flops on after that Good Friday victory.

And I'd decided to articulate my frustration.

In hindsight I should have named names. Leon Osman later took me to task pointing out that he had made only the third of what would become 357 starts he would ultimately make for Everton at Manchester City that afternoon, and expended every last ounce of effort he possessed that day.

He was right. I was wrong to have generalised. But I believed my basic argument was sound.

Not that any of the playing staff saw it that way.

I was on holiday with my family in Cornwall that summer when one of the Everton media guys called me to inform me that the Echo was banned from the training ground and I was persona non grata.

It had been a gloomy summer holiday anyway. This was the summer that the picturesque port of Boscastle was washed away in a storm and as Melanie, Daniel, Scarlett and I drove further south, the black, foreboding clouds looked like we were heading into Hades.

The hellfire was still to come.

I was told that Alan Stubbs had been acting as a kind of dressing room shop steward, photocopying the article, distributing it amongst his team-mates and telling them 'this is what people think of us.'

As a piece of pre-season psychology it was inspired.

After losing heavily on the opening day to Arsenal, and having sold Rooney to Manchester United, a belligerent siege mentality set in at Everton. It was a siege mentality which saw Everton start the season magnificently and actually lie second in the table by Christmas.

It was a staggering retort.

It came as no surprise that Stubbs eventually became a manager who guided a Hibernian team to their first Scottish Cup success for 114 years.

He was even asked by David Moyes to conduct the manager's press conference alongside him after Everton had beaten Middlesbrough in September to make the club's best start to a season for 26 years.

"What do I put it down to?" said Stubbs, as he sat behind the small table in the old press room at Goodison. "Hard work, a great bunch of lads and turning all the rubbish that's been thrown at us into a positive. From day one of pre-season basically it's been like that.

"We've played some decent teams up to now. Every other press man was linking us with going down. We were going to be the team that was one of the three. It's nice to make you eat your words."

Moyes added: "I know the players and myself had a long, old summer and it was mainly because of the way we played and the way we finished the season. So why should we not be quite pleased with ourselves now because we all suffered long and hard through those months?

"The only way we could put it right was when we came back and to be fair to the boys they have been extremely honest in their work.

"It doesn't matter what level of ability you've got, if you do it to the best of your ability nobody can complain."

Quite.

On May 7, 2005, just 53 weeks after posting the lowest

points total in the club's history, those same group of players secured the club's highest in the Premier League era and finished fourth.

Actually it wasn't quite the same. Rooney had gone, Thomas Gravesen followed him out of the exit door in January – replaced by Marcus Bent and Tim Cahill – but the transformation was remarkable.

It was still a little unsettling to read that my 'Taking the P***' column was still resonating almost a year later.

In the match day programme for the visit of Newcastle, which clinched Everton's fourth-place finish and led to the surreal sight of David Moyes toasting the achievement with a glass of champagne in a beige cardie, Steve Watson said: "The last game of the season at City was as embarrassed as I've ever felt after a football match. We were shattered after that game and we got some stick in the local press for going away as a group as soon as the season finished.

"The way the criticism of the lads was worded was scandalous because we knew that there wasn't a group of players that cared more about their football or were more genuine than we were. The stick we took hurt us."

Actually, the stick wasn't for going away as a group. It was for pulling on their flip flops before they flew out to Marbella and for casually frittering away the last 12 points.

And not all the individuals involved deserved that level of criticism. Watson certainly didn't. But in my new role as chief sports writer I had started to offer comment and analysis, and Everton was the club I cared about most. Mind you, my role was to offer analysis of events on both sides of Stanley Park.

# A GRAND OLD TEAM TO REPORT

It was a true test of journalistic impartiality with Everton and Liverpool locked in a battle for England's fourth and final Champions League place.

In truth it wasn't really a problem.

If anything I erred too far on the side of looking for good in Liverpool's performances in a bid to avoid accusations of bias.

And in my first meeting with Gerard Houllier I thought I might as well lay my cards openly on the table.

I bought him a bottle of red wine. Decent red wine from Australia. Brown Brothers were the vintners and the label contained the word "Everton" in bold print.

Gerard laughed and then decided to show me an incongruous piece of office furniture which, in hindsight, would probably have proved quite useful.

On the bottom shelf of the TV cabinet of the Liverpool manager's Melwood office, underneath the video player, was an antique helmet from a medieval suit of armour.

Gerard even tried it on for me – and began to explain the problems he had dealing with criticism.

"It is ex-players," he explained. "We have lots of former players who are jealous and undermine our work." Then he put on a video of Alan Kennedy previewing a fixture at Blackburn Rovers for Sky TV, by way of explanation.

Alan's critique was hardly withering.

He basically shrugged and laughed when asked about the potential for attacking football that day.

"See! See!" said Gerard, appalled. "That is what we have to deal with."

I laughed nervously.

Houllier certainly didn't need armour plating for those kind of barbs, but just a couple of years later he was under fire from all quarters – including many Reds fans.

His reaction during a UEFA Cup exit at Marseille's Stade Velodrome, when a little known centre-forward called Didier Drogba won a penalty against Igor Biscan, an incident which saw the Reds defender red-carded, was telling of his personality.

At half-time, with his team down to 10 men, tactical tweaks surely necessary and an inspirational team-talk required, what was Gerard Houllier's first priority?

Not the Stade Velodrome dressing room, as you'd expect.

Houllier headed for the Channel Five TV gantry to watch a re-run of the controversial penalty incident. To many people it looked like a manager trying to get his excuses ready, while there was still half-a-match to play.

Two months later he was sacked.

He didn't even have that bottle of Everton red wine to drown his sorrows. When I handed it to him he declared: "I will share it out with every member of the coaching staff."

He wasn't taking the piss. Gerard Houllier was a decent man but our paths crossed only briefly.

Besides, I had Everton players to upset once again.

## Chapter Twenty-Five

# HERE WE GO, AGAIN

JOLEON Lescott was sat to my right, flanked by Phil Neville and Davey Weir.

Leon Osman was to my left – squeezed in the corner between Tony Hibbert and Alan Stubbs.

Lee Carsley, Tim Cahill and Tim Howard were spread around – and they were all looking intently at me, all apart from a seemingly disinterested Andy van der Meyde who was carefully scrutinising a tattoo on his arm.

In fact, the entire Everton first-team squad was arranged around Everton's Bellefield dressing room, waiting for me to speak.

It's the kind of dream I might have had as a 10-year-old, waiting to go out to battle with my beloved Blues.

Except the circumstances this time were very different.

No-one wanted to go out to battle with me. In fact one of them actually wanted to fight me.

As ever, it was my Friday Echo column which had caused the rift – a column I'd allowed emotion to cloud.

Under the headline 'Labby's legacy', it was written on the

Thursday – four days after the lovely, the noble and the down-right decent Brian Labone had passed away on his way home from a Supporters Club presentation at the Winslow Hotel.

I loved Brian – as did pretty much every Evertonian who had made his acquaintance.

His beaming smile looks down on me from my office wall as I write these words, one arm around my wife the other around another outstanding Evertonian, Dave Hickson – as he and Melanie hold the silver trophy still presented in Melanie's grandad's name.

Brian had suffered a heart attack on the way home from the event on Sunday night, the same function that Tim Cahill had also been asked to attend.

Cahill didn't turn up – on club physio's advice – because he had suffered a knee ligament injury against Birmingham City on the Saturday.

Now, most reasonable supporters would accept that explanation. Brian certainly would have understood – as would any journalist. Except I wasn't aware that Cahill had cried off through injury – but was aware that he had been out on Saturday night in the city's trendy Newz Bar.

His presence was the talk of everyone who had been in there, because Cahill and the group of Everton players he had been with had become embroiled in an argument with some of the city's less savoury characters and had ended up making a hasty departure.

So I penned a self-righteous article comparing the attitude of former footballers like Labby to modern day counterparts.

Under the headline 'Labby's legacy', it read: 'Brian Labone's final night on this earth was spent in the shadow of his beloved Goodison Park, spending time, sharing drinks and swapping anecdotes with fans.

'He might have chosen to join other former players and their wives at the Empire Theatre, watching a special performance of Blood Brothers laid on by Bill Kenwright.

'Instead he had agreed to give up his time to present trophies to Everton's Players of the Year at the Winslow Hotel.

'James Vaughan turned up to collect his Young Player award. Tim Cahill, however, couldn't be present to accept the main award because he was injured.

'For me that item of news underlined the gulf which currently exists between modern players and their old-time counterparts.

'While Labone will be fondly remembered as a man of the people, a player with such generosity of spirit he would spend hours every day talking football with those who idolised him, too many modern stars have lost touch with the ordinary supporter.

'Cahill couldn't be at the Winslow on Monday night because he was injured. There is no doubt the problem is a serious one. It may even prevent him from taking his place at the World Cup finals this summer.

'But the problem wasn't serious enough to prevent Cahill allegedly being involved in an altercation with Reds fans at the city centre Newz Bar on Saturday night.

'Labone could also be spotted regularly in the city's pubs and bars – The Exchange and the Pig and Whistle were favourites – but he was never involved in altercations.

'A lovely tribute was paid to him by a Liverpool fan this week 'Labone liked a drink and you'd often see him in a city centre pub. But he was never obnoxious and he was never drunk.'

'Labone never enjoyed the material wealth of modern footballers, but the love and affection in which he is held can be measured only on a Richter scale.

'Modern 'stars' like Cahill would do well to consider that fact.'

I didn't suffer the fall-out. Initially.

My long-suffering colleague Dominic King was the Blues man on duty at Middlesbrough the next day when he was told that no Everton player would be speaking to him after the match and that the Echo was banned. Indefinitely. Again.

The trip to Teesside was the penultimate match of the disappointing 2005/06 season, so the 'ban' endured until the following season.

The impasse was helping neither party, so eventually I was asked by a member of Everton's media team if I would be prepared to come down to Bellefield to explain myself to the first-team squad.

I did.

Hence the surreal moment of sitting in a dressing room surrounded by Premier League footballers, while club masseur Jimmy Comer strode in with two pairs of boxing gloves, grinned and said, "Will we be needing these?"

Acting ability clearly runs in Jimmy's family. His daughter Jodie won a BAFTA for her delicious depiction of the psychopathic serial killer Villanelle in the Killing Eve series.

At least I hoped Jimmy was joking.

Tim Cahill didn't. A man who regularly boxes corner flags as part of his goal celebrations, waved him away – fixed me with a stare and spat: "What you wrote was fucking disgusting. Why did you write that about me?"

He was leaning forward, aggressive, and my response wasn't perhaps as conciliatory as it could have been either.

Words were exchanged, Scott McLeod, a former colleague and the press officer who had invited me down, looked unsettled. This clearly wasn't going as he had intended.

Then Phil Neville, not yet the Everton captain, showed the qualities which would see him very soon installed as Blues skipper.

"Hold on boys, hold on," he said, and without ever once giving the impression he was in any way sympathetic to my corner, poured oil on troubled waters.

"Maybe we should give Dave the chance to explain why he wrote what he did."

Cahill's attitude went from confrontational to merely bristling.

I spoke. He spoke some more.

The atmosphere was becoming almost conciliatory.

Then Cahill rapped: "I can't believe you brought Brian Noble's name into it."

I froze. The press officer froze.

Then Tim repeated: "I can't believe you did that. I have the utmost respect for Brian Noble."

I'm sure Tim's respect for Brian Labone was sincere.

Maybe it was the charged atmosphere that led to him getting his name wrong. Twice. Maybe.

I didn't challenge him. I didn't sneer. I caught Scott's eye and he raised an eyebrow.

I prefer to think it was diplomacy. Maybe I just bottled it. But the moment passed and we ended with an uneasy truce.

"How do we know you're not going to go away and do exactly the same thing again in a couple of weeks' time," asked Davey Weir, not unreasonably.

And the truth is, I couldn't offer that guarantee.

The Echo would be banned again.

I ended up in front of Everton managers again, but I genuinely believe that was because we cared.

The Echo sports desk is traditionally made up of journalists who have begun their lives watching either Everton or Liverpool.

They learn journalistic impartiality, they understand how to bury their feelings when they're working in a packed press box and they don't allow affiliation to a football club to cloud their judgement. But deep down they care about the clubs they're reporting on. It's the same across the country.

I poignantly recall the day Blackburn Rovers unfeasibly won the Premier League title at Anfield and Rovers boss Kenny Dalglish looked up and gestured to the Lancashire Evening Telegraph's long-time Blackburn correspondent Peter White, sitting at the front of the press box.

Peter was trying his darndest to put on a stoic mask, but after Kenny gestured he broke and wiped away a tear.

In regional journalism we're all a bit like that – football fans first, reporters second.

I reckon we've got it the right way round.

## Chapter Twenty-Six

# A MATTER OF LIFE AND DEATH?

I AM convinced Bill Shankly did not intend his now infamous "matter of life and death" statement about football to be interpreted literally.

Sure, he was obsessed with football. It was his reason for living.

And when he prematurely resigned as manager of Liverpool in 1974 it left a void in his life that he could never adequately fill.

But Shankly was also an intelligent and supreme media manipulator. And, like so many of his best quips, I believe that particular catchphrase was designed to reinforce Liverpool Football Club's position at the centre of the universe, a sentence uttered to stoke the intense idolatry which already existed on the Kop and influenced so many football matches.

Shankly's most recent successor, Jurgen Klopp, does exactly the same, but even more cutely and more cleverly. But Klopp also delivered a much more accurate assessment of football when he described it as "the most important of the least important things in life."

# A MATTER OF LIFE AND DEATH?

Football matters. It matters massively. But not as much as people's lives, livelihoods and feelings.

That was underlined dramatically when, as I wrote these words, the 2019/20 football season closed down as a result of a worldwide coronavirus pandemic which cost thousands of lives.

It was another way of reminding us that football really is just the most important of the least important things.

It is a message which has been re-emphasised to me many, many times during my career.

Writing about football is a wonderful way to earn a living. But it's really not that important.

I had the good fortune not to cover the 1989 FA Cup semi-final at Hillsborough. My best pal was getting married later that summer and had staged a stag weekend in France on Saturday, April 15. As a result I was enjoying a weekend off in Calais, while his brothers were both in Sheffield, standing on the Leppings Lane terrace.

I witnessed first hand Simon's desperate attempts to ascertain the safety of beloved family members in the pre-mobile phone and internet age; in truth his experience was nothing compared to what others were subjected to in South Yorkshire that horrible afternoon.

I was back in work on Monday, witnessing the moving work produced by my then colleague Brian Reade for the Daily Post, and taking pride in the Echo's challenge to the vile perpetrators of The Lies published in two national newspapers and several regional newspapers at that time.

Football gave support to a grieving community back then. It

was appropriate that Liverpool's first match back following the disaster should be against Everton, Liverpool fans supported by neighbours who had shared the pain of their fellow supporters.

Football could offer comfort and support back then, as it did throughout the 1980s when Merseyside was exposed to the prospect of a 'managed decline' by a cynical Tory government.

But despite its influence, football wasn't strong enough to protect individuals from personal torment.

I knew exactly where I was when the Hillsborough tragedy unfolded, and I know exactly where I was 22 years later when I learned that Gary Speed had taken his own life.

I was at home, standing in my conservatory, when the phone rang and the hideous news was delivered.

So shocking, so unexpected and so inexplicable was the news that I started to have irrational thoughts myself.

I'd spoken to Gary just three weeks earlier.

He was a visitor to Anfield for a match against Swansea and he was with his young son as he shuffled past the front of the Press Box. He stopped and chatted and we joked a little.

Gary was famously a lifelong Evertonian who had once been Kevin Ratcliffe's paper boy and I joked: "What are you punishing your lad for, bringing him here?"

Gary, then the Wales national team boss, joked: "I'm working (there were several Welsh internationals in the Swansea line up that day) and besides, he's a Liverpool fan!"

With wit as sophisticated as a sledgehammer I replied: "What? He's a Liverpool fan? You've failed in your responsibility as a parent. I hope you're proud of yourself!"

It was a joke. A poor one. But Gary politely laughed. That lovely, infectious, little chuckle he had. Then he stared briefly into the distance.

At least I imagined that he did. He probably had significantly more important things to worry about like the performances of Joe Allen and Ashley Williams than a local journalist's crass jokes.

But when news of his untimely death was delivered to me, my mind immediately flashed back to that moment and I couldn't help thinking that my words could and should have been more delicately chosen.

He probably never gave my insensitivity a passing thought. After all, this was a man who had thrived in professional football dressing rooms where the 'banter' is fierce. But really none of us ever know what's going on in somebody else's head.

I'd already discovered that with Speedo.

When Howard Kendall made him club captain at the start of the 1997/98 season I would speak to him regularly to gather his thoughts for his captain's column in the programme.

And I've already related how he told me, "You know why I want to go," in 1998. Except I didn't, really.

No-one knows what goes on inside another man's mind, and equally few of us know about the very real pressures a life in the public eye places on professional footballers.

It wasn't long after Gary's passing that one of his team-mates came to see me at the Echo offices in Old Hall Street.

He arrived unannounced, sat down with me in reception, and initially asked about the prospect of the Echo helping him to write and publish his autobiography.

During the course of that conversation, however, a harrowing tale of personal torment was revealed – anguish which had culminated in his planned suicide.

He had actually gone as far as connecting a rubber tube to his car exhaust in his garage, sitting behind the wheel, turning the engine on and waiting for the end.

Fortunately a family member found him before that irrevocable step was taken.

The dreadful tale was delivered in such matter of fact fashion that it was even more unsettling.

Happily he has now completely conquered those personal demons, is content, relaxed and embarrassed to even look back on that bleak chapter of his life. The autobiography wasn't ever a realistic proposal, I think the man concerned just wanted to talk.

But it underlined again that there are so many more important matters in the world than the game we love so much.

A matter of life and death? It's much, much less important than that.

I personally found that out the hard way.

On March 11, 2000 Everton played Chelsea at Stamford Bridge. The same night Shea Neary was due to defend his WBU light-welterweight title against Micky Ward at nearby Earls Court. So it made sense to cover both, stay over and drive back the following Sunday morning.

Just three months earlier my dad had been diagnosed with cancer, a cancer so advanced it was untreatable, and he was being cared for at Queenscourt Hospice in Southport.

My dad was old school, male working class. He didn't believe in being ill and even when he was he didn't believe in visiting doctors.

This was a man who once had the heavy metal fork from a fork lift truck drop on his foot, but refused to remove his boot to check on the damage until he'd completed his day's work and driven home.

The accident happened in the morning. I removed his boot at half past six that night – when the pint of blood I poured from his boot made a hospital visit a non-negotiable decision.

He had several toes amputated from a crushed foot, spent two weeks in a hospital bed and wasn't back behind the wheel of his lorry for months. So, around Christmas 1999 he self-diagnosed the pain he was experiencing in his stomach as a pulled muscle and sent my mum to the doctors on his behalf.

Frustrated physicians were understandably unable to agree on the correct course of action because they couldn't actually diagnose him in person.

When he finally relented and agreed to see a doctor it was too late. The tumours found on his liver were secondary tumours and he was starting to look jaundiced as his liver began to fail.

This was in January, so on March 11 – just six weeks later, and a week after his 61st birthday – I still believed we'd have some time in the future to at least sit and talk and engage.

But as a proper wordsmith from around these parts once wrote: 'Life is what happens when you're busy making other plans.'

Life. And death.

On that March Sunday morning I received a call from my mum. The hospice wanted us there as soon as possible.

Naively I believed it might have been a change in his condition. Maybe they wanted to move him to another room? My endlessly-wise wife Melanie knew better. She told me I needed to get back as quickly as possible, and to prepare myself for the worst.

So I drove back. As quickly as the Echo's pool car would manage, which was well over 100mph all the way and enough to later land me in court on a speeding offence.

I still arrived minutes too late.

Eric William Prentice, the former merchant seaman, the devoted Duke Haulage shop steward, the man adored by my mum, Laura, the man who my brother Stephen worked proudly alongside and the man who utterly idolised my little sister Gillian, had passed peacefully away.

And I'd missed spending one last moment with him because I'd been watching Everton earn a draw at Stamford Bridge.

You don't need to ask where I'd rather have been. Sometimes football really isn't that important at all.

## Chapter Twenty-Seven

# A COLLECTION OF MEMORIES

THE thing which initially struck me when David France first presented himself at the Echo's reception desk in the summer of 1995 was his surname.

I'd never met a man whose last name was a country before.

Alan Brazil, Mike England and Joe Jordan were the only others I could quickly conjure up who enjoyed such a distinction. And I'd never met any of that trio.

But I quickly discovered that David's surname was the least interesting aspect of a truly remarkable man.

We quickly became pals. He still starts and ends all his correspondence to me with the phrase 'T'Other', to indicate that we were both christened David.

But that's where the comparison ends. Because T'Other David has achieved more than I could ever dream of in the support, celebration and contribution to Everton Football Club.

Way back in 1995, over a lunch at a long since vanished steak house called The Albany in Old Hall Street, David wanted to pitch an idea about creating an American-style Hall of Fame, a pantheon of deserving individuals who have contributed to the history of Everton.

I was sceptical, but agreed to help out.

And not for the first time David was right and I was wrong.

The Gwladys Street Hall of Fame became a hugely successful concept, initially inducting 75 players and five club officials into its ranks – and culminating in a riotous annual celebration at the Adelphi Hotel.

Len Capeling, my former Daily Post sports editor and a man whose cynicism made Lee Van Cleef resemble your grandma, wrote this about the first dinner.

'If heartfelt aspirations were Premiership points Everton would be so far ahead in the title race that the rest would have given up by now. That much was clear from the intoxicating act of worship that saw 84 Goodison greats being ushered up the royal blue carpet into Gwladys Street's Hall of Fame.

'More than 500 Evertonians dined on a meal of Premiership chicken from which the wishbone had been removed, followed by generous portions of pie in the sky, all washed down with jeroboams of pure adrenaline.

'This is not to be cruel. It was a memorable, memorable night, with due honour being accorded to a pantheon of Goodison gods.'

They weren't just evenings of orgiastic adulation – although there was plenty of that – they were fundraisers for another of David's bright ideas, the Everton Former Players' Foundation.

And they became even more adrenaline-charged and successful.

Every year, usually March-time when dreams of any silverware had been dashed for another 12 months, more and more passionate fans would be shoe-horned into a huge dining room which health and safety had surely only stipulated could house barely a quarter of that number.

They would be joined by scores and scores of former players And when one of Dixie's last surviving team-mates, Gordon Watson, walked into the dining room unaided holding the FA Cup, just 12 months after he had been pushed in seated in a wheelchair, the roof nearly came off the building.

No, the evening hadn't suddenly generated sufficient energy to suddenly bestow Lazarus-like qualities on its guests, but the money it did generate allowed David's latest initiative to offer medical care and attention to former heroes who wouldn't previously have been able to receive such assistance. And Gordon, a player who had earned £8 a week during the playing season and £6 a week during the summer, the maximum allowed by the Football League until 1945, had been one such recipient.

It was a wonderful symbiosis of supporters paying homage to their heroes and in so doing paying their medical bills.

David had insisted on the Foundation becoming a registered charity, and convinced me to sit as one of the first trustees.

The model proved so successful that the idea spread across Europe and was swiftly embraced by giants like Barcelona, Real Madrid and Bayern Munich.

Then David, as was his wont, stepped quietly into the background to work on other projects.

These included books, by last count he had 17 with his name on the spine – every single one about Everton – creating the Everton Heritage Society, commissioning portraits of the founding fathers of Merseyside football and, of course, compiling the truly astonishing Everton Collection.

Words cannot do justice to the scale, breadth and quality of the hundreds of thousands of items David collected over the course of several decades, artefacts which effectively charted the history of Everton Football Club.

During that first meeting he casually showed me a medal with a Liver Bird in the centre which had been presented to one of Everton's first league title winners in 1891.

I gasped. This was a piece of Everton's very early history. But medals – at least one from every trophy lifted by an Everton captain until 1985 – made up only a fraction of the collection. There were programmes; an unbroken sequence stretching back to the pre-Football League era and including editions for the first matches ever played by some of world football's biggest names like Manchester United, Tottenham Hotspur and our old friends from across the park. There were photographs, letters, football shirts, international caps, the original tenders for construction of a new stadium at Anfield, but perhaps most significantly of all, the official Everton boardroom minutes from 1886 to 1964.

These hardbacked volumes with ornate fountain pen script etched onto every page are the DNA of Everton Football Club, and as far as David could ascertain were tossed away by the club, possibly when the Megastore was constructed.

David spent more than a decade tracking them all down.

Auctioneers Sotheby's valued the collection in its entirety at a conservative £1.6million – probably more if it was split up and sold individually at auction.

David preferred to undertake a long and arduous campaign, almost as exhaustive as putting the collection together, to chase charitable trust funding to allow the collection to remain intact and ultimately become available to the people of Merseyside.

As he so often is, he was successful. Eventually.

The David France Collection is now known as the Everton Collection, is still being added to by the redoubtable Lord Grantchester and resides in the Liverpool Record Office where it can be inspected by anybody who wishes to make an appointment. It even has a website dedicated to it www.evertoncollection.org

But there was much, much more to David France than his crack-level addiction to collecting.

Many years after that initial introduction in The Albany he asked if I'd mind proofreading his autobiography 'Everton Crazy' and offer some independent criticism.

What began as a chore for a pal became a truly thrilling read.

I knew David was a gas fitter's son from Widnes, I knew he'd endured learning difficulties as a youngster and I knew he'd overcome those challenges to become some kind of NASA boffin in the USA and made a fortune.

But there was so much more he'd left unsaid or hidden in his typically self-deprecating fashion.

Based in the USA for decades, he became a transatlantic Toffees traveller, clocking up more than two million miles during his 60 seasons of watching the Blues. Or the equivalent of a journey four times to the moon and back.

Ill health proved no bar to his obsession. He once discharged himself from Reading Hospital where he had been treated for a heart attack, to watch Duncan Ferguson's return from a jail sentence to play for Everton reserves.

Just a few days after an emergency operation at the Countess of Chester Hospital, which left him with a stomach wound requiring 38 staples, he attended a UEFA Cup tie against Brann with a catheter strapped to his right leg.

David considered each sacrifice worthwhile: Ferguson scored twice in a 5-0 win and Brann were dispatched 6-2.

It came as no surprise to me when he was invited to Buckingham Palace in 2012 to accept an OBE for 'Services to Football' – and no surprise at all that as he kneeled in front of Prince Charles and gazed wistfully at the latest medal added to his collection, he quipped: "I'm very proud, Your Royal Highness, but don't you have one with a blue ribbon?"

My only surprise was that I was there to witness the moment. David had asked me and his close friend Norman Jones to join himself and his wife Liz to share the experience.

It was memorable.

David does not flaunt his success or the kind of wealth which once allowed him to offer £78,000 for Tommy Lawton's washed out England shirt, but he proved the most amazing host that weekend.

We dined at The Savoy Grill the night before the Royal Appointment, then after the occasion he took us to Rules, which those who watch closely during the James Bond movie Spectre will know is the London restaurant where M takes his supper.

I felt like a film star that day.

Norman took his leave late afternoon, David and Liz retired to their hotel and I decided to meet up with an old Echo colleague in Hampstead.

Keith Kendrick's career path had been almost as diverse as David's.

He was the UK's Young Journalist of the Year when he worked at the Echo, won a scholarship to work at the Washington Post, was headhunted by the Echo's old editor Chris Oakley to work at the Birmingham Post, became editor of Loaded, switched from the notorious lads mag to Woman magazine – and is now editor of the BBC's Food Magazine from where he floods Instagram with pictures of cheese.

He's a dear friend, despite supporting Manchester United. And we enjoyed an excellent evening, walked back to his home in Hampstead and much, much later I caught a cab back to the hotel booked for me by the Echo, sited on the North Circular Road and a building which closely resembled an Eastern European detention centre.

Fortunately, the quantities consumed during the day and night meant I was oblivious to the seedy room, traffic noise outside and threadbare carpet held together by masking tape until I awoke the next morning.

Sadly I was all too acutely aware of the events at the match I was covering that day. David's Palace visit had coincided with FA Cup semi-final weekend – and after leading Liverpool at half-time and looking set to finally banish their then six-year derby hoodoo, Everton did what Everton do in big matches against their near neighbours and imploded.

The least said about that day the better.

If only someone had shouted "Behind you!" to Sylvain Distin. Which is a link about as subtle as a bite to the arm.

Because the number of people who present themselves at the Echo's reception desk is vast.

And another well meaning philanthropist to call on Old Hall Street and pitch an idea to me was how I ended up treading the boards at the Royal Court Theatre alongside a team of former Everton players, my wife, Elton Welsby, Billy Butler, local comedian Mickey Finn and Kenneth Cope of Randall and Hopkirk Deceased fame.

An Everton pantomime was the brainchild of former boxer Brian Snagg.

Again I was sceptical. Again I was wrong.

A career in regional sports journalism takes you in many unexpected directions.

The week-long production attracted sizeable crowds to the Royal Court Theatre, raised decent funds for local charities and raised a few laughs and smiles along the way.

Although the last laugh was on me.

On the last night of Snow Blue and the Seven Blues Noses, friends, family and partners were all invited to attend. Melanie was already there on stage with me. As a drama school-trained student she was completely at home playing the Good Witch and opening the production, while I tried to untie my stomach from knots before delivering the one line I had to utter alongside Dobbo, Rog, Bails and Telf – yes, fellow thespians Martin Dobson, Roger Kenyon, John Bailey and George Telfer were now my fellow cast members.

I'd got on particularly well with George during the week and on that last night he walked past me through the stage door, Mrs Telfer on his arm, and said: "Evening Dave, this is Pam, my wife. Is she still gorgeous?"

She was. But how on earth did George know that as a match-going 14-year-old me and my mates used to rate the players' partners who featured with their husbands in a popular feature in the matchday programme, and that Pam Telfer – who appeared in a programme when Middlesbrough were the opposition for a 1977 League Cup tie – was by a country mile the most drop-dead gorgeous?

Was he a secret mind reader? Had I drunk one too many in a post-performance session and confided in him?

Neither, it turned out.

"H-h-how do you know?" I stammered, face colouring brightly.

"Because you wrote about it in a Football Echo feature years ago you daft bastard," he smiled.

Fortunately the Telfers had laughed it off.

It always pays to be aware of – and remember – exactly what you've written.

I learned my lesson. Years later I knew exactly what Danny Williamson was referring to when he knocked on a team bus window outside Elland Road, made the writing gesture people in restaurants often employ to ask for the bill, then made another gesture with his other hand which was altogether more threatening.

Williamson had been an underwhelming Howard Kendall addition to the squad in the summer of 1997.

He ran with a flat-footed gait, which was appropriate given

the lack of impact he had on the side, and my reports had reflected that fact.

Slaven Bilic knew him from his West Ham days, sat next to him on the team bus and kindly nudged his mate to point out my presence loitering outside.

Fortunately Danny seemed content just to make his displeasure known through sign language.

Slav, meanwhile, proved an immensely interesting character.

A trained lawyer, fully conversant in several languages, he was effectively signed by the club chairman after Joe Royle had been mutually consented. For several weeks he looked every inch a cultured Croat, but then as his discipline deteriorated and he somehow collected three red cards and eight yellows in 27 matches he looked more and more a barmy Balkan.

He once agreed to conduct an interview, which he suggested should take place in the bar of a budget hotel opposite the Jolly Miller near Everton's Bellefield training ground.

We sat down and he offered me a Camel cigarette. I don't smoke. He ordered a brandy and asked if I'd like one also. I do like brandy, but not at lunch time.

So he shrugged, lit up, sipped his brandy with a fiercely intense coffee accompaniment and proceeded to tell me how he'd turned down Real Madrid to play for Everton.

I was sure he was spinning me a line so I never used that information in the subsequent article but in truth it didn't need outlandish claims.

Slaven was – and still is – a wonderfully engaging individual, the kind of person a career in football journalism allows you to rub shoulders with regularly.

# A COLLECTION OF MEMORIES

Caressing century old football medals, treading the boards in panto and turning down brandies from a man who would achieve notoriety in a World Cup semi-final, it's been an interesting career path.

And it would take even more unexpected routes.

## Chapter Twenty-Eight

# A FRAUD IN ISTANBUL

DAVID Fairclough sometimes delivers delicious home-made banana cake to our house.

Which is a sentence I never imagined I would ever write.

Certainly not in the spring of 1976, when all the teen-age Supersub was cooking up were more and more unlikely matchwinners for Liverpool Football Club, including one of the most extravagantly crafted individual goals ever seen in a Merseyside derby. It was a goal which happened to coincide with my first ever visit to Anfield.

I stood against the wall in the Paddock, woollen blue and white scarf wrapped around my neck and one silk scarf tied to either wrist, and the goal traumatised me so much I cried.

So, too, did my school pal, Dave Abbott. But at least I was spared the ignominy of my distress making the national news-papers. Seconds after Fairclough's goal a quick-thinking pho-tographer had spun and snapped the distraught Everton fans ranged along the front row of the Paddock, so David found his teary visage plastered on the back page of the Daily Express, while I was just out of shot.

My distress was more enduring. I hated Liverpool's flame-haired young forward that day. So, too, did my future Sunday League team-mate, Dusty Miller, who was something of an Everton-supporting Cantril Farm hardcase in 1976; which is why Fairclough spent that evening sat at home with his mum and dad watching Match of the Day rather than out celebrating, because Dusty had threatened to "get him" and David took the threat seriously.

I know this because years later David became a neighbour and friend who would send me reminder text messages on the anniversary of that derby, and occasionally drop off some of his fine home-made baking.

Such friendships are possible on Merseyside. Just as the most successful captain in Everton's history, Kevin Ratcliffe, could befriend Everton's nemesis Ian Rush and even give him a lift home after the most harrowing Goodison derby of modern times, just as Jamie Carragher could follow Everton with the same kind of intensity he later showed as a genuine 24 carat Liverpool FC legend, and just as his best pal Steven Gerrard could be pictured reluctantly wearing an Everton kit to pose for a photo with the last league title Everton won in 1987.

Everton and Liverpool's rivalry is a weird dynamic.

Both clubs' fortunes have been intertwined ever since one club begat the other back in 1892 and continued until the famous cup finals of the 1980s.

Yes, Evertonians hate everything about Liverpool FC – and vice versa – but their fans also love their city and their shared heritage more.

It's impossible to articulate accurately, unless you come from

Liverpool. It manifested itself most obviously in the 1980s, when the city was under threat from outside agencies like the government, the national media, the establishment, heck, the rest of the country, and fans of the best two teams in the country circled the wagons and fired back.

Maybe it's why the derby atmosphere soured in the noughties, as more and more supporters from outside the city started to attend matches?

But prior to that Everton fans could be spotted congregating on the Kop when it was an all-standing terrace, and Liverpool fans could celebrate a Liverpool goal at Goodison – on the Gwladys Street – and both sets of fans preferred to sing "Merseyside" at Wembley in the 1980s.

It's a weird dynamic. Still is. But there are limits.

Which is why I was the most sanguine observer in Istanbul in 2005 when heads were falling off all around me.

By this stage I was the chief sports writer of the Echo, and was at Anfield for the night of the 'ghost goal' which overcame Jose Mourinho's Chelsea and took Liverpool to their first European Cup final for 20 years.

Sure I could appreciate the incredible atmosphere. Obviously I could feel the suffocating tension in the air as Eidur Gudjohnsen's last-minute shot ripped past the far post (idiot). And there is no doubt that I could embrace how important such a moment was for the city as a whole.

But I didn't feel 'part' of it like many of my colleagues.

I remained collected and professional and wrote reams and reams of words about the power of Anfield and the debilitating impact of more than 40,000 screaming, hollering hordes.

But I was emotionally detached, just as I was in Istanbul almost a month later.

I've had worse gigs. I was invited out the night before for an evening meal by some of my national newspaper colleagues, to a restaurant near Besiktas' ground, when an Australian radio station wanted to speak to me about Harry Kewell. So I left the table to take the call on the balcony of the 21st-floor restaurant and looked out at the shimmering lights over the Bosphorus, discussing a man who would limp off after 20 minutes of the following night's final.

You all know what happened. It was apparently the greatest Champions League final ever staged and I was privileged to be present.

Just as I was two years later when I was in Athens and Liverpool faced AC Milan again.

That trip underlined the curious Everton-Liverpool dynamic even more.

Jimmy Case had long been a bete noire of the Everton fanbase, ever since he ended Geoff Nulty's career with one particularly brutal challenge in a Merseyside derby. In fact his name is rarely uttered by Blues without the prefix 'Shithouse!'

Yet on this trip I discovered that Jimmy was actually a nice guy. Deaf in one ear, engaging, liked a pint or two and very good company.

He was co-commentating on the next day's match with Mike Hughes, like myself a Blue, and Mike had invited me out to dine with them.

It was an interesting conversation when my daughter Scarlett called to proudly tell me she'd passed an audition to appear in a Christmas pantomime and I had to explain who I was dining with.

Like I said, the Everton and Liverpool dynamic is unique.

Which is perhaps why now is the right time to hold my hand up and admit to hoodwinking the most one-eyed, bitter and resolute Red of them all, Tommy Smith, a.k.a. the Anfield Iron.

In the 1990s Tommy had been employed by the Echo to act as an independent (ha! ha!) arbiter of the Football Echo's letters pages.

If he agreed with the letter writer he would award a 'Fair Tackle', if he disagreed he could go 'Over The Top'. It was an interesting concept, but obviously it was unpopular with many of the Everton-supporting readers.

So I decided to go into bat for them.

In the days when letters arrived through the post and would be opened by the sports editor's secretary Barbara, I would write out faux correspondences and slip them into Barbara's pile.

The first one inquired, innocently, 'Dear Smithy, Could you settle an argument amongst some of the drinkers in Hartley's in Formby. Exactly how many times did Duncan McKenzie nutmeg you in the 1977 FA Cup semi-final?'

Smithy bit. Boy did he bite. His response was something along the lines of 'One nutmeg, but I won umpteen tackles, we drew the match 2-2 and the score in the replay was Liverpool 3 Everton 0 when McKenzie didn't get a kick.'

Obviously Smithy went 'Over the Top' on me.

My Blue-tinted colleagues Ric George and Phil McNulty

were in on the subterfuge and suggested more and more convoluted letters to wind up Smithy – and to add to the conspiracy all the letters were addressed from S Bland, Redgate, Formby, my Liverpool season-ticket-holding best mate.

The most spectacular reaction came when Simon innocently inquired: 'Dear Smithy, Could you settle another argument amongst some of the drinkers in Hartley's Formby? Do you really think Vinny Jones is as hard as some of the players you played against? Obviously the Wimbledon midfielder is a hard man, but unlike footballers of your vintage Jones can play a bit too.'

That last line was magnificent.

Smithy's reaction was Krakatoa-esque.

Poor Ken Rogers, who would sit alongside the Anfield Iron and type out his replies, needed ear muffs.

And obviously a simple 'Over The Top' tackle wouldn't suffice for the reply to that query.

Smithy invented a new category called 'Wipe Out!'

It was all innocent fun, inspired by an irritated young Evertonian. I later became friendly with Smithy and, strange as it may sound, he really was a generous, warm-hearted soul with a good sense of humour, unless you mentioned Emlyn Hughes.

I never did own up to those letters, though.

## Chapter Twenty-Nine

# GLASS CEILINGS

AT the end of David Moyes' first full season as Everton manager, the club's PR department sanctioned the release of a video summary entitled: The Magnificent Seventh.

For fans old enough to remember title triumphs, like myself, it was a little cringe-inducing to be perfectly honest.

But it also underlined exactly how far Everton had fallen since the 1980s, and where expectation levels were now at.

Nevertheless, with a shrewd recruitment policy and a zealous work ethic, Moyes did stabilise Everton quite superbly.

He didn't even need the midfield talents of Momo Sissoko, a man his honesty actually cost him the chance of signing.

When I returned to the Echo offices in Old Hall Street one morning, to file a transfer story that Moyes had confirmed to me, our Liverpool correspondent, Chris Bascombe, was an eager eavesdropper. When he saw the identity of the player I was writing about he instantly called his own contact, the Liverpool manager.

"Yes Rafa, they're about to sign him. Yes, you'll have to move quickly. No, he hasn't signed anything yet."

Which is how Liverpool hijacked Everton's attempt to sign a player Rafa Benitez had mentored at Valencia.

It was a blow, but Moyes made up for it by snapping up a Manchester United hero a fortnight later who went on to make 303 appearances and captain the club impressively.

Phil Neville's Mancunian associations mean he is still not as widely appreciated by Evertonians as he ought to be, while Sissoko suffered a dreadful eye injury in 2006 and made just 87 appearances for Liverpool.

Maybe honesty was the best policy for Moyes in that instance.

After that mid-table campaign of 2005/06, David conjured up a spectacular level of consistency from his squads.

League finishes of sixth, fifth, fifth, eighth, seventh, seventh and sixth was a mile away from the relegation escapades of the era which immediately predated his arrival.

But it was also never quite good enough to crash through the glass ceiling and into the Champions League places which would have seriously changed the club's outlook.

Those two fifth-placed finishes ensured Europa League football for the Blues, but after that fleeting 2005 experience the chance of Champions League football was never even close. Liverpool were 11 points distant in fourth place in 2008 and in 2009 Arsenal were nine points clear.

A new moneyed elite had developed in English football, bolstered by billionaires like Roman Abramovich and Sheikh Mansour, and Everton were not part of it.

Evertonians had to get their kicks elsewhere.

The 2008 UEFA Cup campaign was one such avenue. After overcoming the trauma of missing two penalties at home to

Metalist Kharkiv to go to Ukraine and win a thriller 3-2, Everton topped an engaging five-team group which included a legendary trip to Nuremburg, became the first team to win in Alkmaar for 32 matches – and scored a goal against the Cypriot side Larissa which was a flashback to something Howard Kendall's wonderful team might have conjured up.

David Moyes was often accused of creating an Everton team which was pragmatic and played route one football.

But the goal curved in with the outside of Leon Osman's right boot, on the run, was a culmination of a move which had the School of Science blueprint stamped all over it.

Think Carlos Alberto's legendary World Cup final strike for Brazil, but in Royal Blue.

Tim Cahill played the Clodoaldo role, collecting the ball in his own half and releasing Leighton Baines, the full-back romping down the left like a greyhound released from a trap, before he speared a pass infield to Steven Pienaar.

The South African's instinctive backheel was a delight and invited Osman to play a return pass to his midfield partner, but Osman had other ideas. He strode forward purposefully then struck a shot which veered a yard outside the goalpost at the Gwladys Street End, then faded unerringly back to ripple deliciously into the net.

That Europa League campaign ended with the best – and worst – of David Moyes' Everton.

On a rocking, roaring night at Goodison Park, Mikel Arteta almost broke the sonic boom with a steamroller of a shot to cap a 2-0 victory over Fiorentina.

But that only led to a penalty shoot-out because in the first leg the Blues had produced a limp, lacklustre performance and lost 2-0 and, well, you all know how Everton and penalty shoot-outs end.

But there are exceptions which prove the rule.

After winning the first ever penalty shoot-out to be staged in the European Cup against Borussia Moenchengladbach in 1970, the Blues promptly lost their next five.

That record stabilised a little under Moyes, beating Newcastle and Bristol City in the League Cup but losing to Middlesbrough and then Fiorentina...before THE big one.

Wembley 2009 and an FA Cup semi-final against Manchester United.

This was an occasion when I was able to behave entirely unprofessionally – and with a clear conscience.

When your career entails writing about football for a living, the rites of passage that most men take for granted, like taking your son to a football match, are denied you.

As a result I'd accompanied Daniel to a football match just twice before his 14th birthday, once when he was a toddler and Paul Gascoigne was making his Everton debut in a preseason friendly at Tranmere, and once when Andy van der Meyde made one of his two meaningful contributions as an Everton winger and crossed a corner for James Beattie to score against Middlesbrough.

Daniel had clearly picked up bad habits watching football without the authoritative presence of his old man alongside him. Shortly after that goal I caught him making obscene hand gestures towards the away fans in the Bullens Road.

But we won the match. So I didn't tell his mum.

Not that she'd have minded. After all, her granddad once belted a fan at White Hart Lane who'd been abusing him all match, and received a nod of recognition from a patrolling policeman.

But when another victory over Middlesbrough in 2009 ensured an FA Cup semi-final, I declared my intention to watch the match with my lad, as a fan.

Well, sort of.

I bought Club Wembley tickets. It was a far cry from my own first visit to Wembley in 1977 as a 14-year-old when, as I walked up the rear staircase heading to Wembley's East Upper Standing enclosure, I had to negotiate a waterfall of urine from pissed up fans relieving themselves on the stairwell.

In 2009 I was able to purchase a pie and a pint – for £7.50 mind. A slice of pizza cost six quid, a pint of bitter £3.80, and if I'd have fancied a pint of black velvet (in a chilled tankard) it would have set me back a whopping £13.

But there was a moment at the end of that day which was utterly priceless – a moment money couldn't buy.

Like my first visit to Wembley, the match ended 0-0. And like in 1977 not much happened on the pitch.

But unlike in 1977, this time there was a penalty shoot-out to decide the outcome.

Tim Cahill skied the first effort over the crossbar but I should have remembered that whenever Everton miss the first kick in a shoot-out, they win.

Joe Royle was thwarted against Moenchengladbach, David Unsworth saw his first kick saved at Newcastle, Steve Watson's was saved at Bristol City. Now Cahill had joined that illustrious group – except I wasn't enjoying that kind of confidence at that precise moment; I was thinking more along the lines of 'you stupid Aussie bastard!'

I needn't have worried. Dimitar Berbatov decided to imitate Diana Ross at the 1994 World Cup with his penalty and Rio Ferdinand wasn't any more accurate.

Leighton Baines, Phil Neville and James Vaughan – nervelessly in his first match for five months – were, and then Phil Jagielka stepped up for the money shot.

His understated reaction to confidently clipping the ball past Ben Foster's limp dive was in stark contrast to the undiluted explosion of ecstasy which ignited the Everton supporters.

I turned to Daniel, anticipating some kind of meaningful father-son exchange, a rite of passage where I imparted some kind of message about always believing, never, ever, ever losing faith in the Blues and never fearing the worst, no matter how bleak a situation might look.

But Dan was several rows down and several seats across, crowd surfing with total strangers and hugging anonymous Evertonians with uncontrolled glee.

I preferred it that way.

It was spontaneous, it was natural – and it meant he got it.

He was an Evertonian, for better or worse.

I couldn't call in another favour for the Cup Final and so I was back in the Press Box for the showdown with Chelsea.

It started well enough with Louis Saha's laser-guided left-footer after 25 seconds.

If you look back at it, that was a goal which in the current world of VAR lunacy would probably have been disallowed, because Steven Pienaar's left shoulder was offside before he clipped the cross in. But that merely underlines the inefficiency of that flawed system rather than any grave injustice. And in any case, Chelsea came back to win.

Frank Lampard scored his customary worldie against Everton with Tim Howard a little leaden footed, and the Chelsea midfielder repeated his old man's FA Cup semi-final celebrations of 1980 by running round the corner flag, to rub salt into a smarting wound for older Evertonians.

That afternoon was almost a summary of Moyes' time as Everton manager – close but no cigar.

A League Cup semi-final the previous season ended in similar heartache, Chelsea again inflicting the pain, then there was that 2012 abomination against Liverpool at Wembley.

When it mattered most, Moyes couldn't quite get over the line.

And when he was frustrated it would usually be us in the media who got it in the neck.

When I enjoyed my first pre-season tours with David Moyes' squads, I visited Scotland and Austria, nothing further than a couple of hours' plane ride away.

My successors as the Echo's Everton writer visited the west coast of America, Tanzania and Australia!

But at least the players were speaking to me on my tours.

Greg O'Keeffe was the Echo's Everton writer in the summer of 2010, when he picked a short straw stuffed into the pack by me once again – that's if travelling halfway around the world to one of the planet's most famous tourist spots to be blanked by the manager and players really was that short a straw. After all, he did have the Sydney Opera House and the Great Barrier Reef for distraction.

But professionally the trip was a nightmare.

The problem this time, bizarrely, was a subhead on a newspaper story published 11,000 miles away from Everton's Sydney training base.

This was the summer when contract talks between the enormously influential Mikel Arteta and Everton had reached a precariously delicate stage.

Indeed some national newspapers had declared that Arteta was nailed on to return to his native Spain as a result of medical issues with his partially sighted son.

So Everton granted Greg an interview with Arteta – with one colossal caveat. Any questions about the future of the best little Spaniard we knew, or the prospect of him signing a new contract, were off the table.

Imagine the boost an exclusive interview with Mikel Arteta would have given that day's Echo sales? And imagine the reaction from the readership if there was no mention of his future or his contract?

So we reluctantly agreed to the chat, but I insisted on including a paragraph in the paper detailing that questions about the player's future had been ruled out by the club.

Remember the Men At Work chart topper? 'Do you come from a land down under? You better run, you better take cover.'

David Moyes combusted. And Greg was banned. Eleven thousand miles away from home and he was being snubbed by the very people he was travelling with.

If that seemed like a heavy-handed over-reaction to simply telling Echo readers the truth, that was the world we now inhabited.

Fortunately the ban was short lived because I followed Bill Kenwright's advice. Eventually.

"Just apologise, son," he advised.

"But we haven't done anything wrong," I ranted.

"Just say 'David, I'm truly and deeply sorry,'" he purred.

"But I don't even talk like that," I raged. "Apologise? For telling people the truth? That's ridiculous."

It was. But I did.

I told David I was truly and deeply sorry. And he forgave us and embraced Greg back into the fold.

Life had been much, much easier when you could ask a footballer if he wanted to give an interview and then quote him accurately.

But those days appeared to have gone for good.

## Chapter Thirty

# LONDON CALLING

IF you've never read Simon Barnes' 'The Meaning of Sport', I'd urge you to.

It's a book which is a celebration of life as much as sport – and it's written by a proper writer who has attended far more meaningful sporting events than I could ever dream of.

Simon has covered more Olympiads than I have FA Cup finals (that Chelsea experience was my third) so his views on covering Olympic Games are worth noting.

So when I was told to forget about football for a month and attend the 2012 Olympics in London to report back on the exploits of the Merseyside sporting contingent, I noted his advice.

'At Olympic Games, the two things that worry you most are the nature of your cell and the efficiency of the transport,' he warned.

My 'cell' was a houseboat on the Thames, an enormous Dutch barge, hired for less than the cost of a cut-price hotel, and moored just round the corner from Kew Gardens.

And the overland train service from Kew Bridge to Hackney

Wick could have me from my floating haven to the Olympic Stadium in a little over an hour.

It was a route which worked well for four days, until the athletics began. Then the return trains late at night were so packed it was almost impossible to squeeze on board.

So I hatched a different plan.

I took a couple of London buses from Kew High Street to the media centre behind the Natural History Museum – then used the media shuttles to the Olympic Park, the North Greenwich Arena for the gymnastics or the ExCeL Exhibition Centre for the boxing and the taekwondo.

They were long days, but memorable.

I'd sit on the deck of my Dutch barge in the morning, drinking coffee and catching up with the morning papers, while looking out on the Thames at the herons, foxes…and parrots.

Yes there were wild parrots in the trees. Local rumour had it that because the Humphrey Bogart and Audrey Hepburn classic, The African Queen, was filmed on the same stretch of water, wild birds were brought in for realism escaped, bred and have remained ever since.

I'd leave mid-morning by bus, always on the top deck to enjoy a tourists' guide to London, watch some of the greatest sporting events in the world in the afternoon and evening, file my reports, then make the long journey back to the houseboat, arriving usually after midnight for a couple of cold beers then bed.

It wasn't entirely idyllic.

While much of the country was gripped by an evening which became known as Super Saturday, watching Greg Rutherford,

Jessica Ennis and Mo Farah all win gold medals inside one hour at the Olympic Arena, I was round the corner at the Aquatics Centre watching our swimmers try to keep their heads above water.

Metaphorically, obviously.

But the reckless joy being enjoyed inside the Olympic Arena was in stark contrast to the depression which enveloped Team GB's swimmers that summer.

I was there to pay particular interest to Michael Rock, a possible medal contender from Allerton, and Fran Halsall, a nailed on medallist from Southport.

A teenage silver medallist at the 2009 World Championships, Fran wasn't just a world class swimmer, she exuded a vibrant world class personality.

Brought up just down the road from me in Southport, and schooled just up the road in Crosby, I'd written plenty about her before she deservedly became a darling of the national media.

The Times' Matthew Syed once had to publicly apologise to his girlfriend after going overboard in one print eulogy to Fran.

But she was an incredibly easy sports star to like, and I desperately wanted her to succeed in London where she was a realistic contender for gold in the 50m and 100m freestyle.

In the end she reached four finals, but two fifth places were the closest she came to a medal.

And as I skulked around the mixed zone after her last chance of a medal had gone, Fran approached the waiting journalists looking a little red-eyed.

I'm not a swimming correspondent. I don't write about swimming regularly. I presumed it was the water which had reddened her eyes.

Then as she approached she suddenly ducked out of view behind a temporary wall.

I was puzzled and concerned.

Had she fainted? Had she slipped on the surface?

Then she bounced back into view, beaming that dazzling, trademark smile.

And I realised.

The poor girl was heartbroken. She'd seen her lifetime's dream dashed. But she was composing herself before fulfilling her media duties – the last thing in the world she must have felt like doing.

What a trooper. What a totally professional reaction.

So I behaved completely unprofessionally.

I put my arm around her and let her sob briefly on my shoulder.

Then she still gave me the interview I needed for the following day's newspaper, as I stood there uncomfortably, feeling like a prize heel.

It was an Olympiad for tears.

Just two days previously I'd had a pair of gymnasts break down in front of me.

The City of Liverpool Gymnastics Club made up three-quarters of the women's GB team in 2012, but while Beth Tweddle triumphantly brought home a bronze, one member, Hannah Whelan, had fallen from the horse and seen her hopes of a medal extinguished with that solitary error.

She emerged in the mixed zone with her team-mate, Rebecca Tunney, at 15 the youngest member of Team GB, for support.

It's clearly unrealistic to expect a schoolgirl to stand in front of a dozen strangers and articulate her thoughts on the most pressurised, emotional moment of her young life.

But that's what journalism is today.

We don't just paint a picture of what we've just seen. Given the all pervading presence of the TV camera in this digital age everyone has seen it anyway.

We want words and reaction and sound bites.

So Rebecca started to try and deliver what modern journalism demands, but when she started to talk about Hannah she burst into tears.

That set off Hannah – and I was faced with two sobbing youngsters in front of me, thinking to myself, 'what kind of job is it that reduces a pair of schoolgirls to tears?'

The only conscience salving reply I can offer is that it's a job which also offers you access to some of the most amazing sporting moments in human history, allows you to witness greatness and gives you the opportunity to try and record and recreate that moment for your readership, moments like watching a flesh and blood missile called Usain Bolt running 100 metres in 9.63 seconds.

The 100m final is usually the Blue Riband event of any Olympiad, the coronation of the fastest human being on the planet.

But in London, Bolt's appearance in that final gave it the potential to become one of the moments of the Games, so I arrived early to try and claim a ringside seat.

The previous day I'd managed to commandeer a position barely 50m from the finish line, so I tried again.

This time there were stickers on the Perspex screens containing the names of various sports agencies.

But between Press Association and Pravda, there was a gap.

I asked a steward if it was available and he explained that as long as there was no sticker I was fine to sit there.

So I did.

The seats began to fill around me, but the seat to my left remained empty until, half-an-hour before the big race and before the athletes had even come out to warm up, a huge, bearded Russian made his way ponderously down the steps, sat heavily in the seat next to me, grunted – and then fell asleep.

It was a surreal moment. Was he the world's most relaxed sports journalist? Had he been overworked into a stupor? Or was he just pissed?

I had no idea of the protocol which existed amongst athletics correspondents but as the sprinters took their places on the blocks I decided I had to act, and nudged him sharply.

He awoke, nodded at me, watched Bolt make history with his phenomenal performance, then put his head back on his chest and fell asleep again.

I still have absolutely no idea what to make of it all.

But that summer was packed with meaningful moments – and occasional moments which made me smile.

My sports editor decided to call me in the middle of a team meeting back in Old Hall Street and pop me on speaker phone so I could hear the rest of the staff back on Merseyside.

Unfortunately he called while I was at the ExCeL Arena just

as Katy Taylor was about to step into a boxing ring to face our own Natasha Jonas. It was the noisiest event of the Games, with the decibel level recorded at 113.7. A jet aircraft taking off only reaches 140.

Thommo quickly hung up.

I'd now ticked off an Olympic Games, a World Cup finals, Euro 96 and many, many world title fights in my journalistic assignment book.

But in 2012/13 it was back on the tools, which meant the Premier League and Everton Football Club.

## Chapter Thirty-One

# FOLLOWING FERGIE

AS a sports journalist, we're often at a loss to understand why people have reacted the way they have to words we have written.

But I think I knew exactly what to make of the day David Moyes called to deliver an expletive-laden rant about an Echo article in May 2013.

The words weren't even mine on this occasion!

"James Pearce. What a w\*\*ker," was the message shouted down a phone line by the angry Everton manager.

And Jamesy wasn't being accused of winking.

It was an unexpected call.

David didn't often phone me at home. He rarely used industrial language in front of me. And Jamesy has a delightful wife and children, which suggests he doesn't indulge in self pleasure all that much.

But that Monday afternoon the Everton manager begged to differ.

The reason for his anger was a sneering match report James had written on the previous day's Anfield derby match.

Everton had drawn 0-0, Blues chairman Bill Kenwright had punched the air in delight at the final whistle shouting "That will do us!" and in his Monday analysis Jamesy had sarcastically enquired when the DVD would be on sale.

Sure, it was condescending, but it was aimed at the Liverpool supporting readership. Worse things had been written about Everton Football Club in the Echo without their manager taking exception, but this time was different.

Just four days earlier, unknown to all except the man extending the invitation, David Moyes had been summoned to Alex Ferguson's Cheshire home to be told he was the Manchester United manager elect.

David was kicking off with me in the knowledge that he was about to be announced as the new Manchester United manager – replacing a volatile personality renowned for his 'hair dryer' lectures to players and press.

Using my admittedly amateur psycho-analysis skills, was it stretching the imagination too much to suggest that Moyes was already acting out his new role? Was he taking a leaf out of Fergie's book and acting the way he believed his famous predecessor so often did?

Because the outburst was certainly out of character.

Moyes often growled about stories in print. But the only time he'd previously called me at home to do so was when a stroppy teenager called Wayne Rooney had barged into his Bellefield office to accuse him of breaking confidences to me.

In hindsight, that incident should really have given me some insight into the career path Moyes would later take.

That accusation ended up the subject of a legal wrangle. But before I met with his lawyer, David had confided: "I can't let Wayne say things like that about me in a book. Say a club like Manchester United one day want me as their manager? I can't have them thinking I don't know how to handle big name players."

That was in 2007.

But managing a club like Manchester United was clearly an ambition of David's, and Alex Ferguson clearly believed 'The Chosen One' had the ability to handle big name players, even if Rooney was then nearing the end of a stellar United career.

The reaction of the Everton fanbase towards Moyes after it was confirmed he was going to succeed English football's most successful ever manager was a weird one.

They were certainly less angry than the future Manchester United manager had been with the Echo.

Initially supporters reluctantly accepted that the club couldn't realistically hold back his ambitions. I think that after 11 years some privately hankered for a change. He left to a hero's ovation.

Everton had finished above Liverpool for the second successive season, the team was playing a brand of decent, attacking football and the players created a guard of honour for the departing manager ahead of his farewell appearance as Blues boss against West Ham.

The Gwladys Street chanted Moyes' name, but as if to underline their conflicting emotions then asked, "Who the fuck are Man United?"

But the mood was primarily positive.

Moyes lapped the pitch at the end, cupped his hands to his

ears as the fans applauded him and exited with everyone's best wishes.

I witnessed all this from the Bullens Road Stand, alongside our Everton correspondent Greg O'Keeffe and sports editor John Thompson.

We hadn't decided to take a busman's holiday. We'd learned on Friday night that Greg had been banned from the Press Box by the club's always over-sensitive chief executive Robert Elstone, and John had followed the 'one-out, all-out' mantra and told us we'd be watching the game with the fans.

Greg's 'crime' had been to suggest in print that if Moyes had been given money to spend in the January transfer market he may have had second thoughts when United came calling.

It was an honestly expressed opinion, and from what Moyes had told me midway through the season, when he desperately wanted to sign a striker, probably accurate.

But Elstone was always a man to sense a conspiracy when one didn't exist.

So we watched the match and collected our thoughts from the Bullens Road, which at least helped me complete my set of having watched a match from every one of Goodison Park's eight existing stands.

It doesn't do any harm to watch a game from a fan's perspective every now and then – and even now I always go to a handful of away games in that fashion.

But a paragraph in the Monday report I filed from that vantage point still brings a rueful smile to my face.

It read: 'When the visiting West Ham fans tried to taunt the home supporters with a shout of 'Where's your Moyesy gone?'

the Park End responded with an incredulous 'You've got Sam Allardyce!'

'Safe to say Big Sam won't be targeted if Bill Kenwright really is going to listen to the advice of the club's supporters in replacing Moyes.'

Big Sam never was targeted by Bill – even when he ultimately did arrive at the club four years later.

But Bill did, as promised, canvass views from the club's supporters when he ultimately opted for Roberto Martinez to succeed Moyes. He just didn't listen to this one.

My relationship with Everton's impresario chairman – it's the law that Bill has to be described as a theatre impresario, even though no-one really knows what an impresario actually is – goes back 20 years. And we've had a few rocky spells in that time.

For one entire season he actually chose to look the other way every time I entered Goodison Park, in the days when journalists used the main entrance and walked up the staircase shared by directors. This caused a man with enormous generosity of spirit inner turmoil because I usually arrived with Claire Gray, who wrote for club newspaper The Evertonian, and Bill desperately didn't want to be rude to her but equally didn't want to acknowledge me.

But that was many, many moons ago when I was an angry, impressionable young club correspondent and Bill was an emotional owner who couldn't bear to read anything remotely critical of his beloved football club.

We long since buried the hatchet. And when he appointed Roberto Martinez in the summer of 2013 we'd become close.

So much so that I felt comfortable in expressing my reservations about the prospect of appointing a manager who had just won the FA Cup, but taken his Wigan Athletic team down into The Championship with a rearguard which couldn't defend its dinner.

A goals conceded record of 73, 62 and 61 in the previous three seasons concerned me.

"So who would you go for then, son?" Bill enquired.

When I told him, it was as if I'd placed a two-month-old kipper under his nose.

Suffice to say Rafa Benitez wasn't ever going to be the new Everton manager. But for 12 months at least, Martinez's appointment looked an inspired move.

It was a slow-burner, mind. I still clearly recall one supporter bitterly whingeing about "bloody tippy tappy football" to me as Stevenage Borough took Martinez's side to extra time in the League Cup, and then vowed not to renew his season ticket after two goalless draws in the new manager's first four games at the helm.

He was quickly in the minority.

Stylistically Martinez's Everton was a complete contrast to Moyes' more direct methodology.

With inspired additions to the squad like Gareth Barry, James McCarthy and Romelu Lukaku, promising additions like Gerard Deulofeu and Joel Robles and, let's just call them additions, like Arouna Kone and Antolin Alcaraz, Everton started to play with the kind of pizzazz Moyes' sides had rarely shown. A quite stunning derby match late in November was indicative.

Everton were trailing 2-1 when the enormously influential Leighton Baines sustained an injury, so Martinez decided to switch the left-back with a winger, bringing on Deulofeu who promptly went clean through and missed a sitter.

It was a cavalier switch, reckless almost, but it paid off spectacularly.

"I wanted to try and stretch the match," the bold Blues boss later explained.

The game stretched more than credibility in a Carl Hiassen novel, except the match, like most of Hiassen's characters, was actually factual.

Everton led 3-2, conceded a last minute equaliser, then both teams still had three chances apiece to score in time added on. It is still comfortably the best derby match I've ever witnessed, certainly more thrilling than the admittedly exciting but error-laden 4-4 draw of two decades earlier, and pointed to a change of mindset at the club.

Everton ended the campaign with a points haul which is still a Premier League club record of 72. The following two seasons it would have been comfortably enough to ensure fourth place and Champions League football. In 2016 it would actually have been enough to finish runners up to champions Leicester. But 2013/14 was an exceptional season and the Arsenal team who Everton walloped 3-0 in early April recovered to finish fourth with a 79-point haul. No team finishing fourth in the Premier League era has ever collected more.

It was Roberto's misfortune that such a campaign coincided with his first at the helm. But with a new attacking verve welded onto the defensive shield David Moyes had created, and the Gwladys Street singing about the School of Science on its way back, the platform to build on that season looked secure.

But then Roberto's tactics reverted to type.

Ten goals were conceded in the opening three games of his second season, and even when impressive German outfit Wolfsburg – containing a promising youngster called Kevin De Bruyne – were walloped 4-1 in the Europa League, with one full-back actually creating a goal for the other, the game was so wide open it could easily have ended 4-4.

Mo Besic and Samuel Eto'o were new additions to the squad that summer, and while Eto'o was undoubtedly a charismatic signing, his capture pointed to a facet of Martinez's character we hadn't witnessed before.

After recklessly tossing away a two-goal lead against Arsenal in the first home match of the season, Martinez stood at the back of the family enclosure and told a small gathering of Monday newspaper men that he had absolutely no interest in signing Chelsea's free agent Samuel Eto'o.

There had been rumours of Everton interest. But Martinez was categoric.

So no-one reported Everton's interest. Forty-eight hours later Eto'o signed.

So be it. Transfers are complex arrangements which can change quickly. But to have absolutely no interest in a player one day, to suddenly unveiling him as a new striker two days later suggested that Martinez had been economical with the truth.

At the time it seemed a rare slight.

Unfailingly optimistic, a man for whom the words 'phenomenal' and 'pristine' were used more often than 'yes' and 'no' – and certainly more than 'defend!' – Everton's Spanish boss even turned a Ross Barkley penalty miss into a positive. After demanding the role normally adopted by Leighton Baines (15 successful kicks from 16 attempts), Barkley promptly missed. But Martinez cooed: "I'm happier that he missed it because as an experience it doesn't get any better than wanting to take responsibility."

He then went on to compare the young midfielder as some kind of cross between Michael Ballack and Paul Gascoigne.

Bizarre. But hell, if you're going to have a fault, being unfailingly positive is not the worst characteristic to possess.

Initially.

But after a time, unrelenting positivity, especially when results on the pitch are anything but, starts to be seen as insincere.

Our articles in the Echo did not share the positivity and bullishness of the Blues boss.

So I was, let's say, summoned rather than invited with our Everton correspondent Phil Kirkbride to Finch Farm to explain ourselves in front of Roberto.

The Echo's 'crime', apparently, had been to not offer sufficient support to the club at a time of poor results.

But I got the impression Roberto's heart wasn't really in the admonishment and that he was simply fulfilling a request from the other Robert at the club.

When I was personally criticised for a lack of support, I pointed out that I'd actually 'supported' Everton Football

Club since 1975 and would still be at Goodison Park 'supporting' the Blues when Martinez had long since moved on. But we held a duty to our readers to accurately reflect what we were witnessing on the pitch.

I'm not sure he was even listening.

He certainly couldn't reference any individual articles which had failed to provide the support he deemed should have been obligatory from the local paper.

It was a little like that celebrated Denis Healey quote directed to Geoffrey Howe: "Like being savaged by a dead sheep."

But the tide was turning and the Everton fanbase were becoming pricklier.

An inconsistent Premier League campaign was kept just about alive by a promising run in the Europa League – and a last-16 draw against Dinamo Kiev appeared challenging but not insurmountable.

Despite conceding first in the Goodison leg, Everton came back to take a narrow lead to Ukraine – but Martinez then made the baffling decisions to hand Christian Atsu one of his five Everton starts and select Antolin Alcaraz ahead of a fit-again John Stones in Kiev.

Atsu was hauled off after an hour and Alcaraz endured one of those evenings which, in Goodison parlance, can only best be described as Glenn Keeley-esque.

He never played for Everton again which, in truth, was too soon, as Everton were annihilated 5-2.

Those five goals were conceded in the space of 55 harrowing minutes and pack-of-cards collapses became something of a norm in Martinez's third, and final, campaign as Blues boss.

The 2015/16 season started patchily – a home draw with Watford, a wonderful win at Southampton, a home defeat by Manchester City and a goalless draw at Spurs – before a match against Chelsea which contained one of my favourite moments of the Martinez reign.

The Everton fanbase had been slow to warm to Steven Naismith, a free transfer acquisition from Glasgow Rangers at the tail end of the David Moyes era, and some Goodison supporters had been quick to let the Scot know their views.

Unfortunately for some of the more acerbic Evertonians, they were sitting directly behind the striker's feisty wife, Moya, when Naismith came off the substitutes' bench to groans against Chelsea – and scored a perfect hat-trick!

After the matchball-clinching strike, Mrs Naismith couldn't help herself, turned and declared to her husband's detractors: "He's not so shit now is he?"

He never was. But Martinez turned his back on Naismith that season, preferring the more mercurial talents of Arouna Kone. And then in January he splurged £13.5million on one of the most hapless forwards it has ever been my misfortune to witness in Royal Blue. And I saw Brett Angell.

Oumar Niasse, the third most expensive signing in Everton's history at the time, was paraded in front of Evertonians at a night match against Newcastle in early February.

His last match for Lokomotiv Moscow had been on December 10 and he wasn't considered match-fit enough to start an Everton match until April 30.

He finally started against Bournemouth at Goodison Park, didn't touch the ball for six minutes and when he finally did he won a throw in. He then did little for half-an-hour until Everton suddenly launched a counter-attack. The ball made its way to his feet and he turned, looked up to see where his team-mates were, and passed the ball straight to Harry Arter, who plays for Bournemouth.

Evertonians laughed. After all, light relief had been in short supply that season.

But worse than an inability to pass the ball accurately, Niasse looked well short of fitness. A man who had spent three months building up his stamina, frequently stopped to place his hands on his knees and suck in deep lungfuls of air.

For 30 minutes he bore all the hallmarks of a Bernie Wright for the millennium.

If you are unaware of the cult hero called Bernie the Bolt, he was a centre-forward signed from Walsall in 1972 and proved a rumbustious character. Bernie Wright tales are legion – and mostly true – although this one I'm about to relate may be apocryphal.

Legend has it that on one of his rare Everton appearances Wright paused from chasing down a defender to put his hands on his knees, relieve himself of the contents of his stomach on the side of the pitch, then turned and carried on as if nothing had happened. Niasse wasn't quite that knackered. But he was certainly no better.

He eventually wore down Evertonians – and won them over – with a handful of goals, a cordial personality and watching an away match at Old Trafford with the away fans.

Nice guy though he may have been, he was a dreadful foot-baller in a team performing dreadfully.

This wasn't the relegation threatened dreadfulness of the 1990s, but more mid-table mediocrity dreadfulness.

Just after Christmas, Everton showed colossal character to pull back a 2-1 deficit and lead Stoke City 3-2 at Goodison, then showed colossal crassness to lose 4-3.

They scored what appeared to be a 90th-minute winner at Stamford Bridge, then conceded a 98th-minute equaliser.

Then came West Ham, an afternoon which seemed to underline the chaos of Martinez's management.

This was a day Evertonians craved a little what-we-have-we-hold mentality.

Instead they got more gung ho madness.

Romelu Lukaku scored early. Well it was West Ham. Kevin Mirallas got himself stupidly sent off but Aaron Lennon still made it 2-0 early in the second half.

Then when Everton were awarded a penalty with 21 minutes remaining it just needed the cherry placing neatly on the top of the cake.

But Lukaku missed, and with 14 minutes remaining Martinez made the substitution which effectively sounded his death knell.

With the game crying out to be blunted and magnificent midfield enforcer Gareth Barry on the substitutes bench, Martinez took off Aaron Lennon, and replaced him with Oumar Niasse.

Now, we're all amateur tacticians inside football grounds but even by Martinez's standards this looked reckless, rash, unnecessarily bold.

It looked ridiculous when Michail Antonio pulled a goal

back, then Diafra Sakho levelled, and when Martinez finally, belatedly, introduced Barry for Lukaku, Dimitri Payet scored the winner in time added on.

Goodison Park can be a wonderfully atmospheric old arena, just as it was a week later in the FA Cup when Chelsea visited, but that afternoon it was ugly. The mood was critical, toxic and recrimination-seeking.

The fanbase was turning against Martinez. Then came Leighton-gate.

That's not a curiously-named successor to the wonderful Welsh winger Leighton James, but the moment Martinez decided to pick a public fight with the most respected, decent and experienced member of the Everton first-team squad, Leighton Baines.

Everton had lost 1-0 at Old Trafford, the same opposition were looming in an FA Cup semi-final and Baines stood in the tunnel at Old Trafford and told my colleague Phil Kirkbride: "I don't think there is anyone expecting to have their name pencilled in for that game.

"But the motivation should be getting your name there.

"I just don't feel as though the chemistry is quite there with the team on the pitch at the moment, and it hasn't been for a while.

"We are maybe leaning too heavily on individuals to come up with something."

Maybe Martinez was seeking recriminations of his own because he responded by forcing Baines to apologise – and then criticised the Echo for 'misinterpreting' Baines' words.

It was pure psychobabble.

Baines spoke honestly and candidly, and his words were represented accurately.

So I had a pop back in print.

'Roberto Martinez has blamed referees this season, he has blamed bad luck and he has blamed his players – now it appears to be our turn,' I wrote.

'Leighton Baines delivered a typically honest assessment of Everton's insipid defeat at Old Trafford on Sunday.

'The comments weren't analysed. They weren't 'interpreted' by us. They were delivered as an accurate representation of an honest footballer's thoughts following another disappointing defeat. Yet Roberto Martinez declared today that Leighton Baines has been 'misinterpreted' – and has 'apologised'.

'So what was the 'misinterpretation?' Clearly a lack of 'chemistry' amongst a group of players reflects badly on a manager.

'Did Baines choose the wrong word? If so, he did so three times. Did we 'misinterpret' Baines? Have our readers 'misinterpreted' Baines' meaning?

'Or is Roberto Martinez seeking another avenue to apportion blame? Is there chemistry on the pitch? If so, it is not being reflected in Premier League results.

'Baines has been 'misinterpreted' before. A typically honest interview he gave cost him his place at a World Cup in South Africa. But we don't believe he has been on this occasion.

'Perhaps there should have been other apologies forthcoming.

'From Romelu Lukaku for undermining his team-mates by saying 'it would be nice to play in the Champions League from next season.' Clearly that won't be with Everton.

'And from Roberto Martinez for the worst run of home results in living memory.'

I didn't hear from Martinez. But unexpectedly I did receive an intriguing message from one of his backroom staff.

Reflecting on that Leighton Baines comment piece he messaged: 'I am happy to see the veil of illusion is slowly being lifted. Everton is a great club and I hope it finds its principles again soon. My only surprise is that it took so long for people to see the manager as he really is! I have met many people in my life and none quite like him.'

It wasn't just the fans and a member of his backroom team who were becoming disillusioned by Martinez. A month later he was the former Everton manager.

But not before an FA Cup semi-final exit to Manchester United and one of the worst Anfield performances it has been my good fortune to miss.

Prior to Wednesday April 20, I hadn't missed a Merseyside derby for 24 years. But this match had been rearranged to a date when I'd planned to take my son, Daniel, to Berlin for a few days.

I had to end that derby sequence some time. I was just concerned that Everton would choose that night to end their long run of not having won at Anfield.

I needn't have worried.

Hertha Berlin were at home to Borussia Dortmund in the German Cup that night in front of 76,233 fans but Dan and I chose to pass up that opportunity to sit and watch the derby in a Berlin bar, just in case Martinez could pull off some kind of miracle.

By half-time it was quickly apparent we'd made the wrong decision.

The moment the final whistle blew on a soul-shredding 4-0 embarrassment, we left the bar where there really were Liverpool fans wearing replica kits watching, to find the nearest non-television possessing pub.

The Klo Bar, which we genuinely stumbled into by accident, was the perfect antidote.

It has been described by The Guardian as: 'The most bizarre drinking experience ever. Red wine in blood transfusion packs, electric shocks from tables, rotating bar stools, a tarantula in a glass case, a flasher at the entrance... and not too expensive either! Has to be seen to be believed,' and it was marginally less surreal than a season under Roberto Martinez.

This was the season that Everton beat Manchester City in a League Cup semi-final first leg, when Mo Besic looked every inch the World Cup midfielder who had shackled Lionel Messi, but lost the second leg 3-1 (although myopic Martin Atkinson played a more than pivotal role in that exit).

It was the season Everton beat Chelsea in an FA Cup quarter-final in one of Goodison's truly great atmospheres, then meekly surrendered in a semi-final at Wembley.

And it was the season Everton waved a white flag at Sunderland to save Sam Allardyce's record of never having taken a team out of the Premier League – a statistic we'd dearly come to regret not having ended 18 months later.

Martinez was sacked, Unsy came back in with Big Joe for one match only, and won 3-0, and there was a new man right at the very top of the club...Farhad Moshiri.

## Chapter Thirty-Two

# SO FAR,
# SO GOOD

THE 1955 autobiography of legendary Newcastle and England inside-forward Len Shackleton famously contained a chapter titled: The Average Director's Knowledge Of Football.

It consisted of a blank page.

This chapter will contain a little more. But not much.

But for very different reasons to Shackleton's scathing critique.

Because Everton's current majority investor is not your average football club director, and Farhad Moshiri gives very, very little away.

Farhad is a guarded individual.

I've been in his company several times now, but he has remained resolutely circumspect every single time.

So here's what I do know.

He was announced as Everton's new majority investor on the eve of the 2016 FA Cup quarter-final against Chelsea – and he couldn't have chosen a better game in which to make his bow.

There are some afternoons when Goodison truly rocks, occasions which caused Sir Alex Ferguson to once memorably quip: "It is always a nightmare going there and it wouldn't matter whether it was Dixie Dean playing for us. The atmosphere is fantastic."

It certainly was that day, and Romelu Lukaku helped create it with one of the finest individual goals even The Old Lady has ever witnessed.

Lukaku was just 22 years old at the time and could easily have gone on to become a 24-carat Everton legend, the latest in a long line of truly great Goodison centre-forwards containing names like Dixie Dean, Tommy Lawton, Alex Young, Joe Royle, Bob Latchford, Andy Gray and Graeme Sharp.

But he chose not to.

And the circumstances surrounding his exit underlined some of the problems the men who had stepped into my club reporting role now faced, problems I couldn't ever have contemplated a decade earlier.

In March 2017, Greg O'Keeffe was the Everton correspondent who had been invited down to Finch Farm, along with his national newspaper rivals, to listen to Lukaku explain why he was on the brink of signing a new, £130,000-a-week, five-year deal with the Blues.

Except Lukaku sat down with the guys, trotted out a handful of lame platitudes, then as soon as Everton's media officer left the room, he pounced. Well, he was a world class striker. As soon as his marker found his attention diverted, Lukaku struck and intimated to everybody he had no intention of signing.

Cleverly he didn't actually use the words "I want to leave" that came a few months later but his actions, his facial expressions, his body language all made it clear.

And then there were the words he did utter.

"Can I be one of the best in the world? Definitely. But to do that, you need the platform to show yourself. Then you are talking about Champions League and whatever types of games."

And: "Sometimes I speak to Vincent Kompany, who was at Manchester City when it all happened. He said, 'Rom, one summer I just came in and boom, boom, boom…Robinho from there, this guy came in, this guy came in'. Everyone was criticising them but, at the end, there are two league titles, FA Cup here, League Cups there. That is what we want as players."

Then: "Stuff is happening but there were some players we could have got, that I knew the club could have got and they didn't. And they are playing in this league. I'm not saying names but they are doing well."

Lukaku had made it obvious to everybody in the room he wanted to be somewhere other than Everton. Somewhere where top players could be attracted. Somewhere capable of playing in the Champions League straight away. Somewhere like Manchester United, in fact.

The press officer returned and sensed something was afoot. But Greg and the guys already had their tale. 'Romelu Lukaku claims Everton's lack of ambition is why he wants to leave in the summer' was just one headline.

Except nobody wanted to believe them.

Even Everton's CEO Robert Elstone continued to say that he believed the striker would sign.

Of course, he didn't.

Predictably it was the journalists who put their names to the stories who were in the firing line.

"Shit-houses stirring things up." "The Red Echo trying to force out Lukaku." "Manc* twats writing falsehoods." Just some of the less extreme reactions. (*The Echo has never moved from Liverpool city centre since the paper was launched in 1879, but the paper is printed on the Mirror presses in Oldham, which when any reader has a beef with the Echo makes us Manc twats. Go figure).

And now readers are able to let us know their views with a couple of ill-thought through stabs of their finger on a mobile phone.

It was easier popping out for a pint in Liverpool city centre in the 90s and noughties, explaining your articles face to face with fans. But social media has taken journalists' accessibility onto a whole new level. And try defending yourself in 280 characters or less to hundreds of snipers, on a social media platform where herd mentality is evident.

Greg needed a thick skin that spring. Until he was proved absolutely correct when Lukaku signed for Manchester United in July for £75million.

But once the messenger has been shot, no-one bothers to patch them back up again. Certainly not on Twitter anyway.

A year later Farhad came up with a more convoluted reason for Lukaku's departure, reasoning which did not reflect well on the Everton owner.

But the occasional AGM gaffe apart, Moshiri has been an undoubted force for good at Everton Football Club.

Bill Kenwright's '24-7 search' for an investor might have

gone on far too long for some supporters' liking. But there is no doubt that his quest was well worth the wait.

It always irked me that when Bill was receiving flak from some sections of the fanbase, it was because he was 'too much of a fan' and not as rich as Roman Abramovich.

In truth Everton needed – and still does – a fan at the helm, someone whose every waking minute is wrapped up entirely in the football club he truly loves.

But Everton also needed an investor with the clout to significantly improve the club's lot, and crucially wasn't in it for financial reward.

In Bill and Farhad they have got both.

And as a result they haven't lost the sincere family values which make Everton such an appealing club.

In the same summer in which Liverpool took advantage of the government's furlough scheme – then hastily backtracked – Everton announced voluntary pay reductions for their manager, first-team squad, backroom team, the nine members of the club's executive leadership team and the board of directors. In some first-team footballer cases, voluntary deferrals of up to 50 per cent were agreed for three months. Heart-warming.

And it is worth noting that during that painstaking and often frustrating quest for an investor with Moshiri's credentials, Everton stabilised superbly from the traumas of the 1990s to become a football club lauded for over-achieving.

They turned cutting their cloth into an art form.

Many football clubs did find new owners in that timescale – but plenty of them ended disastrously...the Leeds United catastrophe, the burial of Blackburn Rovers, Cardiff's colour switches, Glasgow Rangers going into administration, Newcastle, QPR, the Tom and George debacle across the park.

After the scare of the Peter Johnson years, Everton never flirted with financial ruin as closely again. But they never had the money to compete with the nouveau riches of Chelsea and Manchester City and the established Champions League regulars of Arsenal, Manchester United – and belatedly Liverpool.

Bill waited and waited, then waited some more before finding his man – and Farhad Moshiri quickly proved he was worth waiting for.

His recollection of Kenwright selling the Blues to him bears repeating.

"The day I went to Bill's office was a very special day," said Moshiri.

"I had looked at a number of clubs and I'd been at Arsenal for a very long time as a minority shareholder and I just wanted to be involved in a club.

"Meeting Bill, and especially in his office, was what had the greatest impression on me. That was a real man, totally obsessed in whatever he's doing. I saw all the photographs of the musicals, the movie productions and the great moments of Everton. His enthusiasm for Everton was infectious.

"You couldn't find anything negative, his heart was Everton and I just found him a guy very much in my own mould in being driven and committed to what he liked.

"He talked about the history, values and heritage of Everton. We kept on meeting each other and we became friends, he met my family, we got to know each other and, after a while, there was no real other option – it was Everton."

That was March 2016.

It was January 2018 before I finally got to sit in front of Everton's new majority investor. Like I said, he's circumspect.

According to most recent estimates, Farhad Moshiri is worth £1.5 billion. So I took along a bottle of £20 red wine to hand over.

It was a gesture. This is a man who has pretty much everything already, including, as he quickly proved, the ability to talk.

I did get a few words in edgeways, but for half an hour Farhad largely did all the talking. I wasn't interviewing him. It was an off-the-record meeting. And maybe he was spiking the chance of me getting any meaningful questions in by talking himself.

But it was a snapshot into the mindset of a man who could significantly alter the entire trajectory of Everton Football Club in a manner which hasn't happened since another wealthy benefactor stepped into the club in 1960.

John Moores still doesn't have any permanent memorial to his name around Goodison Park, the ground he helped redevelop and fill with trophies in the 1960s.

Everton's proposed new stadium simply wouldn't be happening without Farhad Moshiri or the man who introduced him to all things Evertonian.

It is to be hoped that when the Bramley-Moore Stadium does come to fruition, the contributions of the modern administrators who helped to fulfil that dream are not similarly ignored.

## Chapter Thirty-Three

# REVOLVING DOOR POLICY

AFTER two managers in 15 years, Everton then had four in three-and-a-half. Make that six if you're counting caretakers.

And I never really established a rapport with any of them.

Walter and Joe had attended my wedding. Six years after he quit Everton, I sat with David Moyes in the Goodison Main Stand watching a match against Brighton – for 45 minutes, anyway; he moved to a different seat in the second half – and I'd enjoyed many, many beers with Howard.

All were men I'd enjoyed a degree of familiarity with.

But Ronald Koeman, Sam Allardyce and Marco Silva remained steadfastly anonymous.

That had more to do with the changing face of sports journalism – and the intense demands on managers' time now – than their respective personalities. Not to mention my changing role at the Echo.

I'd been Tranmere correspondent, Everton writer, chief sports writer and then deputy sports editor before, on February 11 2016, the following email was circulated around Echo staff.

'DAVID PRENTICE is promoted to Executive Editor (Sport) Merseyside, reporting to Maria Breslin. David will combine the role with his current responsibilities as Chief Sports Writer.'

It didn't have quite the same ring as Echo sports editor, but that's what it meant, only the sixth to occupy that heralded role since Dixie Dean hung up his boots.

I was enormously proud. But it also meant that my opportunities to develop any kind of rapport with players and managers would become even more restricted.

And, of course, the competition was fiercer than ever.

When I started as the Echo's Everton correspondent and enjoyed a daily cup of tea with the boss, my rivals were a handful of national newspaper reporters, two local radio stations and a premium rate telephone service called Club Call.

Within two decades they'd been joined by Sky TV, BT Sport and Amazon, countless websites, numerous independent media outlets plus the club's own burgeoning media channels, all desperate for a piece of Everton action.

That speaks volumes for the way in which football has reinvented itself since the creation of the Premier League, but it also makes it more difficult than ever to enjoy intimacy with individuals at a football club.

Physically it was impossible for an Everton manager to devote time individually to every outlet who wanted to speak to him.

So we started to be grouped together.

Media outlets could only access the training ground by invitation, usually the day before a match, and even then the manager's presser was a carefully controlled environment.

The TV companies would begin by asking their questions, then the manager would be led into a side room for radio interviews, then we'd get our go for five or six minutes, and finally the manager would return to the conference room, which the TV cameras had since vacated, for a national newspaper briefing.

It was an environment which does not encourage intimacy, and given the number of different faces presented to the manager in such a short space of time, not really a situation in which he could become familiar with any.

Mind you, initially Ronald Koeman's introduction to us hinted at a more open relationship.

We all sat around him in a circle at Finch Farm when the new Blues boss made it clear that his assessment of Oumar Niasse chimed with many of our own.

So frank and candid was his assessment that everyone present assumed the words were 'off the record' and didn't report them. But even that wasn't enough to develop any trust between both parties.

A week later Ronald was asked for a 'steer' on a particular story, and when he seemed reticent was encouraged, "Off the record, Ronald?"

He laughed. "Off the record? Really? That does not exist with journalists."

Maybe he'd been stung in the past. He had played for clubs like Barcelona with their worldwide media scrutiny after all.

Often one journalist can develop a rapport with a manager and enjoy a closer relationship than his colleagues. But no-one enjoyed Koeman's ear.

His Everton 'reign' was a short-lived 16 months. It started promisingly, peaked with a joyous 4-0 mauling of Manchester City, and inconveniently ended when I was enjoying an October half-term family holiday in Tenerife.

Mobile phones mean family holidays today aren't anything like they used to be.

"The editor wants a 1,000 word comment piece from you," I was told. But writing a comment piece on a computer screen in the reception area of the Arona Gran Hotel in Los Cristianos, then stepping back outside for a cold beer in 32 degrees pool side is undoubtedly one of the more agreeable ways to have your holiday interrupted.

I chose to reflect on Koeman's inability to communicate with the fans, and his clearly dysfunctional relationship with the club's recently appointed director of football, Steve Walsh.

'The social media mockery of Ronald Koeman in recent weeks has become increasingly cruel,' I wrote, as holiday-makers traipsed past in shorts and carrying towels.

'From lampoons of Eastenders harridan Pat Butcher, to a Flump from the children's TV show.

'Then in recent weeks, when the former Everton manager's unshaven visage reflected the growing pressure on him, he was cast as another desperate character from Eastenders, Phil Mitchell.

'A more accurate portrayal, however, would have been a character from a movie. 'What we've got here is a failure to communicate.'

'It's a famous line from a famous sixties film. And it sums up Ronald Koeman's tenure at Everton perfectly.

'Life has replicated art at Goodison Park, with Koeman cast in the role of Cool Hand Luke.

'The difference is that Paul Newman's character boasted charisma and charm, while Koeman has been aloof, even arrogant – and he never once connected with the influential Everton support base.

'For a man who always spoke openly, honestly and candidly at press conferences, he failed to communicate with the fans.

'There was no sense of the style or pattern of play he was trying to implement. There was no sense of the club's rich and vibrant history; it was always 'Everton' rather than 'we'.

'Then there was that comment last month, when asked about the club's January transfer plans. 'We have Steve Walsh in the club for the long term,' Koeman snapped, the inference being that the three-year term of his contract would be the sum total of his attachment to Everton.

'For a club which has boasted a manager who spoke of being married to the club, and other managers like Harry Catterick, Colin Harvey and Joe Royle who gave most of their lives to the club, it jarred.

'Then there was the telling contrast between Duncan Ferguson bouncing up and down the Goodison Road touchline like Tigger on acid following Oumar Niasse's unlikely equaliser against Bournemouth, while Koeman trudged in the opposite direction, hands in his pockets.

'Little wonder the Gwladys Street tellingly never once coined a chant for him.

'Even after the harrowing hatchet job performed on his team by an Arsenal side which until that point hadn't won an away game in the Premier League all season, Koeman was pictured out and about – in Manchester – enjoying a meal and a few jokes.

'The choice of venue was significant.

"While his backroom staff chose to live nearer to Merseyside, and in touch with the club's supporters, Koeman chose to reside in Alderley Edge, Cheshire. 'In my position it is better to stay outside and focus on your job,' he said.

'That choice is understandable given the insane pressures which are inflicted on modern football managers, reflected in the equally insane salaries they are now paid.

'But it also means that a manager loses touch with the man in the street, the people whose lives revolve around the fortunes of their football club and who live, breathe and sleep Everton Football Club.

'Ironically Ronald Koeman never lost the dressing room.

'The players were still running, still chasing, still trying to put into practice whichever new system or formation Koeman had decided to implement in his latest match.

'But he lost the fans. Lots of them. A long time ago.'

If Koeman lost the fans, his replacement never ever had them.

Everton were in the bottom three after the 5-2 defeat by Arsenal which precipitated Koeman's exit – after the toughest set of opening fixtures any football team had ever been handed in the Premier League era, based on the previous season's league placings.

After four league matches with Unsy at the helm again, returning one win, one draw and two defeats, Everton had climbed out of the bottom three but were still too close to the drop zone for comfort.

And Farhad panicked.

He saw his Premier League project threatened, so turned to the closest thing he saw as a guarantee to preserving that position.

Big Sam.

Thanks to Everton's capitulation at the Stadium of Light under Roberto Martinez 18 months earlier, Sam Allardyce still enjoyed the reputation of never having taken a team down from the Premier League.

Talk about being damned by faint praise.

But as if appointing the disgraced former England manager, a manager mocked on the Gwladys Street just three years earlier and a man whose perceived style of football was anathema to the School of Science was bad enough, his assistant was little Sam – Liverpool legend Sammy Lee.

I'd met little Sam several times previously and he's a charming, engaging, decent man. He's also a very talented coach.

But he's also an Anfield icon who had lifted four league titles, four League Cups – one against Everton – and a couple of European Cups, before returning to Anfield as a much loved coach. If Big Sam was never going to be accepted, little Sam alongside him was a match made in Everton footballing hell.

And for six months we were in purgatory.

Unsy was still picking the team and delivering the team talk for a visit of West Ham which lifted Everton up to 13th in the table, with Allardyce watching with relish from the Main Stand.

Football's renowned fire fighter had been enlisted to put out a fire which hadn't really taken hold. He must have been licking his lips with glee.

While Joe Royle had achieved a near football miracle in keeping Everton up two decades earlier, Allardyce only had to achieve mediocrity to maintain Everton's Premier League place.

And mediocrity is exactly what we got. Big Joe decided he didn't want to stick around to watch and promptly retired as the club's professional development co-ordinator.

It was a wise decision.

The football Evertonians endured under Allardyce was attritional.

Sure, a season which had looked like slipping into a relegation dogfight was halted and given some stability.

Everton rose from 13th to eighth, with Allardyce's first seven matches in charge seeing five clean sheets kept, but it was done at a cost, sacrificing any attempt at attacking football.

In truth, the faint prospect of relegation – Everton were five points clear of the relegation zone when Allardyce arrived – was very quickly banished with back-to-back home wins over Huddersfield and Swansea, a draw at Anfield and a win at Newcastle.

But there were no signs of Allardyce removing the shackles.

Everton played five at the back at West Bromwich Albion on Boxing Day, a truly awful goalless draw which saw my Echo colleague Ian Doyle memorably quip: "I can hear a mouse drop a pin. That's how quiet it is now. Fans are comatose."

Everton's new manager knew how to set up a team to grind

out results to avoid the trauma of relegation, but seemed incapable – or unwilling – to move out of that comfort zone and attempt anything even slightly more extravagant.

Watford scored a late winner in February when Allardyce was about to make a defensive substitution to grind out another stalemate.

And Everton's end of season stats reflected that attitude.

Shots on target: 20th

Shots at goal: 20th

Chances created: 20th

Big chances created: 11th

Dribbles: 19th

Possession: 13th

Managing a football club is a supremely difficult balancing act.

Go too gung ho and you're labelled a naive idealist like Roberto Martinez. Go too far the other way and you become a dour, defensive dudgeon, like Allardyce.

Some media pundits, clearly out of touch with the atmosphere at Goodison, asked: "I don't know what Everton fans want."

The answer was obvious: Entertainment. Ambition. And just a little aspiration would have been nice.

Or how about home matches which would have made the £30 price of a match ticket seem like a decent alternative to wandering around the local garden centre on a Saturday afternoon?

Everton ended their home campaign with a 1-1 draw against Southampton which encapsulated much of Allardyce's tenure.

Tom Davies' added-time equaliser ensured Everton remained unbeaten again, but it was another tough, tough watch.

Everton's last 10 home games of that turgid campaign produced half-time scores of 0-0, 0-0, 0-0, 0-3, 0-0, 0-0, 2-0, 0-1, 0-0, 0-0. And Allardyce was only in charge for 12.

Everton had been safe from the once possible prospect of a relegation fight for some considerable time.

But Allardyce refused to remove the shackles from his side, clinging to Everton's solid home record like a drowning man clinging to a rubber duck.

As ever, another man with the prefix 'Big' to his name summed up the dirge succinctly.

Neville Southall tweeted: 'If I had three minutes to live I would watch a DVD of Everton playing this season. It would seem like I had a lifetime left.'

It was clear Allardyce had very little time left.

By the time the players returned to the pitch for the traditional end-of-season lap of appreciation after that last match draw with Southampton, Goodison Park was a largely deserted arena – barely a quarter full.

Apathy is an even more worrying reaction from supporters than frustrated anger, but there were plenty of examples of that too.

Players, partners and children all paraded around the pitch. But there was notably no sign of the manager or his coaching staff.

There weren't many fans either.

We had to remain in our seats to record what was taking place.

And at the end of the match the supporters who remained made their feelings known, calling for Sam Allardyce to, well, let's politely paraphrase, exit the club rapidly.

Those chants had been unprecedented in my then 43 years of watching football at Goodison Park.

Everton fans have audibly called for a chairman to quit the club in that time and many, many players to never darken Goodison's doorstep again.

But not managers. Even the hapless Mike Walker didn't endure that ignominy.

Sam Allardyce was a first.

And after an unedifying defeat at David Moyes' West Ham the following weekend he was quickly relieved of his role.

No tears were shed.

Everton's media officer Brian Doogan had been actively trying to set up a 'cup of tea' between myself and the manager in the weeks leading up to his departure but for reasons I was never made aware of it proved difficult to set up.

Then when it finally did it was all a little surreal.

I was invited up to and ushered into a conference room at Finch Farm where Allardyce spent 10 minutes pointing out all the positives of his period as Everton manager – 10 minutes may be stretching it, admittedly – spent a little longer complaining about the Echo's inability, or reluctance, to reflect those points, and then got to his feet and left without shaking my hand.

And I never got my cup of tea.

At least his sacking at the end of a season meant that we never had the need for a caretaker boss this time.

Farhad went directly for the man he'd targeted prior to Allardyce's appointment, Marco Silva.

Phil Kirkbride was then the man in my old Everton writer's role and the man tasked with building a rapport with the Blues boss – a task he achieved better than any other reporter.

But I did manage one lengthy sit-down chat with Silva, again effected by Brian Doogan.

There was none of the blustering braggadocio of his predecessor. Silva was polite, charming and decisive in his answers.

But he was also personally guarded. Any attempts to steer him towards anecdotes about family life were swiftly dismissed, and he refused even to admit to where he lived and whether he bumped into Evertonians as part of his daily life outside football.

The game was definitely changing. Not entirely for the better.

But there is still room for a little old-school common touch.

Marco Silva lasted just 18 months as Everton manager. Barely 12 months to the day after an Everton side under his stewardship had produced an inventive, enterprising and ultimately unlucky display at Anfield – Jordan Pickford's youthful zest leading to an unnecessary and fatal last-minute error – another Everton side produced a sloppy, uncommitted, disorganised display at the same venue and were walloped 5-2.

That was an eighth league defeat in 11 matches and he was sacked.

Duncan Ferguson then showed that while he was reluctant to speak publicly, privately he could speak articulately, passionately and convincingly.

Bill Kenwright bumped into Big Dunc at Finch Farm in the minutes after Silva's sacking and asked him what he would do with the team for the visit of Chelsea.

His response was so stirring Bill asked him to repeat it in front of Farhad, which is how Ferguson became the caretaker manager for four spirit-lifting fixtures.

Chelsea were blown away on a tide of passion, enthusiasm and emotion, Manchester United and Arsenal were held when Ferguson displayed his tactical acumen – and love of substituting a substitute – and while Leicester utterly outplayed Everton for more than an hour in the Carabao Cup, spirit and endeavour, plus a last-minute humdinger from Leighton Baines, got the Blues back in it and ensured a penalty shoot-out – which, of course, we lost.

But Ferguson had more than done his bit and ensured that a platform had been constructed for a new manager to step onto.

The new appointment was inspired.

Carlo Ancelotti is a boss who belongs in the very highest echelon of modern European managers, one of only three coaches to have won the UEFA Champions League three times, with two different clubs, and one of only two to have managed teams in four finals. I was in Athens for his third in 2007 when this time Liverpool actually performed much better than they had two years earlier, but lost, which made for a nice ice-breaker when we were first introduced.

He has won the FIFA Club World Cup twice and is also one of seven people to have won the European Cup or Champions League as both a player and a manager.

That is managerial royalty.

Yet when he arrived at Everton he was quickly spotted shopping at Bootle New Strand, counting the Iron Men on Crosby beach and shopping in my local supermarket.

To paraphrase Kipling badly, if you can walk with kings but not lose the common touch…you'll be a manager the fans can relate to.

Ancelotti is a supremely successful modern football coach, but some of his values also hark back to the days when I first started in journalism.

I dearly hope he's successful with that approach.

## Chapter Thirty-Four

# TIMES THEY ARE A-CHANGING

MY first article for the Echo was published in April 1989.

The world was never the same again.

Not because of anything I rattled out from my Old Hall Street desk, obviously. The man who caused the whole world to shift dramatically on its axis was a fella who wrote coded computer programmes rather than thousand-word features. Tim Berners-Lee invented the worldwide web in March 1989.

In time, the whole world would change irrevocably. Not least, journalism.

"People will always want news," Gordon Lee had mused to me in his Preston North End office almost a decade earlier – and he was right.

But the means of accessing that news changed dramatically.

In 1990 the Liverpool Echo sold 200,000 copies of a printed newspaper every day, editions rolled off the printing presses in Old Hall Street at 11.30am, 12pm, 12.30pm, 2pm and finally at 3.30pm.

You could get a good story overnight and still preserve its exclusivity until the paper hit the streets the following day.

In 2020, pre-Coronavirus lockdown when football matches were still being played every three or four days, barely 30,000 copies of the Liverpool Echo were being printed.

But crucially, the Echo attracted more than two million readers to its website every single day, with 900,000 readers alone clicking sports stories. If there was a big match that night you could effectively double those figures. These were stories which could be uploaded within seconds of having been created.

More people are reading the Echo's journalism today than ever before – from all over the world – but in keeping with that changing world it's a different kind of journalism.

In 1990 a thousand-word 'think piece' was a lofty ideal.

But the internet didn't just change the way news was delivered, it altered the way we read.

In 2017 Twitter decided to extend the length of permitted tweets from 140 characters to 280, but it actually made no difference to the length of people's thoughts.

A year later only one per cent of tweets actually hit the new, extended character limit, while only 12 per cent were longer than 140 characters.

In the modern world, it seems, brevity is all.

Progress of a match was delivered in a series of tweets rather than a report, 'Five Things' replaced thousand-word colour pieces and managers' press conference quotes were delivered verbatim rather than described with a sense of mood and atmosphere.

It was the same with the sports themselves.

The sports we loved for decades changed. And all because organisers do not believe modern spectators have the attention span to concentrate for longer than short, snappy, excitement-charged chunks.

Society gets the media it deserves. Likewise, we get the sport we clamour for.

Football doesn't do replays any more. Cup ties are resolved by a penalty shoot-out.

Snooker has swapped the best of 31 frames format for one-frame shoot-outs, a shot clock to speed up play and theme tunes for the players as they approach the table.

Then there is cricket – perhaps the longest, most complex and most subtle of all sporting challenges.

A sport which can take five days to complete, and still not produce a winner, has now been pared down to a 20-over-a-side slog…and we love it.

But even that format proved too lengthy for some modern attention spans. In 2016 The Hundred was introduced, an inter-city tournament of 100 balls – which if you do your maths is less than 17 overs. Then in August 2018 the ICC officially sanctioned a T10 League. Yes, 10 overs a side – the time it would usually take Geoff Boycott to settle himself at the crease – was deemed sufficient to complete an entire innings.

It's a symptom of our world – a world where we do not switch off for a minute, but rapidly chop and change from one task to another.

We text message, answer emails, change channels, tweet and try to conduct our regular daily lives while (hang on while I get that text) not spending longer than 20 minutes on any one single task.

Newspaper, or should that now read website, articles reflect that switch. We are encouraged to write short and snappy articles, lists have proliferated everywhere, all modern life is instant and disposable – even in sport.

Is it any better? You tell me. It's certainly different.

But it's what the readership at large seem to want so we'll give it to them.

## Chapter Thirty-Five

# THE DAY THE MUSIC DIED

I STARTED this personal odyssey twenty-something years and over 300 pages ago with an anecdote about an Everton chairman who treated me like faecal matter.

Perhaps symbolic of how far my Everton journey has taken me was that in 2019/20 I watched each of the 16 matches played at Goodison Park – before a sinister virus put the world into lockdown – in the second row of the Goodison Directors' Box.

My wife was alongside me, resplendent in Royal Blue coat, and we were guests of the current Everton chairman, usually after we'd dined and exchanged bon mots in the Goodison boardroom.

The venue is significant.

As you already know, Mrs P is the granddaughter of the club's most iconic player, and poignantly that incredible man took his final breath in that very same room.

How curiously appropriate was it that the greatest player in Everton's long history should have drawn his final breath at Goodison Park, watching his beloved Everton Football Club play their fiercest rivals, having earlier in the day had a stirring eulogy delivered by Liverpool's greatest ever manager – a tribute which ultimately became his obituary?

It's all a little surreal.

But Dixie's daughter Barbara, my mother-in-law, who drove her dad to his last match that fateful day, firmly believes that "he stage-managed the whole thing."

Maybe he did. Because everything about March 1, 1980 was unusual.

Everton were playing Liverpool in the 136th Merseyside derby and while Dixie played in 17 of these tribal conflicts and scored 19 times in them, he had never visited one as a spectator.

Not one, until that fateful Saturday afternoon.

But on March 1, 1980, Dixie agreed to attend a launch of that year's Everton and Liverpool club annuals at the now demolished Holiday Inn on Paradise Street, enjoy a lunch with his good friend Bill Shankly, then go on to the match. A derby match.

In preparation Barbara, who had lived with and cared for her dad since he lost his wife Ethel in 1974, polished the one shoe he then wore, after having his leg amputated in 1976.

"I got him all spruced up, polished his one shoe and drove him to the hotel. But as we got him into his wheelchair I noticed he still had his slipper on!" she recalled.

"He said not to worry, but it had drops of tea and bits of biscuit on it and I always liked him to look his best. So I ran to the toilet and wiped it with some tissue. It was a leather slipper and he probably felt more comfortable in it.

"I was due to start work at Clatterbridge, where I was nursing, and as I left he shouted me, I turned around and he said 'Don't worry about me, I'm going to be alright.'

"Then he gave me a thumbs up.

"He didn't usually do that. I think he knew."

But that was only the start of the day's unusual events.

If Dixie knew, Bill Shankly, who passed away himself the following year, certainly didn't.

Yet he delivered the most eloquent and moving eulogy to his pal sat alongside him during that Holiday Inn lunch.

He got to his feet and in that resonant brogue declared: "We have in our midst today, ladies and gentlemen, a man who was the greatest at what he did. You can't say that about many people in history, whatever branch of life you're talking about. But you can say that about Dixie Dean.

"Oh yes. His record of goalscoring is the most amazing thing under the sun. Nobody will ever come near to equalling his fantastic feat of scoring 60 league goals in a season.

"I played against him a few times when I was with Preston. He was a big, cocky, confident man, arrogant in his approach to the game. That is the hallmark of a great player and Dixie was the greatest centre-forward there will ever be.

"Nobody who's ever been born could head a ball into the net like him. When he connected it frightened people. You couldn't stop him scoring. He belongs in the company of the supremely great…like Beethoven, Shakespeare and Rembrandt."

John Keith, the former Daily Express journalist who penned a Dixie Dean biography and who had invited him to that launch, recalled: "As Shankly was spellbinding his audience, a tear fell down Dixie's cheek. It was a moving, cameo moment which, for me, remains frozen in time."

Dixie Dean, the footballing-warrior never booked nor sent off and who once lost a testicle in a match without demur, shedding a tear?

It truly was a strange day.

Then there was Doctor Ian Irving, Everton's respected long-serving physician who retired in June 2017 after almost 40 years of sterling service, who was on matchday duty for the first time at Goodison Park.

One of his first duties in a long and storied career with the Blues was to attend to the club's greatest ever player after he had taken ill in the Main Stand towards the end of the match.

Dr Irving recalled that he tended to the stricken star after he had been taken into the club's boardroom, but that nothing could be done.

And he was bitterly upset that some members of the media had become aware of what had happened. He desperately wanted to protect the family from discovering the dreadful news second hand.

Melanie had lived with her granddad all of her young life. They were pals and partners in mischief-making as well as grandad and granddaughter. In 1980 Melanie was a naive 13-year-old watching the match from the Gwladys Street End with family friends.

She was aware that something had happened, because she could see her granddad being taken into the Main Stand before the match had finished, but didn't know exactly what.

She was driven back to the friends' house in Claughton Village and while she was aware of a subdued atmosphere in the house, and the knowledge that something strange had happened because she was unexpectedly served her tea there, she was spared the fate of discovering the sad news over the airwaves.

Barbara was not so fortunate.

On duty at Clatterbridge Hospital, Everton's club chairman Bill Scott had immediately set off in his plush car to deliver the sad news in person. But as he arrived at the hospital the news was already being broadcast on the television.

"It was a terrible shock," recalled Barbara, "but Mr Scott couldn't have done more. He drove me to pick up Melanie, then he drove us home. And because my car was still at Clatterbridge he arranged for us to be taken back there on the Sunday to collect it.

"Then on Monday I had to go to the mortuary at Walton Hospital to identify my dad."

So William Ralph Dean, the footballer who illuminated Goodison Park so many times during his stellar playing career, saw his life's light extinguished there.

And he has remained there ever since.

Following his funeral service on Friday, March 7, at St James' Church in Birkenhead, the church where he had been baptised and married, Barbara insisted on scattering his ashes along the halfway line at Goodison Park.

The very next day, in an uplifting epitaph, Everton won a famous FA Cup quarter-final there.

The derby match at which Dixie had died was a grim ugly

affair, a game which saw Everton defender Geoff Nulty's career ended by a crude tackle.

But seven days later, against a wonderfully gifted and attractive Ipswich Town team which had won 4-0 at Goodison Park just a month earlier, Everton triumphed. They won with a goal from their then celebrated centre-forward Bob Latchford, a proud Dixie successor, and a goal from another man who had worn the number nine shirt for the Blues, Brian Kidd.

I was there that day as a fan, unaware that almost two decades later Dixie's granddaughter would become my wife.

Several years later Liverpool songwriter Gerry Murphy penned the moving Ballad of Dixie Dean.

It's a stirring, evocative anthem and opens with the words: 'On the banks of the River Mersey, it is morning in the street. There's a boy in a football jersey...playing music with his feet.'

Dean created an orchestral symphony with those feet – and that anointed head – creating a goalscoring record which still stands almost a century after it was set, and which will surely never be broken.

Dixie Dean scored 60 goals in a single league season, scored 383 goals in an incredible Everton career, scored 18 goals in 16 England appearances, and made supporters' spirits sing everywhere he played.

And if March 1, 1980, was the day that music died, that night's Match of the Day, for the first time in the programme's history, also silenced its famous theme tune at the end of the show.

A black and white image of the great man filled the screen instead – accompanied by a powerful, poignant silence.

It really was the day the music died.

And both Melanie and I think of that moment every single time we step into that Goodison boardroom.

Forty years after his passing Melanie's granddad still arouses intense interest, and still possesses the capacity to make people smile, sometimes in the most unexpected of circumstances.

Some time ago an award-winning English film producer, then based in Hollywood, contacted Barbara to discuss the possibility of making a film about her dad's incredible life story – or more specifically an untold area of his life which only Barbara and Ethel were aware of.

That led to a series of meetings, usually in our local pub, with an array of film 'people'. We met producer Orian Williams, who worked on the wonderful Joy Division biopic Control, director Simon Aboud, who was also Paul McCartney's son-in-law and many, many potential investors.

Then in 2018 Sara, the English film producer whose burning passion for the Dixie film project meant she has long since become a family friend, contacted Barbara to say she had an actor lined up interested in playing the part of her dad.

Except this time, we couldn't possibly meet in The Freshy because the actor was too well known.

"So come on Barbara, who is it?" we asked excitedly.

"Oh, I'm not sure now," she replied. "I think Sara said Toby something."

I racked my brains for cinematographic Tobys.

"Toby Jones?" I mused. Great actor but at five feet four that was ambitious casting.

"No, no, not him." Phew.

"Toby Stephens?" Well he has the chiselled good looks, but wasn't he a baddie in a Bond movie?

"No, not him either."

"Toby Maguire?" I ventured, running quickly out of Tobys.

"Yes, I think that was it," declared Barbara.

"Oh my God, Bibs," I said. "He's Spider-Man! No wonder we can't meet in The Freshy."

For a lifelong Marvel geek this was akin to an audience with the Queen. Or Bob Latchford.

So we trooped around to Barbara's the following Sunday morning in a state of mild foment, all set to meet a Hollywood superstar who was keen to play Melanie's granddad in a movie.

Daniel and Scarlett hadn't been in long after a Saturday night out and were still hungover, which probably added to their confusion when they were introduced to a tall, handsome, six-foot-plus actor who actually bore a physical resemblance to Melanie's granddad, but who clearly wasn't Toby Maguire.

Toby Kebbell was physically imposing, he was engaging, charming and he was clearly interested in playing the part of Dixie Dean in a movie, not least because the great man ended his English league career in Toby's native Nottingham, playing for Notts County.

But given his acting credits included playing Marvel villain Doctor Doom, in which he donned an iron mask, Koba in Dawn of the Planet of the Apes, wearing simian face make-up and the role of a heavily made-up orc in Warcraft, we might have got away with a pint in The Freshy.

Several years later investment is still an issue for Dixie The Movie but who knows?

One day we may get to see Toby strutting his stuff with a Brylcreemed centre-part. Toby Maguire would never get the Birkenhead accent anyway.

Almost 50 years after taking possession of a handful of Everton programmes, my Royal Blue journey had now led to me sitting down on a Sunday morning talking about the club's greatest ever player over coffee and croissants with a celebrated thespian.

## Chapter Thirty-Six

# WHAT EVERTON MEANS TO ME

MANY years ago I was asked to contribute to a book called 'Scousers', a collection of articles celebrating civic pride, published by the Echo, which contained reminiscences from people like Faith Brown, Tommy Smith, Ricky Tomlinson, Gerry Marsden and Colin Harvey.

Part of my brief was to answer the question: 'What does a lifetime of following Everton Football Club mean to a man?'

To be honest I didn't give it a huge amount of thought.

It was a work obligation. So I trotted out the obvious answers, like worry lines, sleepless nights – and the occasional dizzying, soaring, giddy highs which make all the tribulations seem almost worthwhile. Almost.

I rabbited on about Bob Latchford (any excuse!) and I ended with: 'So what does Everton mean to me? A job, a wife, a myriad of memories – and no reason whatsoever why I should forget my wedding anniversary or my mother-in-law's birthday.'

It was a trite sign-off.

Melanie and I married on April 29, which was the date Dixie Dean captained Everton to an FA Cup victory in 1933, becoming English football's first high-profile number nine in the process, and the same date when, 50 years later, big bad bustling Bob proved he was at least half as good as Dixie by scoring his 30th league goal against Chelsea.

But that wasn't the reason we married then. April 29 wasn't just Barbara's birthday, it was also the date of her dear mum's funeral. Dixie lost his beloved wife Ethel in 1974 and we wanted to garnish that date with a little more positive symbolism. It was also a Sunday, so the wedding breakfast venue was a little cheaper.

So Everton meant all that to me, and more, but let's try and answer the question a little more fully now. What exactly is Everton?

The Everton which fills our consciousness isn't even in the geographical region of Merseyside which bears its name.

Is it the football team? If so which one? Hundreds of footballers have represented Everton in the past 142 years so it can't be any one team. Is it Goodison Park? Clearly not, because Everton have played at different stadia before and will hopefully do so again in the very near future. So is it the fans? Maybe we're getting a little closer now.

Yuval Noah Harari, in his bestseller 'Sapiens', evocatively explained how thousands of years ago Homo sapiens were able to differentiate themselves from other related species by their ability to believe in common myths. He explained that any large scale human co-operation, whether a modern state, a medieval church, an ancient city, or a historic football club, is rooted in common myths which exist only in people's collective imaginations.

Yuval then went on to use the car manufacturer Peugeot as an example of a figment of our collective imagination, an entity which wields immense power, even if it doesn't physically exist. He might have used Everton Football Club.

Everton doesn't physically exist. The football club we worship is an imagined reality, but it exercises more power than we can possibly imagine.

Everton has saved lives through its powerful work in the community, it has provided solace and comfort in times of trial, it has provided an excuse for wild celebration – and it has caused us pain and distress.

Its meaning is different to every single Evertonian.

For me, it has permeated and dominated every facet of my entire life. I have supported Everton, worked for Everton, prayed for Everton, cried for Everton and celebrated wildly thanks to Everton. I have paid my daily bills writing about Everton and found personal happiness as a result of Everton.

So yes, it's a Grand Old Team to report, but it's also much, much more than that. Everton is a concept which is part of my being and I'm far from alone. There are tens of thousands of us just like that all around the world. Everton gives me a kinship with strangers all over the planet.

Bill Kenwright frequently extols the virtues of his Everton Family and he's absolutely right.

What is Everton? I honestly don't know. But I do know that in the words of the song, they are my Everton, my only Everton, they make me happy when skies are grey, they'll never know how much I love them, but please don't take my Everton away.